Lost
Languages

by P. E. Cleator

 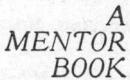

A MENTOR BOOK

PUBLISHED BY THE NEW AMERICAN LIBRARY

© 1959 BY P. E. CLEATOR

All rights reserved. This book, or parts thereof,
must not be reproduced in any form without permission.
For information address The John Day Company,
62 West 45th Street, New York 36, New York.

Published as a MENTOR BOOK
By arrangement with the original publisher,
The John Day Company

FIRST PRINTING, JUNE, 1962

MENTOR TRADEMARK REG. U.S. PAT. OFF. AND FOREIGN COUNTRIES
REGISTERED TRADEMARK—MARCA REGISTRADA
HECHO EN CHICAGO, U.S.A.

MENTOR BOOKS are published by
The New American Library of World Literature, Inc.
501 Madison Avenue, New York 22, New York

PRINTED IN THE UNITED STATES OF AMERICA

TO

ACKNOWLEDGEMENTS

Thanks are due to G. Chesterfield, whose idea this story of the recovery of lost languages and forgotten writings was, and to those scholars and decipherers who contributed to the telling of it by their generous response to requests for information and illustrative material. In particular, I am indebted to the following for allowing the reproduction of photographs and sign lists from specialised accounts, and for providing copies of some of these items: Sir Alan Gardiner (*Egyptian Grammar*); Professor I. J. Gelb (*Hittite Hieroglyphs*); Dr. C. F. A. Schaeffer, the British Academy, and the Oxford University Press (*The Cuneiform Texts of Ras Shamra-Ugarit*); Dr. Emmett L. Bennett and the Yale University Press (*A Minoan Linear B Index*); Dr. David Diringer and Hutchinson & Co. (Publishers) Ltd. (*The Alphabet*); Dr. John Chadwick, M. Oliver Masson, Professor Carl W. Blegan, and the Syndics of the Cambridge University Press (*Documents in Mycenaean Greek*); and K. W. Marek (C. W. Ceram), M. G. Scheler, Professor H. T. Bossert, Sidgwick and Jackson Ltd., and Victor Gollancz Ltd. (*Narrow Pass, Black Mountain*). Other photographs and drawings appear by kind permission of Macmillan & Co. Ltd. and the Executors of the late Sir Arthur Evans (*Scripta Minoa*); George Allen and Unwin Ltd. (Thor Heyerdahl's *Aku-Aku*); and Routledge and Kegan Paul Ltd. (G. R. Hunter's *The Script of Harappa and Mohenjodaro*). Yet other illustrations were provided by Glyn Edwards, by the New York Metropolitan Museum of Art, by the Chicago Oriental Institute, and by the British Museum.

Much literature has been consulted, including sundry issues of the *Journal of Hellenic Studies*, the *National Geographic Magazine*, *Acta Congressus Madvigiani*, *Studia Orientalia*, *Syria*, *Archaeologia*, *Antiquity*, *Revue Biblique*, *Bib-*

liotheca Orientalis, and the *Bulletin* of the American Schools of Oriental Research, not to mention such well-known publications as the *Cambridge Ancient History*, Black's *Bible Dictionary*, William L. Langer's *Encyclopedia of World History*, and a representative selection of other standard works of reference—*Americana, Britannica, Chambers's, Collier's, Compton's, Everyman's, Funk and Wagnall's,* and *Universal*.

A comprehensive list of other sources of published information will be found in the Bibliography (pp. 178-181), and to the anonymous army of librarians who located and supplied these works (on occasion, only after months of searching); to the linguists who assisted with transliterations and translations; and to my wife and my old friend, W. H. Browning, for their diligent reading of the proofs, I am also much beholden.

P. E. CLEATOR

CONTENTS

CHAP.		PAGE
	Acknowledgements	vii
I.	The Confusion of Tongues	13
II.	The Egyptian Hieroglyphs	29
III.	The Key to Cuneiform	65
IV.	Some Subsidiary Systems	113
V.	Among the Undeciphered	161
	Bibliography	178
	Index	182

LIST OF ILLUSTRATIONS

PLATES

between pages 96 and 97

1. The Rosetta Stone
2. Bushman paintings
3. Papyrus gathering
4. Clay tablets from Jemdet Nasr
5. Egyptian hieroglyphs
6. Official hieratic
7. Cartouche of Amenemhet I
8. Demotic script
9. Book of the Dead
10. Ruins of Persepolis
11. Inscription from Palace of Darius
12. Behistun—general view
13. Behistun—close-up
14. Sennacherib's prism
15. Tell el-Amarna tablet
16. Hittite hieroglyphs
17. Hittite cuneiform
18. Avenue of inscribed stones at Karatepe
19. Ugarit account book; Will of citizen
20. Cretan hieroglyphs
21. Linear B tablets
22. Page-form tablet from Pylos

NUMBERED FIGURES IN TEXT

1. Map: The Eastern Mediterranean and the Near East — xii
2. Egyptian writing — 55
3. Uniconsonantal signs — 57
4. Niebuhr's "B" and "G" inscriptions — 74
5. Persian cuneiform — 95
6. Development of cuneiform — 104
7. Monumental and cursive Hittite hieroglyphs — 120
8. Hittite hieroglyphic syllabary — 125
9. Ugaritic syllabary — 141
10. Linear B—the grid — 151
11. Linear B—syllabic sign list — 155
12. Linear B—list of ideograms — 157
13. Writing from Byblos — 160
14. Linear A—sign list — 163
15. Phaistos disc — 165
16. Cypro-Minoan sign list — 167
17. Etruscan inscription — 169
18. Mayan glyphs — 171
19. Indus Valley script — 173
20. *Rongo rongo* script — 175
21. Early Proto-Elamite — 177

Fig. 1. The Eastern Mediterranean and the Near East.

CHAPTER I

THE CONFUSION OF TONGUES

I

Inasmuch as the active application of language is speech, it is upon speech that writing, essentially a secondary means of communication, is dependent. The pedants, it is true, have long fostered the misconception that everyday speech is to be regarded as inferior to the written word, that the one constitutes a base and corrupt form of the other. As to this, there is no doubt that writing is much more conservative than speech, upon which it exercises a powerful and restraining influence. But the fact, nevertheless, remains that mankind has been possessed of language since time immemorial, whereas even in these days of universal progress and enlightenment, some two-thirds of the population of the world are still unable either to read or to write. Very evidently, language is what is spoken, rather than what is written.

But although as a means of communication language is preeminent, there are, of course, various other ways in which living creatures contrive to make known their feelings and intentions to one another, from the antennal activities of ants to the courting posturings of birds and the oral exchanges of the anthropoids. In the absence of a vocabulary, however, the higher apes must be considered incapable of discourse, while it would be too much to suppose that the parrot, able though it is to reproduce noises which are strange to it, including the sound of the human voice, can have the slightest understanding of anything that it repeats, even when a premonitory cry of "Fire!" happens to coincide with the fall of a burning coal upon the hearthrug. In short, only man is properly describable as a talking animal, and he alone can claim to be a conversationalist.

In pondering this remarkable circumstance, the ancients were content to explain the phenomenon of speech as a ready-made gift from the gods, the identity of the divine bestower varying from one geographical location to the next—in Egypt, Thoth; in India, Indra; in Palestine, Yahweh; in Greece, Hermes; and so on. Modern enquiry, it need hardly be said, unhesitatingly rejects all such naïve and improbable notions, and leaves the question of origin unanswered, though by no means unguessed at. Thus, according to what has been somewhat jocularly termed the Pooh-pooh theory, man's first meaningful words were uttered instinctively, and thereafter came to symbolise the particular situation which gave rise to them. The Onomatopoetic (*alias* the Bow-wow) theory, on the other hand, holds that primitive speech resulted from attempts to imitate animal and other sounds, while advocates of the so-called Yo-ho-ho theory would have us believe that undue muscular exertion, by provoking heavy breathing, caused an involuntary vibration of the human vocal chords. . . .

All such explanations have encountered objections of one sort or another. The Bow-wow theory, for example, at once comes up against the fact that even among uncivilised peoples, imitative words such as "cuckoo" and "whip-poor-will" make up a relatively small part of the vocabulary. There is thus raised the further problem of how speech movements and their accompanying sounds gained meaning, and here, too, our ignorance is both lamentable and profound. We cannot even explain why the product of twice two is termed "four" in preference to "six," though we can say with some assurance (it being a matter of much more recent history) how it happens that we are content to munch what we call sandwiches, but steadfastly decline to make a meal of cardigans or wellingtons.

That the first words actually distinguishable as such were in some way related to animal sounds and gestures appears likely enough, as does the suggestion that in all probability human speech did not develop until men began to live in communities, and so experienced the need to indulge in an exchange of ideas. But was this development monogenetic or polygenetic—did speech, that is to say, have a single or a multiple beginning? And if, with the late Alfredo Trombetti, we favour the theory of a solitary origin, how then do we satisfactorily account for the great diversity which now exists among the languages of the world?

As late as the start of the 19th century, such questions had yet to be given serious consideration, for the Mesopotamians were then unrecognised as the authors of the legend of the Tower of Babel, and the belief was still widespread that all languages were Hebrew in origin—the contradictions inherent in the proposition that any tongue could antedate that supposedly spoken in the Garden of Eden were simply dismissed as inconceivable.

To-day, however, blind conviction has been replaced by admissions of uncertainty, and it is generally acknowledged that final answers cannot be expected in regard to events which may well have occurred a million or more years ago. It is accepted, in short, that there is a complete lack of data about the beginnings of language, and that any study of its subsequent evolution must be confined to those later stages of the process which took place during the historic period. And by the time this limited aspect of the enquiry was begun, scholars found themselves faced with hundreds of different native tongues, the precise number of which could not be agreed (estimations still range from 2,500 to 7,000) because a conflict of opinion at once arose concerning exactly what constituted a language, and over the inclusion or otherwise of this or that dialect.

Despite the evident complexities of the situation, various classificatory schemes have nevertheless been devised, among them the morphological. Under this arrangement, three (in some systems four or more) main divisions of language are recognised—an Inflectional type, an Agglutinative type, and an Isolating type. The last-named is characterised by monosyllabic roots, the same word playing the role of verb, adjective, adverb, and noun. Chinese, for example, exhibits no grammar apart from syntax, the precise meaning of a word being determined by its place in the sentence, and (when voiced) by subtle variations in tone and pitch.

In agglutinative languages (such as Turkish and Japanese), the meaning of roots is modified by prefixes (*ab*stract, *bis*cuit), by suffixes (prow*ess*, wood*en*), and by infixes (mes*sen*ger, from message). Many English words are agglutinated (aforementioned, matter-of-fact), and in extreme cases of the phenomenon, the verb may absorb all other parts of speech, so that a single word comprises an entire sentence, as exemplified by the name of the Aztec ruler Montecuzomai-thuica-mina (Montezuma), meaning "When-the-chief-is-angry-he-shoots-to-heaven."

Latin and Greek provide typical examples of inflectional languages. Here, words are modified by alterations in noun forms (declension) and verb forms (conjugation) by the addition of one or more letters (cow, cows; ox, oxen; plough, ploughs, ploughed). Changes may also occur within the words themselves (woman, women; ran, run), and such internal variation constitutes an important feature of Semitic languages, all of which display a marked preference for verbal roots made up of three consonant sounds. Thus, in Hebrew, the triliteral root *k-t-b* is the basis of words associated with writing, which are derived therefrom by the addition of vowels (*cf.* rang, ring, rung).

Inflecting languages contain both monosyllabic and agglutinative words, and it was long considered that in the course of development, languages went through isolating and agglutinative phases before emerging as fully inflectional. This evolutionary idea continued to command support until the disconcerting discovery was made that monosyllabic (and supposedly primitive) Chinese, though now an essentially isolating language, was at one time inflectional!

The fact that all languages undergo continuous change (compare the English of to-day with that of Chaucer's time, or even of Shakespeare's) is the basis of the genetic system of classification, which seeks, by a tracing back process, to uncover family relationships. Technically, a relationship between two languages is said to exist when, and only when, it can be shown that both of them have a common ancestor, which may, or may not, be known. Thus French and Italian (together with Spanish and Portuguese) are derived directly from Latin, familiar as the now defunct language of ancient Rome, while Hebrew and several allied tongues have been identified as the offspring of an unknown parent, provisionally termed Proto-Semitic.

It will be evident that if this genealogical investigation could be carried back to what the monogeneticists regard as its logical conclusion, it would lead to the discovery of the father of all languages. To this end, and after revising an earlier attempt, Trombetti announced in 1929 that he had succeeded in reducing the total of the world's language groups to nine—Caucasian, American Indian, Australo-Dravidian, Munda-Polynesian, Indo-Chinese, Hamito-Semitic, Bantu-Sudanese, Uralo-Altaic, and Indo-European. More conservative authorities, however, are inclined to place the number of apparently distinct linguistic families as high as 200 or more, though of the aforementioned nine divisions, there is at any rate no dispute about the merits and importance of the last-named.

As early as 1786, Sir William Jones, in an address to the Asiatic Society of Bengal, made the surprising prediction that future research would provide proof of the common origin of Sanskrit and the chief languages of Europe, including English. Subsequent enquiries not only confirmed this prophecy, but they brought to light evidence which pointed to the one-time existence of a relatively small tribe, speaking what has been styled primitive Indo-European. Not later than 2000 B.C., it would appear, this community began to break up, and a series of migrations scattered many of its members throughout Europe, and took others across Asia Minor to parts of Asia itself.

In the centuries which followed, several hundred differing tongues developed as a result of this dispersion. But the collective term "Indo-European," which Thomas Young applied to them, is somewhat misleading, in that a number of European languages (including Estonian, Finnish, and Hungarian), and several Indian languages (such as the Dravidian tongues of South India), undoubtedly belong to other linguistic groups. Again, there are some Indo-European languages, *e.g.,* Persian, which are at home in neither of the geographical locations in which their family name suggests they might be expected to be found. The term, however, is now firmly established by long usage.

Apart from their language, no trace of the original Indo-European-speaking people remains, though philologists have nevertheless been able to build up what is believed to be a reasonably satisfactory picture of where and how they lived. Thus many verbal trails appear to converge upon the plain of central Europe, a fact which suggests that it was from somewhere in this vicinity that the parent language spread. Moreover, when it is found that its many offshoots have what is virtually the same name for various plants and animals, it is reasonable to suppose that the people who first used these words must have been acquainted with the things so described. This in turn suggests that their homeland was the habitat of certain prescribed forms of life, a circumstance of assistance in assessing the merits of this or that proposed location.

In sum, these and other considerations point to the fact that the ancestral land of the Indo-European-speaking people was situated some distance from the sea, that it enjoyed a temperate climate, and that in all probability it extended from what is now Lithuania to the vast uncultivated plains of southern Russia.

II

The dawn of recorded history is an occurrence so comparatively recent that perhaps a million or so years went by before *Homo sapiens* learned how to represent speech in the absence of a speaker. But although writing is thus to be regarded as a secondary means of communication, its importance can hardly be overestimated. Prior to its advent a few millennia ago, the knowledge and recollections of mankind had to be handed down by word of mouth alone, and were moreover subject to all the vagaries of the human memory. As a result, and notwithstanding any aid which may have been derived from such mnemonic devices as notched message sticks and knotted cords, much that we should be most interested to know about the activities of our remote forebears is irretrievably lost, and we can now do no more than speculate about such tremendous happenings as the discovery of fire, the invention of the wheel, and the introduction of agriculture.

The art of writing, however, presupposes some knowledge of writing materials, and here we are reasonably well informed, in that examples of the one necessarily provide us with evidence of the other. Thus, one of the forerunners of paper was papyrus, an aquatic plant which once grew in abundance along the lower reaches of the Nile, and which is still to be found in the Sudan. The antiquarian Varro, a contemporary of Cicero, claimed that papyrus was not used for writing before the time of Alexander the Great, but ancient Egyptian manuscripts have since been found which prove that it was so employed between 4,000 and 5,000 years ago.

The Egyptian discovery that a thin vegetable membrane made an admirable writing surface led to the widespread use of papyrus for this purpose. In the preparation of the material, its soaked fibres were laid vertically, and on top of them another layer was placed horizontally, an adhesive being used to bind them together. Pressure was then applied, and this operation was followed by a drying process, whereafter the side of the sheet on which the fibres ran horizontally was polished in readiness for use by the scribe. The finished product was made into rolls (some of them more than 120 feet in length) by fastening sheets one to another, and a reed pen, complete with an ink composed of an aqueous mixture of gum and lampblack, were other standard items of writing equipment.

No less important as an early writing medium was wet clay, extensively used by the Babylonians and their predecessors. This substance, often in the form of cushion-shaped rectangular tablets, was indented with the aid of a wedge-like stylus, and then baked hard. And as a precaution, messages were placed in protective envelopes bearing a duplicate imprint—the equivalent of our carbon copy! But the first writing material of all was probably slate or stone, its use inspired by the pictures which Palaeolithic man scratched and painted upon the walls of his caves. It is a moot point, indeed, whether these drawings were executed merely for amusement, and thus represent the beginnings of art, or were intended to record events, and so constitute an attempt at writing.

However this may be, the first true writing took the form of pictures which did no more than represent the objects shown—an eye was an eye, a dog was a dog, and a circle was the sun. Although a vivid portrayal of scenes and events was thus possible, the limitations of the procedure for purposes of narration will be evident. The position improved as the drawings gradually developed into ideographs or ideograms (word-signs), and so came to represent not so much the objects themselves as the ideas associated with them—an eye with seeing, a dog with hunting, a circle with warmth or daytime. Considerable powers of imagination were thus invoked, with consequent pitfalls for the would-be interpreter of some of these conventionalised images. During a study of North American Indian ideography, for instance, it transpired that whereas an eagle, understandably enough, indicated bravery, life was represented by a snake, thanks to a popular belief that this reptile was capable of living for ever.

In pictography, any connection between the depicted object and the spoken name for it is lacking, and it was the eventual establishment of such a link which led to the development of phonetic writing. Some understanding of how this far-reaching innovation may have come about is provided by the rebus, in which pictures of objects represent, not the objects, but sounds associated with them. By this means, it is possible to communicate proper names, and to express abstract ideas, *e.g.*, the notion of treachery could be conveyed by a drawing of a bee in company with a sketch of a salver, signifying "betray."

A feature of the ancient Egyptian hieroglyphic writing was a combined use of ideograms (sense-signs) and phonograms (sound-signs), the pictorial representation being shown in two sizes, the one large, intended for visual interpretation only, and the other small, explicable in terms of language. Some of the phonograms, moreover, were polyphonic, *i.e.*, they represented more than one sound, while other signs, known as homophones, had the same phonetic value, but stood for different objects, and thanks to these devices, the range of expression was very wide. But the next advance, entailing the complete replacement of sense signs by sound elements, was a step which the ancient Egyptians failed to take, and throughout its centuries-long history, their script remained what was essentially a picture-writing assisted by sound signs.

Writing in which the symbols stood for syllables such as *za, me, pag, mar,* however, duly made its appearance in Mesopotamia, and from this syllabic script there was eventually developed an alphabetic system composed of a relatively small number of signs, each representative of one or more single sounds (in English, for example, the letter *b* stands for the sound *b,* and the letter *c* for the sounds *k* or *s*). It has long been customary to attribute this revolutionary culmination to the Semites, four main divisions of whose so-called alphabet—the Ethiopic (a descendant of the South Semitic branch) and the Aramaic, the Canaanite, and the Palestinian (offshoots of the North Semitic branch)—were in use about 1000 B.C., each consisting of from 22 to 30 signs, all of them expressing consonants. This Semitic practice (subsequently abandoned) of omitting vowels in writing was almost certainly copied from the ancient Egyptians, who had earlier distinguished 24 uniconsonantal symbols which were likewise hailed as alphabetic at the time of their discovery more than a century ago. But as I. J. Gelb maintains in his penetrating analysis, *A Study of Writing* (London, 1952), and in support of which contention he produces convincing arguments and evidence, it is difficult to escape the conclusion that the early Egyptian and Semitic writings were in fact syllabic, and that their phonetic signs represented not merely consonants, but consonants plus any vowel—as is undoubtedly the case with Mesopotamian cuneiform writing, in which the sign for *wa*, for example, also transliterates as *we, wi,* or *wu,* as the context requires. It would thus appear that it was the Greeks who evolved the first true alphabet, the Semitic origins of which, however, are clearly to be seen in the names given to its signs—*alpha, beta, gamma, delta* . . . (Greek); *aleph, beth, gimel, daleth* . . . (Semitic)—a borrowing openly acknowledged by the Greeks themselves, who described their writing as Phoenician.

Apart from introducing vowel representation, the Greeks made several other important alterations to the Semitic writing, including a change of direction. The Semitic version read from right to left (a convention supposed to indicate that its forerunner was a carved script, and designed to suit the convenience of the engraver). At first, Greek inscriptions did likewise, but a period of experimentation followed, during which a boustrophedon (plough-wise) arrangement was adopted, the lines of script running alternately from right to left, and from left to right. The left-to-right-only style (obviously better suited to right-handed scribes of a pen-and-ink era) did not appear until the beginning of the 7th century B.C., whereafter signs such as ᗺ eventually became established as B. Meanwhile, in all probability by way of the Etruscans, the art of alphabetic writing reached Rome, whence knowledge of the invention spread throughout Europe and the rest of the Empire.

The original Etruscan alphabet contained 26 letters, of which the Romans borrowed 21—A B C D E F Z H I K L M N O P Q R S T V X. Subsequently, the 7th symbol (Z, with the sound of G or K) was replaced by G, and later still, in order to assist the transliteration of certain Hellenic vocalisations, the Greek letters Y and Z were adopted, and placed at the end of the Latin alphabet, the classical version of which thus contained 23 letters. The expansion of V into U and W (double U), and the differentiation of I and J, were later developments which took place in the 10th and 14th centuries respectively.

In picture writing, the number of different signs which

are needed may amount to thousands, and the overwhelming superiority of the alphabetic system lies in its representation of a relatively few speech sounds by letters which can be combined to form as extensive a vocabulary as is desired. The undoubted advantages of the process have been recognised for many years by most countries, a notable exception being China, though even here members of the State Council have recently approved a programme of language reform, which includes the adoption of the Western alphabet for use as a phonetic auxiliary. A Chinese student, meanwhile, needs to know about 3,000 different signs to enable him to read an ordinary book, while a more profound display of learning on his part would call for the memorising of some 40,000 other characters!

The introduction of phonetic writing served to draw attention to the fact that all the significant sounds which are made during speech can be assigned to one or other of two categories—vowels and consonants. Of these basic components, vowels are produced by the voice, *i.e.,* by the vibration of the vocal chords, whereas consonants are not so produced, and are merely sounds which accompany the vowels or sonants (hence *con*sonants). Linguists term the constituent sounds of a language *phonemes,* and it has been shown that their number may range from 2 to 12 vowel phonemes in association with 12 to 50 of the consonantal variety. Ideally, an alphabet should have one separate sign for each distinct sound into which the language it serves can be analysed. But apart from an International Phonetic compilation, far too cumbersome for everyday use, no such alphabet exists. The familiar Roman version is essentially a makeshift affair, adapted to the varying requirements of many different tongues, and on occasion no more than half meeting their needs. Thus in English, 26 letters have between them to represent no less than 47 phonemes (12 vowel sounds, 26 consonant sounds, and 9 diphthongs), a situation which has been met by resorting to such expedients as the use of combinations of letters (*ch, sh, th*), and by assigning more than one sound to the same letter.

Inasmuch as letters originated as phonetic symbols, it may be conjectured that there was once a time when a reader could accurately pronounce any unfamiliar word at sight, and spell it correctly on first hearing it said. But this happy state of affairs is far from being the case with the majority of languages to-day, and the eccentricities of English spelling in particular are notorious. Here, not only are identical symbols used to express more than one sound—at, ate; cough, enough; new, sew—but the same sound is expressed by different symbols—blue, blew; tome, ptomaine; night, knight. And further to add to the prevailing confusion, words with different sounds and meanings are written in the same way—refuse (reject); refuse (dross); refuse (melt again).

The reason for all this is not far to seek. A language is a living thing, and in the normal course of its growth and development, words alter their meaning, or fall into disuse, to be replaced by other expressions, either newly coined or borrowed from some alien tongue. And also subject to change are the language users themselves. They come and go in an unending procession, and with each transmission of speech from one generation to the next, subtle alterations in pronunciation inevitably occur. Compensatory modifications in spelling, however, are made only at rare intervals, with the result that writing tends to become cluttered up with such terminological unrealities as cough for *kof,* naught for *nawt,* knock for *nok,* and bough for *bow.* In effect, failing periodic adjustment, alphabetic writing gradually reverts to ideography, in that its words eventually cease to be phonetic elements, and so require to be learned one by one.

III

It has been said that a language grows and develops. It must be added that, in common with other living things, it is also apt to wither and die. Thereafter, as circumstances dictate, the memory of it may be preserved (*cf.* Greek and Latin), or all recollection of it may be forgotten. But even so, a vanished language is not necessarily lost beyond recall, if it happened that during its lifetime, in addition to being spoken, it was also committed to writing. For the probability is that at least some of these records will have survived, and that if they are not already known and available for study, they will sooner or later be brought to light, and so claim the attention of scholars and savants.

Just as different languages share the same writing (*e.g.,* English, French, German, and Italian, among others), so the same speech can be expressed in more than one script, and Turkish, which now makes use of the Latin alphabet, in accordance with a decree issued by Mustapha Kemal in 1928, was formerly written in Arabic characters. Hence, four possibilities face the would-be reader of a specimen of ancient writing, arising from the fact that either it or the language it expresses may be known or unknown. The prospect of decipherment, as it applies to each of these situations, is as follows:

Language	Writing	Decipherment
Known	Known	No problem
Known	Unknown	Relatively easy
Unknown	Known	Difficult
Unknown	Unknown	Impossible

If examination reveals that both the writing and the language are familiar, there is, of course, no difficulty. In cases where the language, but not the writing, is known, the decipherer will make use of the cryptographic technique of simple substitution. But he must first establish the identity of the known language that is concerned, and determine the nature and direction of the unfamiliar script. As to this, assuming the available material is sufficiently representative for a reliable estimation to be made, the number of different characters which the writing displays will give an indication of its nature, *e.g.*, if it is alphabetic, the number will be small. It may, however, proceed horizontally in either direction, or ploughwise in both directions; it may run from top to bottom, in vertical columns which progress to the left or to the right; it may follow a curved path (as on the Phaistos Disc), or form some pattern or other, not necessarily in any particular order at all. Nothing, indeed, can be taken for granted. The early investigators of cuneiform writing were at first misled by a series of window inscriptions, which were observed to run up one side of the openings, across the top, and down the other side. Because it was not appreciated that the wording was intended to be read like the legend on a coin (and that, in consequence, two-thirds of the characters appeared to be lying on their sides), it was wrongly assumed that the signs could face in any direction. Much confusion resulted from this fundamental error, which among other things added greatly to the supposed number of signs. On the other hand, it may happen that the enquiry will be greatly assisted by a prior knowledge of what the unreadable writing has to say, if, for example, some war of conquest necessitated the issuing of an official proclamation in more than one form, *i.e.*, in the guise of a multi-lingual document such as the Rosetta Stone, one of the several versions of which could be read and understood without difficulty.

To assist proof of the concealment of a known language by an unknown script, consideration will need to be given to the land of origin of the writing: this may, or may not, be that of the country in which it was discovered. The next step will be to assign a date to the find, use being made of any available archaeological evidence, in conjunction with such clues as may be provided by the writing itself—its nature, its style, and the kind of material upon which it is recorded. Thereafter, in the light of the known history of the region concerned, it should be possible to name the probable authors, and so identify the language used.

The mode of attack is now two-fold, both the so-called analytical and probable-word methods being employed. Of these, the former calls for an exhaustive analysis of the unknown writing (signs, words, contexts) and the experimental substitution of phonetic values, followed by a check, if possible with new material. In the process, certain recognisable features of the known language may be expected to reveal themselves. Thus, if the language happened to be English, and the writing alphabetic, the letter which occurred most often would almost certainly be *e*, the next in order of frequency being *t, a, o, n, i, r, s* . . . Furthermore, all single letters would be either *a, i,* or *o*, and any two-letter words confined to a short list which included *as, at, be, by, he, if,* and *in,* doubles might be expected to be *ee, ff, ll, oo,* or *ss,* while in any three-letter construction of the type *xyx, x* must be a vowel if *y* is a consonant, and *vice versa*, as in the case of the words *aga* and *gag*. In all languages, word patterns also tend to form stable and recurring groups. Thus *ant*, in association with *hill* and *bear*, is encountered in English as *ant-hill* and *ant-bear*, but never as *hill-ant* or *bear-ant*. The construction of sentences is likewise governed by established procedure, and though the three words of the phrase *Rest in peace* might conceivably assume the form *In peace rest,* they would not normally be found in arrangements such as *Rest peace in, Peace rest in,* or *In rest peace.*

The usefulness of such characteristics as an aid to decipherment will be apparent, as will the incidence of proper names (*vide infra*). But if only a small amount of epigraphic material is available for study, the probable-word technique is likely to prove more effective. As its name suggests, this procedure relies for success upon an intelligent anticipation of probable words and phrases, having regard for the author or authors of the writing, and for the motives which may have inspired it. And often enough, the circumstances will be such that the need for speculation is not very great. Where a once-imposing tomb is concerned, it may be safely assumed that any accompanying inscription will contain the name of some royal personage or other, and proclaim his many virtues and list his numerous triumphs. Hence the search would here be for such time-honoured titularities as "Father of his people," "Beloved of the gods," "Defender of the faith," "King of kings," and so on. Admittedly, the method is essentially one of trial and error, and success in its application requires a certain amount of luck. But human vanity being what it is, that amount does not need to be unduly large. It would be a sorry epitaph, indeed, which, in naming some all-powerful monarch, denied him a mention of his imposing array of titles, or failed to append an account of his many accomplishments, real or supposed. And it would be a singularly incompetent philologist who did not take full advantage of the situation as he found it.

The problem of decipherment where the writing is known, but the language is not, is a much more formidable affair, as the continued failure to gain a satisfactory understanding of Etruscan goes to show. In the absence of a suitable bilingual text, internal analysis, as exemplified by the so-called Combinatory method of G. Passeri, offers the only direct means of approach. Relying on clues as to the nature of the wording (*e.g.*, votive, sepulchral, numerical), there is entailed a tabulating of inscriptions of a like character, and the extracting therefrom of all proper names. An attempt is then made to arrive at the meaning of the remaining words by a careful study of their dispositions (frequent or infrequent appearance; predominantly initial or final; a tendency to be found in pairs), particular note being taken of the occurrence of suffixes, indicative of inflexions of cases (if nouns) or forms of conjugation (if verbs). Tentative meanings can then be assigned to selected words in all the passages in which they appear, in the hope that chance associations of the assumed interpretations will make sense.

The adventitious nature of the procedure will be evident, and any hope of success is small unless there can be discovered a known language with which its unknown counterpart can be compared. To this etymological end, the decipherer seeks to identify the unknown tongue with those of a particular racial group, on the basis of verbal consonance; or, alternatively, the existence of consonance is first assumed, and a search for possible meanings made among languages containing words which express sounds similar to those of the unknown form of speech.

As for the situation in which neither language nor writing is known, so long as this remains the case, the difficulties cannot be regarded as other than insuperable. Nothing, after all, can be made out of nothing. But as recent progress with two examples long considered to be in the insoluble category —Cretan Linear B and Hittite hieroglyphic—has shown, once even some slight point of contact can be established, unravelment may well be rapid.

Irrespective of whether it is the language or the writing which is unfamiliar, not only the amount of material available for examination is important, but also its age and reliability. Apart from the bearing which the state of preservation may have on legibility, the age of specimens is of concern because, where a literature has been in the course of development for many centuries, early examples of it may bear little resemblance to subsequent versions, and the decipherer is likely to find that he faces not one problem, but several. As for the question of accuracy, the possibility of the existence of errors in the original material, or of their introduction into copies of it, must always be kept in mind.

As is now realised, the lengthy inscription on the famous Rock of Behistun, in Persia, contains not a few mistakes and, as it cannot readily be studied *in situ* owing to its inaccessible position, there is always the chance that, to the errors of the engraver, those of a copyist have been added. This problem also applies to writings on the clay tablets and papyrus rolls which have been collected in their thousands from sites in Babylonia, Egypt, and elsewhere. For even when the actual documents are available for study, there is often no certainty that the version before the student is an original text; it may well be a copy of a copy, to an unknown degree. In such circumstances, the possibilities of corruption are considerable. If the copyist of an original text makes a mistake once in 100 times, and a second copyist goes wrong twice in 100 times, the relative correctness of the three sets of writing will be 100, 99, and 98, assuming that none of the errors have cancelled themselves out. But if the second copyist had used the defective product of the first, his percentage would be only 97.02.

Finally, a reference must here be made to the vexed question of transliteration. Even when scholars are able to understand a long-forgotten language, and to write it with fluency and ease, it by no means follows that they are able to speak it. Nor is the difficulty merely that there are sounds in every language for which the phonetic elements of some other tongue are bound to be inadequate. Rather is it likely to be the case that it simply is not known how the ancients pronounced many of their words. This is certainly true of the Egyptians who, in their writing, as already noted, anticipated the early Semitic habit of omitting vowels. Thus a word such as *pet* would appear as *pt*, the speaker supplying the missing vocalisation. But to the often baffled scholar of to-day, *pt* might equally well stand for *pat*, *pit*, *pot*, or *put*, or for any other permissible combination of vowels and the consonants *p* and *t*.

Several thousand years hence, when phoneticists of the future are busily engaged in making a study of 20th-century speech sounds, they should encounter no such difficulty —thanks to the advent of the magnetic tape recorder. But whether they will be able to comprehend the verbal macaronics of the moment ("It's the most—but what's with the square?") is, of course, another matter.

CHAPTER II

THE EGYPTIAN HIEROGLYPHS

I

There is evidence that the language of the ancient Egyptians is related not only to Arabic, Hebrew, Babylonian, and other Semitic tongues, but that it is also akin to certain African speech forms, a possibility which lends colour to a tradition, long held by the peoples of the Nile, that the home of some of their ancestors was the mysterious Land of Punt, now identified, after much conjecture and disputation, as Somaliland.

The spoken language appears to have been reduced to a readable script, by way of the usual pictographic-ideographic route, long before the rival kingdoms of Upper and Lower Egypt were united under Menes, the first of the dynastic rulers. This federative event nevertheless constitutes a notable philological landmark, and an early attempt to determine the date of it (though not, of course, for linguistic reasons) was made by Herodotus when he visited Egypt about the middle of the 5th century B.C. On being informed by the priests that no less than 340 other kings had occupied the throne of that ancient land, the Greek historian, by a process of simple if somewhat misleading arithmetic (he allowed a period of 100 years for every three generations), reached the conclusion that the royal line extended back almost to 12000 B.C.!

More precise information on the point was subsequently

provided by Manetho, high priest of Sebennytos, who compiled a history of his native country at the command, it is said, of Ptolemy II Philadelphus. Of this extensive work, no more than a few extracts now remain, but a known feature of the undertaking was its arrangement of the Pharaohs (as they had come to be called) into thirty royal houses or dynasties, beginning with that of Menes. More or less credible details of individual reign lengths were appended, and thus aided, modern enquiry has lowered the date of the start of the dynastic period very considerably. After making due allowance for the practice of co-regency, Flinders Petrie ascribed the event to about 5000 B.C., and still more recent research has indicated that in all probability even this is much too high a figure, and that 3000 B.C. would be nearer the mark—with which estimation results independently obtained by means of the new radio-carbon dating technique have shown themselves to be in close agreement. Thus the Vizier Hemaka, a contemporary of King Udi of the 1st dynasty, was dated 2850 ± 200 B.C. by this method.

The dynastic period of Egyptian history witnessed in turn the rise of the Old Kingdom (an era terminated by a series of internal disorders at the close of the 6th dynasty); the emergence of the Middle Kingdom (a restorative epoch, embracing the 11th and 12th dynasties); and the appearance of the New Kingdom (which flourished throughout the 18th to 20th dynasties). There then began a final collapse, heralded by a succession of invasions from Libya, Nubia, Assyria, and Persia (22nd to 30th dynasties), which culminated in the bloodless conquest of Egypt by Alexander the Great in 332 B.C.

For the whole of this period—a matter of some 3,000 years—hieroglyphic writing was in use, at first for general, and later for specialised, purposes. But in the absence of any general system of education, few Egyptians can have understood "the god's words," nor was it ever intended otherwise. A knowledge of the hieroglyphs was reserved for the priests, who established their own schools for the tuition of initiates and the many scribes needed to undertake secretarial duties, including the producing of ecclesiastical works such as the so-called Book of the Dead.

Associated with the hieroglyphic writing was a cursive script known to the Greeks as hieratic. This offshoot, which also made its appearance in very early times, resulted from the use of reed pen and papyrus as an adjunct to chisel and stone. Thanks to the nature of the new writing materials, the angular shapes of the conventional characters tended to become increasingly rounded in appearance, until their original pictorial forms were no longer clearly recognisable. Moreover, the direction of the writing, originally vertical, subsequently became horizontal, progressing from right to left. Nor was this all. A much later development took place about the time of the 25th (Ethiopian) dynasty, when there was evolved from the hieratic writing a still more rapid and abbreviated hand, termed demotic. Thus it came about that, during the Greco-Roman period, three distinct styles of Egyptian writing were simultaneously employed, each more or less restricted as to its use—the hieroglyphic for sacred inscriptions on the walls of monuments and temples; the hieratic for priestly purposes; and the demotic for the needs of daily life. Of these three forms, the role of the hieroglyphic (in which all the characters are pictures) has been likened to that of our printed word; the hieratic (in which only the salient features of the pictures are preserved) corresponds to ordinary handwriting; and the demotic (in which the characters have been so modified that they bear little resemblance to the original hieroglyphs) may be regarded as the equivalent of modern shorthand.

With the death of Alexander at Babylon in 323 B.C., his world conquests were divided among his generals, one of whom, Ptolemy the son of Lagus, secured for himself the province of Egypt. Here, after governing as a satrap for nearly twenty years, he finally assumed the royal title, and so founded the 31st or Macedonian dynasty which now bears his name. From the onset, his authority lay in his troops, but prudence dictated that the age-old bond between church and state should be maintained, and he and his successors were careful to cultivate the friendship of the all-powerful priesthood. To this end, rich endowments of corn and money were made to various temples, and others were restored or rebuilt; many new shrines and altars were founded; and enemies of the priests were suppressed. In these most favourable circumstances, it is hardly surprising that the accredited representatives of the high gods enthusiastically endorsed the rule of the intruders, whom they proceeded to deify in accordance with time-honoured practice. And the new rulers, for their part, quickly responded by indulging in the immemorial Egyptian custom of brother-and-sister marriages (the pharaonic law of succession was through the female line), though this did not preclude them from acquiring other wives as well.

Evidence of the state of amity which existed between the temporal and spiritual leaders of the land is provided by a series of official decrees, copies of some of which have been preserved. Thus in 238-237 B.C., the divinity of Ptolemy III Euergetes I was proclaimed by the ecclesiastical authorities, who enumerated his many virtues, and accorded his queen and himself the title Euergtai—Benefactor Gods. This extolment (the Decree of Canopus) was inscribed on stone in Greek and Egyptian, the latter appearing in both demotic and hieroglyphic form, *i.e.*, there were three versions in all. It was a copy of a similar tripartite proclamation, issued in 196 B.C. on the occasion of the coronation of Ptolemy V Epiphanes, then a child of thirteen, which accidentally came to light some 2,000 years later in the vicinity of the Rosetta (western) mouth of the Nile, and so made possible the decipherment of the hieroglyphs. A second, and no less vital, clue was provided by a priestly expression of appreciation of an action by Ptolemy VII Euergetes II, as will in due course be recounted.

During the reign of a 26th-dynasty Pharaoh (Amasis II, 569-525 B.C.) the Greek tongue was brought to Egypt by groups of adventurous merchants and artisans, who had been encouraged to cross the Mediterranean and establish trading posts at Naucratis and elsewhere in the Delta region. And with the advent of the Ptolemies two centuries or so later, Greek became the language of the court, whereafter it was inevitable that it should begin to assume an ever-increasing importance among the Egyptians themselves. Evidence of this is provided by the priestly decrees aforementioned, in that these bilingual inscriptions were first drafted in Greek—an order of events which is revealed by the fact that although the demotic accounts follow the Greek text closely enough, there are not a few misleading improvisations in the hieroglyphic versions. Ultimately, steps were taken to express Egyptian speech in Greek characters, and when it was found that these did not fully meet the needs of the native language, seven additional symbols were taken from the demotic and hieratic scripts. A composite alphabet, consisting of thirty-one letters, thus came into general use.

The rising power of Rome, meanwhile, had begun to cast a shadow over the Ptolemaic domain, though it was not until 58 B.C. that an opportunity for active interference in the affairs of Egypt occurred. In that year, finding himself deposed by a populace grown weary of his many excesses, Ptolemy XI Auletes appealed to Rome for help, and in return for the payment of a staggering bribe (which nearly beggared his luckless subjects), Aulus Gabinus, the Roman pro-consul of Syria, was instructed to assist him. The reinstated monarch died seven years later, naming as joint heirs to the kingdom his children Cleopatra VII and Ptolemy XII. But the two quarrelled, and the brother expelled his sister, whereupon Rome again intervened, this time in the person of Julius Caesar. After the death of Ptolemy XII in the fighting which ensued, Caesar not only restored Cleopatra to the throne, but he presented her with an offspring (Caesarion) as a slight token of his esteem, and then obligingly found her a husband. The son she appears to have cherished, but the husband —a younger brother, Ptolemy XIII—she promptly murdered on learning of Caesar's own assassination. Thereafter, foiled in an attempt to further her cause by the spell she cast over Mark Antony, and failing to captivate by her charms the unresponsive Octavian, she died by her own hand in 30 B.C., and Egypt became a province of Rome.

In the years which followed, the Caesars also set themselves up as Pharaohs, and caused accounts of their activities to be recorded in the mysterious hieroglyphs. But by this time, the number of those who could understand the ancient writing had begun to decline, and it is significant that in his account of a visit paid by Germanicus Caesar to Thebes, Tacitus records that it was an aged priest who was called upon to read to the royal visitor from the monuments: the younger brethren were no doubt more at home with Greek. What led to a final abandonment of the traditional mode of writing, however, was the coming of Christianity. As to this, little is known about the conversion of Egypt, apart from a highly improbable story which tells of a visit supposedly paid by St. Mark to Alexandria in the second half of the 1st century A.D. But that the substitute faith continued to gain adherents is shown by the fact that towards the end of the 4th century, the Christians found themselves sufficiently powerful to enforce the closing of the ancient temples, and with them the schools for scribes. The Egyptian language, meanwhile, expressed by the 31 characters of the expanded Greek alphabet, continued to be employed in this, its Coptic form—so-called because of its use by the Christianised Egyptians, or Copts. Even after the Arab conquest of Egypt (639-642), the followers of Yahweh contrived to live side by side with those of Allah under the Omayyad Caliphate, despite the special tax which was levied on Christians and other infidels. Subsequently, in the face of more oppressive measures, many Copts found it expedient to embrace the Islamic faith. A stubborn minority, however, continued to resist, and a million or more of their descendants reside in Egypt to this day. But their speech is no longer Egyptian, for by the end of the 16th century, Coptic, as a spoken language, had been supplanted by Arabic. As for the ancient scripts, these did not long survive the closing of the temple schools, and the latest example of hieroglyphic writing, found at Philae, is dated A.D. 394. Not long thereafter, it may be surmised, the last surviving exponent of the art was in his grave.

II

In all, knowledge of the Egyptian hieroglyphs was lost for some 1,400 years (A.D. 400-1800), though their study in modern times may be said to date from the publication of G. V. P. Bolzani's otherwise inconsequential *Hieroglyphica* (Basle, 1556). Sundry attempts at decipherment were made by Mercati and others in the following century, but for 200 years these and subsequent investigators were led astray by the often conflicting accounts of the early Greek and native writers on the subject, few of whom seem to have had any real understanding of the picture writing. Whereas some authors were content merely to repeat such information as was given to them, often through an interpreter, others appear to have placed considerable reliance upon their own imaginations, and the result, in sum, was an admixture of not very enlightening fact and profoundly misleading fiction. And an added difficulty which confronted the modern enquirer was the problem of deciding which was which.

Inasmuch as the hieroglyphs, in the later stages of Egyptian history, were employed almost exclusively for religious purposes, Herodotus and Diodorus were to this extent justified in describing them as "sacred letters," as opposed to the "popular letters" of the demotic script, which in later times served business and other everyday needs. It is improbable, however, that either of these historians realised that the two forms of writing, superficially so different, were essentially the same. More knowledgeable in this respect, perhaps, was Chaeremon of Naucratis (1st century A.D.), an official of the great Library of Alexandria. He wrote a treatise on the hieroglyphs, of which work, however, only a few extracts survived. Hardly more helpful to would-be decipherers was Plutarch's *On Isis and Osiris*, in which the author emphasised the mysterious nature of the pictorial script, and likened it to the maxims of the Pythagoreans. But a more useful clue (if it could be relied upon) was provided by Josephus, who implied that historical accounts were to be found among the inscriptions on the monuments, and who, moreover, declared that the celebrated annals of Manetho had been compiled with their aid. The Greek theologian Clement of Alexandria, on the other hand, in making reference in his *Stromateis* to the existence of three kinds of Egyptian writing—epistolographic (demotic), hieratic, and hieroglyphic—was another who described the last-named as "sacred carved letters", and inferred that they were of a purely symbolic character. More confusion still was spread by the outpourings of a certain Horapollo, a native of Phaenebythis, in the nome of Panopolis, renowned in its day as a centre of literary activity. Horapollo is the reputed author of a multi-volume work entitled *Hieroglyphika*, two books of which, purporting to have been translated by one Philippus, are extant. This Greek version, now ascribed by some authorities to as late as the 15th century, contains lists of sign pictures and their meanings, complete with examples of their use, a compilation which in the light of present-day knowledge appears to combine possible erudition with undoubted charlatanry. As to this, it has been suggested that the information was provided for use by manufacturers of amulets and other charms, which would at any rate help to explain how it happens that Horapollo (or Philippus) gives the correct meanings of many of the hieroglyphs, in conjunction with nonsensical interpretations in regard thereto—*e.g.*, that a goose stands for "son," because of that animal's great concern for its young; that a hare means "open," because the eyes of the hare never close; and so on.

Naïve inanities of this sort had a seemingly irresistible appeal to the medieval mind, and Galtruchius and his translator D'Assigny made extensive use of them in *The Poetic Histories* (London, 1672), under the heading *A Short Collection of the Famous Mysteries of the Egyptians named*

Hieroglyphicks, an account interspersed with tales of such kindred marvels as the River Sabbatius, in Syria, so named because, although for six days of the week it flowed seawards in normal fashion, on the seventh day its waters regularly came reverently to a halt; and of another remarkable torrent known as the Virgin's Stream, notable for the fact that it was reputed to have "a pleasant and an excellent virtue upon Maids, whose unhappiness it was to forget themselves, and lose their virginity." Merely by bathing in this salubrious *Virgo Aqua*, it was claimed, the deflowered would forthwith "recover again the stolen jewel, and become as perfect virgins as before." Such were some of the charming irrelevancies which a 17th-century student of the Egyptian hieroglyphs was likely to encounter in the course of his enquiries.

From the beginning of the 18th century, however, there was a growing demand for a sight of the actual writings of the monuments, and P. Lucas, R. Pococke, C. Niebuhr, and other venturesome travellers of the period copied and published examples of many of the inscriptions they chanced to find. Among these visitors to Egypt was F. L. Norden, who made an attempt to date the introduction of hieroglyphic writing by reference to the pyramids. He reasoned (wrongly, as it has since transpired) that because the Egyptians invariably covered their buildings with these symbols, the pyramids, which were seemingly devoid of inscriptions of any kind, must have been constructed before the pictorial script was invented. In fact, the Great Pyramid (of Kheuf) belongs to the 4th dynasty, whereas the hieroglyphs antedate Menes. Moreover, as the subsequent discovery of what are known as the Pyramid Texts has demonstrated, the stonework of some of these structures was not quite as blank as Norden supposed.

In 1636, meanwhile, the Jesuit Athanasius Kircher, among other of his attainments a professor of mathematics, had published a work on Coptic, a study of which had convinced him that it preserved, in alphabetic guise, the language of the ancient Egyptians. This was a realisation of prime importance, but when he then essayed to utilise Coptic (which he termed *Lingua Ægyptiaca Restituta*) to fathom the meaning of the hieroglyphic writing, his results were as worthless as they were ludicrous. Obsessed by a belief in the supposedly sacred nature of the monumental inscriptions, he rendered the seven signs of the Greek title *Autocrator*, associated with the name of Domitian on the Pamphilian Obelisk, as "The author of fruitfulness and of all vegetation is Osiris, whose productive force was produced in his kingdom out of heaven through the holy Mophta." But in other fields, Kircher was an eminent and highly respected man of learning, and if the absurdity of his hieroglyphic elucidations was not apparent to his admiring contemporaries, it was because the depth of his ignorance was more than matched by that of their own. At all events, from 1650 onwards, he published several volumes of this imaginative nonsense, and thereby earned for himself the reputation of being an Egyptologist of outstanding merit, an illusion which persisted long after his death in 1680.

If nothing else, Kircher's misinterpretations at least helped to bring the question of hieroglyphic decipherment to the notice of the scientific world, and throughout the 18th century a succession of savants and scholars—A. Gordon, N. Freret, P. A. L. D'Origny, J. D. Marsham, C. de Gebelin, J. H. Schumacher, J. G. Koch, T. Ch. Tychsen, and P. E. Jablonski among them—grappled with the problem, and hopefully published the results of their labours, which almost without exception were as uninspired as they were in vain. And ironically enough, it was a predilection for the inherited misconceptions of the past which blinded these investigators to the worth of a comparatively accurate translation of the hieroglyphic writing on the so-called Flaminian Obelisk, an authoritative interpretation which was dismissed as undeserving of serious consideration!

The inscribed shaft, nearly 80 feet high, and weighing some 230 tons, had originally been set up by Seti I (*c*. 1300 B.C.) at Heliopolis. Octavian (*alias* Augustus) caused it to be transported to Rome, where in 10 B.C. it was erected in the Circus Maximus in commemoration of the conquest of Egypt. When in the course of time it fell down, it lay hidden beneath the debris from surrounding ruins until it was rediscovered and set up again on the orders of Pope Sixtus V (Felice Peretti) towards the end of the 16th century. In the meantime, the wording it bore had long ago been translated by an Egyptian priest named Hermapion, a rendering which was preserved for an incredulous posterity by the 4th-century historian Ammianus Marcellinus, who quoted it in its entirety. But whereas according to Hermapion the branch and the bee symbol meant "king" (*n-sw-bit*, "he who belongs to the sedge and the bee," *i.e.*, ruler of Upper and Lower Egypt), Kircher translated it as "flytrap"!

The prevailing darkness, however, was not without an occasional flash of enlightenment. The Orientalist de Guignes, though he subscribed to the notion that the Chinese were Egyptian colonists, also expressed the opinion that some of the hieroglyphic symbols were determinatives, akin to the Chinese keys or radicals. And the redoubtable Bishop William Warburton, in his *Divine Legation of Moses* (London, 1737-41), demonstrated by actual quotations from a number of the early writers that, contrary to the contentions of Kircher and his school, the hieroglyphs had not always served an exclusively religious purpose. But the suggestion which was to prove of decisive value concerned the oval rings, or cartouches, which were frequently to be seen in the inscriptions.

As is now known, these rings are representative of a loop formed by a double thickness of rope, the ends of which are tied in such a manner that they appear as a straight line. The area thus enclosed, originally circular, in time assumed an oval shape, a gradual process of elongation doubtless brought about by an increase in the number of the hieroglyphic symbols which it was called upon to accommodate. Significantly, the word which the Egyptians used to describe the cartouche was derived from the verb "to encircle," and it has been suggested that the device was introduced in order that the ruler might be depicted (in the terms of a familiar pharaonic phrase) as the undisputed monarch of all "that which is encircled by the sun." But however this may be, the cartouche was a noticeable feature of hieroglyphic writing, and to at least some of the 18th-century scholars, it seemed reasonable to suppose that the oval enclosure was intended to draw attention to an inscriptional item of particular importance—an idea which occurred in turn to J. J. Barthélemy, de Guignes, and G. Zoega, who conjectured that the item in question might be some sacred formula, or a royal name. Events were in due course to confirm the soundness of this reasoning, but not before the oracular Kircher, on encountering the cartouche of the Pharaoh Apries, proclaimed to the world that its contents signified that "The benefits of the divine Osiris are to be procured by means of sacred ceremonies and of the chain of the Genii, in order that the benefits of the Nile may be obtained."

At the close of the 18th century, the prospect of achieving a genuine understanding of the hieroglyphs seemed as far off as ever. But at this juncture, Napoleon Bonaparte, persuaded of the impracticability of a direct invasion of England, struck at her Indian possessions by way of Egypt, which Turkish domain he reached and temporarily subdued in July, 1798. And in August of the following year, a group of French soldiers, engaged in excavatory work at the ruined Fort Rashîd (renamed St. Julien by the invaders) near the Rosetta mouth of the Nile, chanced to unearth a slab of black basalt, one face of which was covered by three panels of unfamiliar writing. Two of the inscriptions proved to be unreadable. But the third version was written in Greek!

III

The slab measured some 3 feet 9 inches long × 2 feet 4½ inches wide × 11 inches thick, and the importance of the find, notwithstanding its badly damaged condition, was at once realised. Of the three texts, fourteen lines of hieroglyphic writing were uppermost, though each line had lost its beginning and its end, and much appeared to be missing; the middle version, written in a script similar to that to be seen on various papyri, contained thirty-two lines, nearly half of them incomplete; and at the bottom were the Greek uncials, twenty-six of the fifty-four lines of which were mutilated at the ends.

Replicas of the inscription were despatched to Paris for the attention of European scholars, but before the Rosetta Stone itself (as it came to be called) could be transported to France, British intervention in Egypt brought about the collapse of Napoleon's campaign, and the bilingual prize was secured for England. It arrived safely at Deptford in 1802, remained for a while at the address of the Society for Antiquaries, and was then transferred to the British Museum (where it still lies) with the compliments of George III.

The Greek account, which was translated forthwith, told of the endorsement of Ptolemy V Epiphanes by a gathering of priests at Memphis in 196 B.C. And it revealed that among other things, it had been decreed that copies of the proclamation were to be set up in all the temples of Egypt of the 1st, 2nd, and 3rd class. That this very considerable undertaking was fully carried out may be doubted, but it is of interest to note that other transcripts have since been found —one of them, inscribed with thirty-one lines of hieroglyphic text, was discovered at Nubayrah, near Damanhur, in Lower Egypt, in the 1880's.

From the information imparted by the Greek version of the Rosetta Stone, a number of points seemed clear. In the first place, it was evident that the three texts were substantially the same, and that the Greek version of the edict was repeated in the "writing of the speech of the god" and in the "writing of the books"—that is to say, in both hieroglyphic and demotic characters. And this being so, the important fact emerged, not only that the hieroglyphic writing continued to be used and understood in the days of the Ptolemies, but also that it could no longer be regarded as having served an exclusively religious purpose.

Early attempts at decipherment were nevertheless concentrated on the demotic text, the cursive signs of which were widely held to be alphabetic, and were in fact not unlike Arabic. An added advantage was the relative completeness of this portion of the inscription, and in 1802 the oriental scholar Sylvestre de Sacy, with the aid of the Greek account, succeeded in recognising several names, including that of Ptolemy. But even when in possession of the groups of signs thus identified, he failed to establish an alphabet, and finally declared the problem to be insoluble, reportedly saying that it remained as "untouched as the Holy Ark of the Covenant."

The baffled de Sacy handed over to the Swedish diplomatist J. D. Akerblad, who was at that time engaged in studying languages in Paris. Akerblad, a man of considerable attainments, carried on from the point at which his predecessor had left off. By making a judicious comparison of the two texts, he contrived to identify in the demotic version every one of the proper names which occurred in the Greek section, together with a few other words, all of which proved to be alphabetically written. This initial success convinced him of the correctness of the assumption that the demotic writing was alphabetic throughout, an erroneous conclusion which ensured that such progress as he had made promptly came to a stop.

Thereafter, for more than a decade, serious endeavour was almost wholly replaced by the idle speculations of the theorists. Foremost among these was Count N. G. de Palin, who maintained that the act of translating the Psalms of David into Chinese could be relied upon to reproduce the contents of Egyptian papyri. As for the writing on the Rosetta Stone, he claimed that he had comprehended its meaning at a glance, and in making public the results of this lightning interpretation, assured his audience that the very rapidity of his method had "preserved him from the systematic errors that must arise from excessive contemplation." The Abbe Tandeau de St. Nicolas, on the other hand, was convinced that the hieroglyphs were merely a decorative device, and not a system of writing at all, a belief not shared by an ingenious investigator from Dresden, who contrived to read the whole of the Greek text into its fragmentary hieroglyphic counterpart. And in 1806, the otherwise reputable Orientalist Baron von Hammer-Purgstall took the time and trouble to produce a translation of *Ancient Alphabets*, a work containing a supposed explanation of the hieroglyphs which had been written by an Arab charlatan calling himself Ahmed Bin Abuker Wahshih, while as late as 1821, at a time when fact was at last beginning to outweigh fiction, it was solemnly announced that a reading of the inscription on the Pamphilian Obelisk had disclosed details of a victory of the pious over the wicked in the year 4000 B.C.

The problem, meanwhile, had attracted the attention of no less a personage than the Cambridge scholar Dr. Thomas Young, already famous as the propounder of the undulatory theory of light. Young, who was born at Milverton, Somerset, in 1773, is said to have become a fluent reader by the time he was two years old, and to have possessed a knowledge of a dozen foreign languages, including Arabic, Ethiopic, Persian, and Turkish, before he attained the age of twenty. In 1798, he had the good fortune to receive a handsome bequest from an uncle, a legacy which made him financially independent, and he was thus left free to pursue his many and varied interests, which ranged (as his published papers show) from the habits of spiders and the atmosphere of the moon to epicycloidal curves, the theory of tides, diseases of the chest —and hieroglyphs.

The Rosetta Stone and its associated problems were brought to his notice in 1814, when his friend Sir W. E. Rouse Boughton sent him an Egyptian papyrus, written in cursive characters, which had been recovered from a Theban mummy case. Thereafter, armed with a copy of the Decree of Memphis, and with Akerblad's account of his efforts to decipher it, Young went to Worthing and began to study the matter. His first move was to cut up his copy of the three versions of the Decree into pieces, and to paste the thirty-two lines of

42 LOST LANGUAGES

the demotic text on to sheets of paper. Then, having due regard for the fact that the Egyptian writing was known to read from right to left, he apportioned to each group of signs those Greek words which he considered to be their equivalent. He also attempted to repeat the process with the hieroglyphic section, but was greatly handicapped by the fact that it was incomplete, and that it was not known exactly how much of it was missing.

Like de Sacy and Akerblad before him, Young was guided by the existence of identical or similar words in the Greek version, *e.g.*, the 4th and 17th lines contained the names Alexander and Alexandria, and these appeared to be represented by two groups of signs, which closely resembled one another, in the 2nd and 10th lines of the demotic section. Again, the word "king" occurred in Greek no less than thirty-seven times, and could be matched only by a group of demotic characters which were repeated about thirty times. Similarly, there were eleven mentions of the name "Ptolemy," and its Egyptian equivalent could hardly be other than a particular group of characters which occurred fourteen times, though in more than one form, thus (reading from right to left):

$\{y/\!/\!/\cup \!\not\!\!\!\!\!/\,\epsilon\,z\,).$ 1

$\int \varsigma \cup R \wedge \cup \!\not\!\!\!\!\!/\,\epsilon\,z\,).$ 2

From this, it was evident that in the demotic script, the cartouche, though not dispensed with in its entirety, was so abbreviated and amended that it was represented only by its ends:

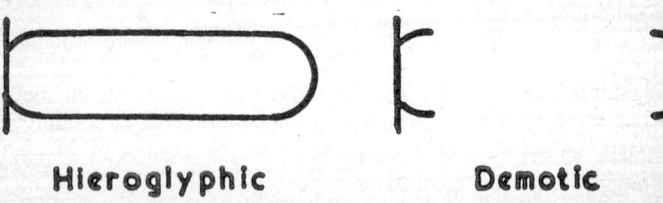

Hieroglyphic   **Demotic**

By providing himself with numerous points of subdivision, whereby all the intermediate demotic sections arranged them-

THE EGYPTIAN HIEROGLYPHS

selves in close proximity to the corresponding passages in Greek, Young was able to compile a Greek-demotic vocabulary containing eighty-six groups, most of them correct, and later in 1814 he ventured to read a complete translation of the middle text before the Society for Antiquaries. This effort, however, was based largely on guesswork, for its author could hardly have been aware that the demotic section contained passages for which there was no Greek equivalent. Nor is it likely that he realised the Decree had originally been drafted in Greek, and that the Egyptian versions were merely paraphrases, though the fact that the proper names did not occur the same number of times in the Greek and demotic texts must have suggested that a literal translation was not concerned. As matters turned out, another thirty-six years were to pass before H. K. Brugsch was able to demonstrate that he had mastered the true principle of demotic interpretation, and it was not until 1880 (by which time the hieroglyphics had been virtually deciphered) that E. Revillout published his *Crestomathie demotique*, in which the entire text was subjected to a word-by-word analysis, accompanied by its Greek rendering and its French equivalent.

During the next two years, meanwhile, Young gave increasing thought to the problem presented by the hieroglyphs, and the idea eventually occurred to him that in a country where such a pictorial script was in use, native scribes, if called upon to write the unfamiliar name of some foreign conqueror, would do so by resorting to the *phonetic* values of some of the characters, without regard to any ideographic meaning which might attach to them. In other words, if (as there seemed to be little doubt), the names of Egyptian kings were distinguished by the royal oval, and if the name "Ptolemy" could be identified in its hieroglyphic form on the Rosetta Stone, it should then be possible to discover the phonetic values of the signs concerned.

That the hieroglyphs might possess alphabetic values had earlier been conjectured by several scholars, but to Young must go the credit for being the first to show that, in respect of some of them, this appeared to be the case. As it happened, Ptolemy's name was the only one which was to be found in its entirety on the damaged upper part of the Stone, though at the time there was no way of knowing this. As Young himself afterwards explained, he experienced considerable difficulty in identifying with this name groups of hieroglyphs which not only varied in different parts of the inscription, but which unexpectedly and most disconcertingly appeared in places where there was no corresponding name in Greek.

In the 6th line of the hieroglyphic text, the following symbols appear in a cartouche (for the sake of convenience, in this and subsequent examples, the direction of the writing has been reversed so that it reads from left to right):

In the same line, however, and again in the 14th line, this same group of signs is repeated, but with additions:

Now, as Young had already noted, the name "Ptolemy" likewise exhibits variations in the demotic text, and the Greek version indicated that the longer form of the name contained titles. He accordingly gave his attention to the shorter of the two cartouches, transcribing its contents thus:

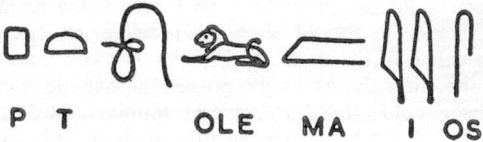

This equating of the Greek P T O L E M A I O S with its Egyptian equivalent was the first promising attempt to decipher any part of the hieroglyphic inscription. Young, however, was unmindful of the Egyptian practice of omitting vowels, and this led him into error. He was mistaken in regarding the 3rd sign as inessential (during the later stages of the writing, it was in fact used in secondary capacity to denote the vowel O), the 4th symbol should have been L, and the last simply S, making P T O L M I S, that is, P T O L (E) M (A) I(O) S. Even so, he was now able to recognise the name Ptolemy I Soter on the ceiling of a temple at Karnak, and correctly assumed that an accompanying cartouche referred to the Pharaoh's wife, Berenice. But in his interpretation of this name, he was less fortunate. As luck would have it, the one symbol which was common to both names led him astray, and apart from misreading B as BIR, the identification of the letter N was all that he achieved. Thus, out of a total of thirteen signs in the two cartouches, he managed to read six correctly, three partly so, and four wrongly. But he was, of course, unaware of this, and these initial errors, though not particularly serious in themselves, inevitably gave rise to yet more mistakes when he attempted to apply his rudimentary alphabet to the contents of other cartouches, with the result that he contrived to read Arsinoe for Autocrator, and Euergetes for Caesar.

Nevertheless, it was Young's discoveries, as outlined in a special contribution to the 1819 edition of the *Encyclopaedia Britannica*, which pointed the way to the decipherment of the hieroglyphs. He not only confirmed that the cartouches contained royal names, and proved that these began at the oval's rounded end, but he also showed the equivalence of the several forms of Egyptian script, established that the writing was to be read in the direction in which the characters faced, and demonstrated the all-important fact of its quasi-alphabetical nature. He was aware, too, that numerals were expressed by strokes, that plurals were formed either by repeating the appropriate hieroglyph three times, or by writing three strokes after it, and that different characters could on occasion have the same sound (principle of homophony), while others (such as the two symbols used in late texts as an indication of femininity) could be employed as determinatives.

It was at this point that Young gave up, contenting himself with the remark that a continued application of his methods would result in the discovery of the remainder of the alphabetic signs. But if he really believed this to be the case, it is difficult to understand why he did not continue his investigations, unless he sensed that he was no longer making any headway. At all events, the success which might well have been his was soon to be achieved by another, and with it, world-wide acclaim.

IV

Jean François Champollion, surnamed *le Jeune* in order to distinguish him from his elder brother, Jean Jacques, was born in 1790 at Figeac, in the *Département du Lot*, and by the time he was twelve years old he had already evinced an unusual interest in oriental languages. At Grenoble, where he had been taken by his brother in 1801, he met the famous mathematician Jean Baptiste Fourier, who happened to have been one of the scientific members of Napoleon's ill-fated Egyptian expedition. Fourier invited the boy to his home, and there showed him his collection of Egyptian antiquities. The examples of ancient writing fascinated the visitor, and on learning that the script could neither be read nor understood, Champollion is said to have made a youthful decision to dedicate his life to the task of its decipherment.

To this end, he intensified his linguistic and historical studies, and eventually accompanied his brother to Paris, where, as a pupil of de Sacy, he became acquainted with the inscriptions on the Rosetta Stone. In 1809, at the age of eighteen, he took up an appointment as professor of history at the Lyceum of Grenoble, only to find himself proscribed a few years later because of his Bonapartist sympathies. He left Grenoble, but was able to return there in 1817, where he served as librarian at the local Academy of Sciences until, once again faced with a charge of treason, he fled to Paris and sought refuge with his brother.

Throughout these troubled years, Champollion's interest in Egypt and its mysterious writings never flagged. But although he was aware that Barthélemy, Zoega, and others inclined to the belief that the ancient scripts were of an alphabetic nature, he himself was for long unable to accept this view. As late as 1821, when he published his *De l'écriture hiératique des anciens Egyptiens*, though he showed that the hieratic writing was merely a modification of the hieroglyphic, he also declared that in his considered opinion, its characters were representative of things, not of sounds. Yet, in the following year, not only did he completely abandon this position, but he exhibited a table of phonetic signs to members of the *Académie des Inscriptions et Belles-lettres*, and read to them his now famous communication to the Academy's Permanent Secretary, in which he announced the alphabetical nature of the contents of the cartouches, and demonstrated his ability to decipher them!

How did this *volte-face* come about? What many critics regard as Champollion's complete lack of candour on the subject of the help he derived from the labours of other investigators, in particular those of Thomas Young, makes this a difficult question to answer. Certainly he did his reputation great (and wholly unnecessary) harm by his disinclination to admit that he owed anything to anyone. But the obvious conclusion—that this sudden conversion to phoneticism was prompted by a belated sight of Young's *Encyclopaedia Britannica* contribution—is not necessarily the right answer, and Champollion himself was subsequently at pains to deny that his method was in any way inspired by the discoveries of his distinguished British contemporary.

That the French scholar had long been familiar with the name Ptolemy, both in its demotic and hieroglyphic forms, there is not the slightest doubt, and it is conceivable that, despairing at last of finding a purely ideographic solution, he eventually decided to proceed on the assumption that the symbols might, after all, be phonetic. However this may be, the solitary word "Ptolemy" was not enough: proof required the identification of a second name, a name, moreover, which contained several of the signs found in Ptolemy, that a comparison might show whether or not similar characters had been used to express the same sounds. The hieroglyphic version of the Rosetta Stone offered no help here, but about this time (so his biographer assures us) Champollion obtained a sight of the papyrus *Casati*. This document was written in demotic characters, and in transcribing them into hieroglyphs, he encountered a name which he had reason to believe might be that of Cleopatra. The correctness of this assumption was soon to be confirmed by way of the Philae Obelisk.

The story of this monument, appropriately enough, begins with the offspring of Ptolemy V Epiphanes—with the daughter and the two sons presented to him by his wife Cleopatra I. Two of these three succeeded to the throne as Ptolemy VI Philomater and Cleopatra II, and this Cleopatra, when her husband was later killed in battle, replaced him by her other brother, Ptolemy VII Euergetes II, alias Physcon (fat-bellied). Any regard the new monarch may have had for his deceased brother's children was overshadowed by his concern over their possible effect on the succession, a problem which he quickly solved by disposing of his young nephew, and by marrying his niece. Cleopatra II thus found herself in the unenviable position of being the wife of the murderer of her son and heir, and of having to share her husband with her own daughter (Cleopatra III).

The combined reign began in 193 B.C., and it was to this triumvirate—"King Ptolemy, Queen Cleopatra the Sister, and Queen Cleopatra the Wife, Gods Euergetai"—that the priests of the great temple of Isis, on the Island of Philae, had occasion to address a petition, requesting relief from the unwelcome attention of an army of state officials and their followers who came in a never-ending procession to Philae, demanding food and lodging at the expense of the temple funds, now seriously depleted. The outcome was the issuing of a royal decree, bringing to the notice of those concerned that the annoyance must stop, and in order that the interdiction might be seen by all future visitors to the island, the grateful priests erected an obelisk (one of an unrelated pair) at the temple entrance, suitably inscribed in hieroglyphs and Greek.

In 1815, some 2,000 years later, a fallen column and its base were found at Philae by W. J. Bankes, who had them sent to Alexandria, and from there shipped them to his home at Kingston Lacy, in Dorset, where the obelisk was re-erected. That the hieroglyphic portion of the inscription mentioned both Ptolemy and Cleopatra by name was inferred from the Greek version, an assumption which was confirmed in part when one of the cartouches was found to be almost identical with the 2nd oval on the Rosetta Stone, already recognised as referring to Ptolemy. Bankes rightly concluded that a companion cartouche must make mention of Cleopatra, and copies of the inscription, on which the name of the queen was pencilled, were widely distributed for the benefit of interested scholars. Ironically enough, although Young was one of the first to receive a copy, he failed to make anything of it. As he later explained in his *An Account of Some Recent Discoveries in Hieroglyphic Literature and Egyptian Antiquities including the Author's Original Alphabet as Extended by Mr. Champollion* . . . (London, 1823), in the lithograph sent to him by Bankes, the artist had inadvertently expressed the first letter of the queen's name with a T, instead of with a K, a circumstance which, though trite enough in itself, was sufficient to discourage Young from pursuing the matter further. In the meantime, a copy of this all-important document had also been sent to J. A. Letronne, by whom, in January 1822, it was forwarded to Champollion. . . .

The Greek forms of Ptolemy and Cleopatra have several letters in common, and the crucial test which Champollion proceeded to apply was designed to show whether or not a corresponding duplication of signs was to be observed in the Egyptian version of the two names. It was necessary to make due allowance for the omission of at least some of the vowels, inasmuch as the ten Greek letters of Ptolemaios were expressed by only seven hieroglyphs, though the name Cleopatra, inconsistently enough, was represented by the same number of letters and signs, if the feminine suffix T and its accompanying egg symbol were ignored. A tentative comparison was accordingly made along the following lines:

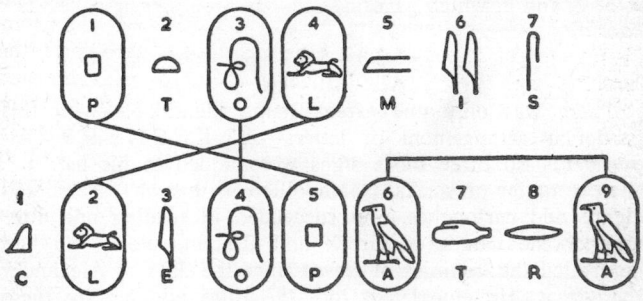

And as was at once apparent, three of the signs belonging to Ptolemy—1st, 3rd, and 4th—were to be found in their correct places in Cleopatra—5th, 4th, and 2nd respectively. Moreover, the first A of Cleopatra (6th sign) was duly repeated at the end of the name (9th sign), though, and rightly, neither this sign nor those representing the letters K, E, and R appeared in Ptolemy. On the other hand, and no less correctly, the hieroglyphs for M, I, and S in Ptolemy had no place in Cleopatra. The only discordant note, indeed, was that introduced by the letter T, which in Ptolemy (2nd sign) different from that of Cleopatra (7th sign), a phenomenon which was with justification regarded as a case of homophony.

Champollion's excitement at this discovery may be imagined. That the Greek names were phonetically expressed by the hieroglyphs there was no longer any doubt. More, he now knew the values of a dozen signs, with the aid of which he would be able to ascertain those of others, a task to which he at once applied himself. He began with the contents of the following cartouche:

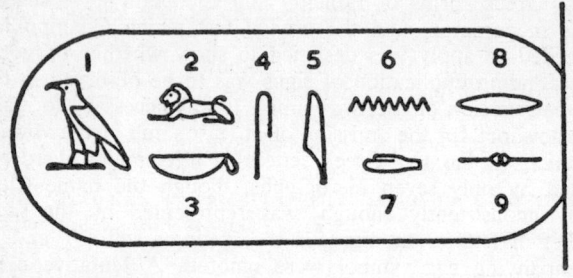

Of these nine signs, he already knew those numbered 1, 2, 4, 5, 7, and 8, which gave:

```
1 2 3 4 5 6 7 8 9
A L   S E   T R
```

There was only one Greek name identifiable with this particular arrangement of letters—ALKSENTRS (Alexander)—so three more signs were added to his list.

In a matter of weeks, Champollion in this way deciphered eighty odd cartouches, and succeeded in reading one after another the names of Greek and Roman rulers who had controlled the destinies of Egypt since the days of Alexander the Great. He elucidated, too, the titles adopted by these monarchs, *e.g.*, Autocrator and Caesar, and as these appellations tended to assume variant forms (Caesar was rendered in half a dozen different hieroglyphic spellings), they added greatly to his ever-growing sign list, which soon passed the 100 mark.

It was by this time clear that the problem, so far as the cartouches of the Greco-Roman period were concerned, had been solved. But what of the pre-Alexandrine Egyptian writing? Young had conjectured that the phonetic hieroglyphs were essentially a Greek innovation, and it was not until 14 September, 1822, that Champollion was able to put the matter to a decisive test. On that memorable day, he received by way of the architect Jean-Nicolas Huyot some impressions of bas-reliefs discovered in an Egyptian temple which unquestionably ante-dated the Greek period. Among this material were several cartouches, and one of them, containing signs with which he was familiar, attracted his attention:

The right-hand character, made up of two identical signs, he at once perceived to be a double form of the letter S of Ptolemy. The middle sign was unknown to him, but it was preceded by an emblem denoting the sun—in Coptic, *Ra* or *Re*. The name thus appeared as R A? S S, a connotation which promptly brought to mind a famous figure in Egyptian history, mentioned in the work of Manetho, and also to be found in the Book of Exodus—Rameses, or Ramesses. Moreover, with the aid of the Rosetta inscription, Champollion was able to associate the unknown centre sign with the Greek word for birthday, and thereby to identify it with the Coptic "be born" (*ms*) or "child" (*mas*), and so obtained a possible explanation of the meaning of the name Ramesses, which appeared to intimate that "Ra begets him," or that the monarch was a "child of Ra."

The probability of the correctness of this rendering was strengthened by his reading of a second cartouche, containing the signs:

Here, two characters encountered in the first cartouche, identified as *mes*, were accompanied by the figure of an ibis, according to the Greeks the symbol of the god Thoth. Hence the name must read T H O T M S S, undoubtedly a reference to the 18th-dynasty Pharaoh Tutmosis, *i.e.*, "Child of Thoth," also mentioned by Manetho.

It was now clear to Champollion that the hieroglyphs were neither exclusively phonetic, nor wholly symbolic, but a combination of the two. A fortnight later, however, when he read to the Academy his *Lettre à M. Dacier relative à l'alphabet des hiéroglyphes phonétiques*, he made no reference to this latest and most important discovery. Instead, it was given to the world in his masterly *Précis du système hiéroglyphique* (Paris, 1824), wherein he announced that the mode of writing employed by the ancient Egyptians was a complex system which was "figurative, symbolical, and phonetic in the same text, in the same phrase, in the same word."

From 1824 until his untimely death eight years later, Champollion laboured incessantly to improve his understanding of the hieroglyphs, first visiting Turin and other European cities to study collections of papyri there, and subsequently journeying to Egypt at the behest of the French Government. He spent two years in Egypt, copying inscriptions, and on his return home began, but did not complete, the immense task of examining and arranging all the material he had gathered. It was while in the middle of this work that he suddenly collapsed and died, whereupon his brother took over, and in due course *Grammaire Egyptienne* (Paris, 1836-41) and *Dictionnaire Egyptien* (Paris, 1843) posthumously appeared.

The worth of Champollion's discoveries by no means gained undisputed recognition during his short lifetime, or indeed until many years after his death. No sooner had he published his *Précis du système hiéroglyphique* than F. A. W. Spohn saw fit to proclaim a belief in the notion that the hieroglyphs were sacred symbols, in which misconception he was supported by G. Seyfarth, while J. Klaproth, at no time a friend of Champollion while he was alive, continued to attack his memory when he was in his grave. And as late as 1860, C. Simonides rejected as fanciful and absurd any suggestion that the hieroglyphs in the cartouches were phonetic, claiming instead that they represented the apophthegms of kings, in support of which contention he extracted from one royal oval a statement to the effect that "The power of truth is everlasting."

But if Champollion had rivals and detractors, he also had advocates and friends. Moreover, his ideas had the great merit that, for the most part, they happened to be right, whereas those of his opponents, in the main, had the misfortune to be wrong, so that in time it was inevitable that he and his supporters should emerge triumphant. Following the appearance of H. Rosellini's *Monumenti d'Egitto e della Nubia* (Pisa, 1832), the eminent Richard Lepsius undertook a detailed appraisal of the situation as it then was. The outcome was the publication of his *Lettre à M. le professeur H. Rosellini* (Rome, 1837), in which he subjected the work of Champollion to a penetrating analysis, and pronounced it basically sound.

Evidence in support of this assessment was later provided

by a party of German savants (and by a coincidence, Lepsius himself chanced to be one of them), who in 1866 unearthed in the vicinity of Tanis a limestone slab, bilingually inscribed —the Decree of Canopus. The upper half of the face of the stele was inscribed with thirty-seven lines of hieroglyphs, and the lower half with seventy-six lines of Greek uncials (a demotic version was relegated to the right-hand edge), and this additional material afforded valuable confirmation of much that had already been surmised about the language and writing of the ancient Egyptians.

The Decree, as elsewhere noted, announced the conferring of certain honours on Ptolemy III Euergetes I by a grateful priesthood. It also revealed that c. 250 B.C. the Egyptian year of 365 days was showing signs of lagging behind the seasons, a defect which it was proposed to remedy by the addition of one day to every fourth year. Curiously enough, another stone, bearing a duplicate of this triple inscription, was found by G. Maspero fifteen years later.

By this time, knowledge of the hieroglyphs had been placed on a much more scientific footing by the grammatical studies of Ludwig Stern and Adolf Erman, and a succession of other important works followed, among them those of K. Sethe, W. Spiegelberg, Sir H. Thompson, H. Grapow, and S. de Buck.

V

In the course of more than 4,000 years, the Egyptian language inevitably underwent considerable change, and the various linguistic stages have been roughly classified as Old Egyptian, Middle Egyptian, Late Egyptian, Demotic, and Coptic. Of these, Old Egyptian almost inperceptibly merged into Middle Egyptian towards the end of the 9th dynasty, and Middle Egyptian, with slight modifications, continued to be used for literary purposes down to Greco-Roman times. Late Egyptian, meanwhile, as typified by the contents of business correspondence and private letters, established itself as the vernacular of the 18th-24th dynasties, while the term Demotic has been reserved for the language used in documents written in the script of that name from the 25th dynasty onwards. Coptic, the Egyptian language in its final form, may be said to date from the 3rd century A.D.

These developments are necessarily reflected in Egyptian writing, the classic age of which is that of Middle Egyptian. The third and latest edition of Sir A. H. Gardiner's monumental *Egyptian Grammar* (London, 1957), which concerns itself with this period, lists some 700 hieroglyphs and their meanings under more than a score of descriptive headings, ranging from Parts of the Human Body (63 signs) and Man and His Occupations (55 signs) to Birds (54 signs), Parts of Mammals (52 signs) and Writing, Games, Music (8 signs). It is thus evident that although the ancient Egyptians professed to believe that the art of writing was bequeathed to them by Thoth, the god of all learning, it was terrestrial, rather than ethereal, affairs which inspired the design of the hieroglyphs themselves. Most of the signs have now been identified, and what Thomas Young vaguely referred to as "a Square, a Semi-circle, a figure often called Feathers, and a vertical line not unlike a Crook" have since been recognised to be representations of a Stool, a Loaf, a Flowering Reed, and a Folded Cloth.

The writing, which is invariably arranged with an eye for decorative effect, appears either in vertical columns or in horizontal lines, and usually reads from right to left, though on occasion it may progress from left to right. On coffins, for example, prayers for the deceased frequently appear as a band of hieroglyphic writing which runs in two directions, beginning at the head of the casket and meeting at its foot, so that half of the invocation reads one way, and half another. Again, there is no separation of words, and unsightly gaps in inscriptions are studiously avoided by a placing of signs in two tiers (if the writing is horizontal) or alongside one another (in the case of vertical columns) in order to utilise as much of the available space as possible. On the other hand, upper signs have precedence over lower, and those exhibiting fronts and backs almost invariably face towards the beginning of the writing of which they are a part, so that the way in which a particular inscription is intended to be read is seldom in doubt, even though the choice may be one of four possible arrangements (Fig. 2).

As a rule, any given hieroglyph may be regarded as coming

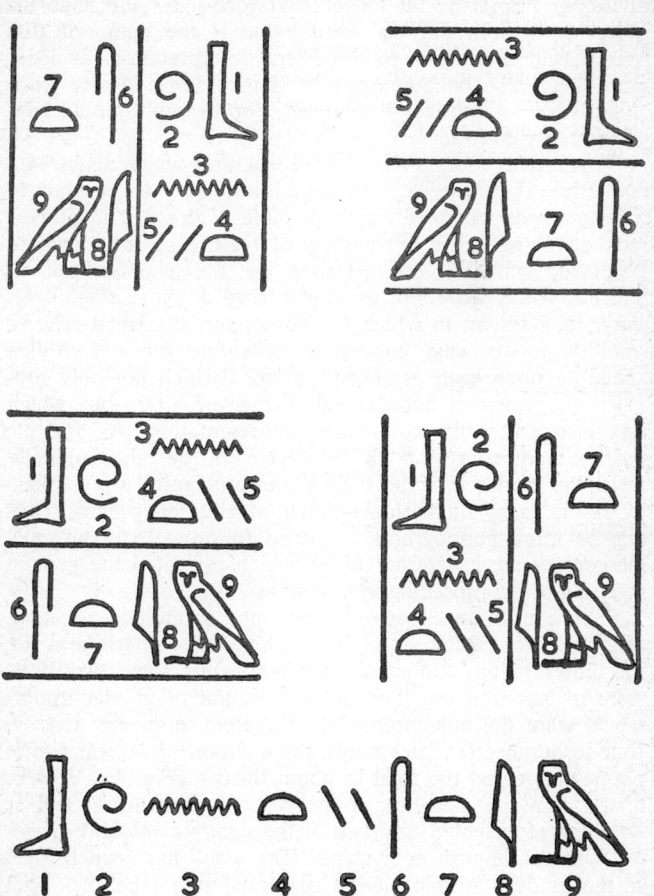

Fig. 2. The four possible arrangements of Egyptian hieroglyphs. The numbering shows the order in which the signs should be read.

under one or other of two main headings—ideograms and phonograms—each of which, however, admits of various subdivisions. Primarily, an ideogram (word-sign) indicates the object it depicts, *i.e.*, its word value is the name of that object. But in addition to this literal interpretation, an ideogram may also be employed to signify some closely associated idea—a musical instrument, for example, could suggest joy or gladness.

Phonograms (sound-signs) are ideograms which acquired a phonetic value when it was found necessary to commit to writing words which it was impossible to draw. The process took advantage of a morphological feature of the Egyptian language, which is characterised by the phenomenon of internal vowel variation, as in the English *sang, sing, song, sung*. In a system in which the consonants displayed relative stability, it was easy enough to substitute for a verb like "heed" a noun such as "head," a word which not only provided the essential consonantal framework—*hd*—but which was also amenable to pictorial representation. As for the possibility of confusion, the context could be relied upon to assist the reader to some extent, and ambiguity was avoided by resort to an increasing number of additional signs. Thus one or more phonograms might be followed by a terminal ideogram (*i.e.*, a determinative) which indicated the general meaning of the preceding sign or signs.

Phonograms are either uniconsonantal or multiconsonantal, otherwise describable as uniliteral, biliteral, and triliteral. Of the biliteral signs (about seventy-five in all) some two-thirds were in common use. Less numerous, but of greater importance, were the uniconsonantal characters, originally twenty-four in number (in later times, the addition of several homophones increased the total to about thirty) (Fig. 3). Vowels, apart from the presence of the weak consonants *w* and *y*, were not represented, and two of the signs—*aleph* and *ayin*— are without English equivalents. The *aleph* has been likened to the modern Arabic *hamza*, or glottal stop (the click produced by a quick compression of the upper part of the throat—a sound encountered in German) and is represented by the smooth breathing of the Greek, and the guttural *ayin*, which has no European equivalent, by the rough breathing. Other of the symbols express sounds which in English can be reproduced only by combinations of two or more letters— *kh, sh, tsh*, and it will be noted that there is more than one form of *h* and *s*.

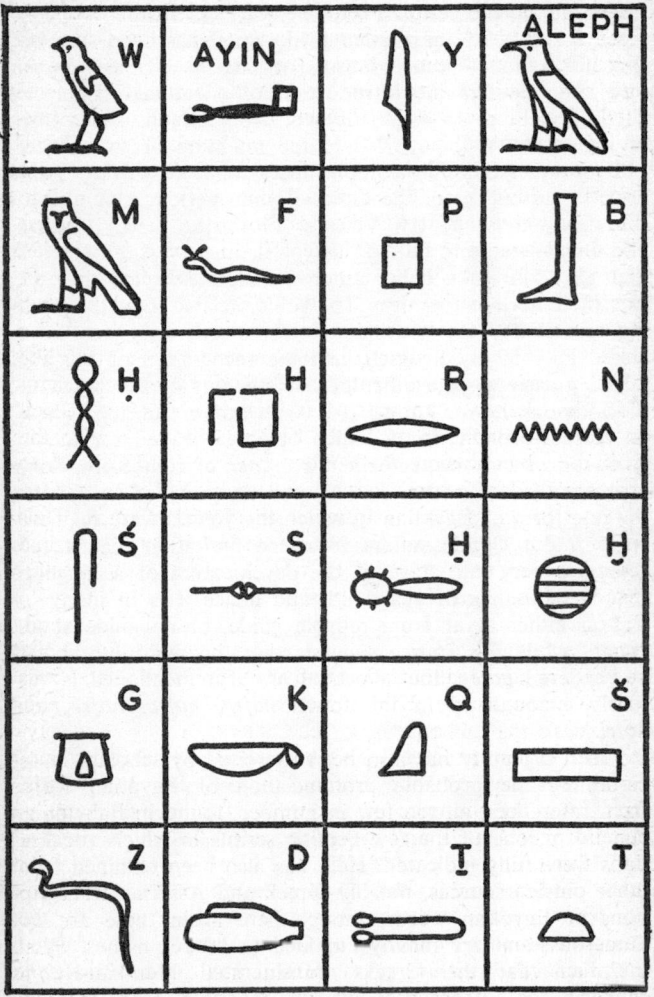

Fig. 3. Egyptian uniconsonantal characters and transliterations.

With this collection of uniconsonantal signs at their disposal, the ancient Egyptians might easily have developed a purely alphabetic script. From the fact that in the course of some 3,500 years they failed to do so, it has been surmised that just as innate conservatism (or extreme laziness) in our own time hinders the introduction of a rational system of English spelling, so in the days of the Pharaohs sheer force of habit may well have led to the retention of so unnecessarily cumbersome and complicated a mode of writing. However, in cartouches of the Greco-Roman period, a number of the signs—those of the Vulture, Flowering reed, Forearm, and Quail—came to be used as vowels, a perversion which at first gave rise to a belief among modern scholars that this was their normal function. The principle that Egyptian writing represented the consonantal framework only was enunciated in 1857 by Brugsch, and the recognition of this fact added greatly to the difficulties of students of the language, for although it was known that the word *nfr* meant "good," its correct pronunciation, which obviously called for the introduction of vowels, remained a matter of conjecture. Some assistance in the matter has since been provided by Coptic, the one form of Egyptian in which the vowels were regularly written. But Coptic suffers from the limitation that it represents a very late stage in the development of a language that is thousands of years old, and hence it is in many instances either a far from reliable guide, or no guide at all. Again, while this source suggests that the word *htp* should be rendered *hotep,* the adjectival *nfr* aforementioned is variously encountered in the forms *nafre, nofra, nofre,* and *nofri.*

Much ingenuity has also been exercised by scholars in ascertaining the probable pronunciation of Egyptian words from references, all too few in number, found in Babylonian cuneiform, one of the few Semitic scripts in which vocalisations were fully indicated. Help has also been obtained from other outside sources, notably Greek and Assyrian transcriptions of Egyptian words, though here again these are not numerous, and are mainly confined to proper names. From the fact that the Greeks transliterated Men-kau-Re as Mykerin (os), it has been inferred that they heard the *ayin* as a nasalised sound.

The problem of determining the position, quantity, and quality of the original vowels in Egyptian words is still far from having been satisfactorily solved, and in the interests of accuracy, meanwhile, it is the modern practice to render the consonants only, so that a phrase such as "the place where it is" appears in the unpronounceable form *bw nty st im*. But since occasions are bound to arise when students of the language find it necessary to refer orally to these skeletal renderings, some method of pronunciation has had to be agreed upon, and the usual procedure is to resort to a liberal use of the English *e*, the only exception to this rule being the replacement of *e* by the French *a* where the letters *aleph* and *ayin* occur. Needless to add, no one supposes that the result of this compromise is anything but a caricature of the ancient Egyptian tongue, but, the circumstances being as they are, it is the best that can be done.

VI

In the days of the later Roman Emperors, Egypt was looked upon as the source of all the arts and sciences, and it was widely held that the mysterious hieroglyphs, everywhere in evidence upon the walls of monuments and temples, gave a summary of all the knowledge that had been acquired in that ancient land since time began. But it was also believed that this accumulated wisdom had been so carefully and so successfully concealed by the priests that its loss must be regarded as irretrievable.

In the event, although the hieroglyphic inscriptions kept their secrets for hundreds of years, their contents were at last revealed, and it then transpired (as might have been expected in so priest-ridden a land) that religious subjects predominated. An early example, known as the Pyramid Texts, belongs to the Old Kingdom, and consists of more than 7,000 lines of hieroglyphs incised on the interior walls of pyramids belonging to five kings of the 5th and 6th dynasties. The Texts, which came to light when F. A. F. Mariette and Maspero discovered the tombs buried in the sand, proved to be incantations designed to ensure that each of the departed monarchs achieved his rightful place in the sky, and enjoyed all the other royal prerogatives which were due to him postmortem.

Another group of spells (12th dynasty), composed on behalf of the nobility and lesser personages, to which the name Coffin Texts has been given, were retrieved from the receptacles after which they were named, and these utterances likewise consist of magical incantations aimed at protecting the nether-world traveller from the anticipated dangers of his extra-terrestrial environment. Yet a third collection, misleadingly termed the Book of the Dead, belongs to 18th-dynasty times, and this, too, provides explicit instructions on how to endure the life-everlasting with a minimum of discomfort and inconvenience.

But notwithstanding the priestly preoccupation with the hereafter, less ghostly matters also claimed the attention of the scribes, particularly during and after Middle Kingdom times, when there was begun the practice of erecting official monuments, often inscribed in the most self-laudatory terms. A classic example is provided by the interminable accounts of Rameses II concerning the part he played in the Battle of Kadesh, in which Egyptian fought Hittite in an attempt to decide the future of Syria, accounts which, though historically of great value, are nevertheless not to be taken too literally (although the outcome of the battle was inconclusive, each side, in the immemorial manner, claimed to have inflicted a crushing defeat upon the other).

Some items of scientific interest have also been found, among them medical and mathematical treatises. There is a 12th-dynasty document of gynaecological import, and a later manuscript (the Ebers papyrus) gives a description of the action of the heart, explains various medical terms, and outlines the treatment appropriate to an impressive list of ailments. Of the mathematical works, copies of the two most important of these are now lodged in London and Moscow. Their concern is not to expound mathematical theory, but to show by example, and among other attainments, it is evident that it was known how to obtain the area of a triangle, while that of a circle was approximated by squaring eight-ninths of the diameter. From these and other sources of information, it is clear that a decimal notation was used, in which one stroke indicated 1, two strokes indicated 2, and so on up to 9. Ten was represented by an inverted U, twenty by two such signs, again up to nine times. Similarly, there were individual signs for 100, 1,000, 10,000, 100,000, 1,000,000, and even 100,000,000. But the system, though effective enough, was extremely cumbersome (no less than twenty-seven signs were needed to write 999!), and while addition and subtraction could be undertaken readily enough, multiplication offered real difficulties. It was contrived by means of a two times table and nothing more, so that the calculation was in effect a continuous doubling operation, the multiplicand being added at the end if the multiplier happened to be an odd number.

General literature takes the form of short stories, fables, admonitions, secular poetry, and hymns. Understandably enough, not very much has survived from the Old Kingdom. There is a book of Proverbs which, though known only from later copies, goes back to 5th-dynasty times, and has been ascribed to one Ptahhopte, a governor of the town of Memphis, who lived during the reign of Dadkere Isesi (Assa), *c.* 2650 B.C. It consists of such familiar father-to-son homilies as the need for diligence, hard work, and the avoidance of women in general, and of those belonging to the households of friends in particular. A similar collection of exhortations, known only from garbled accounts found in the exercise books of New Kingdom schoolboys, is called the Instruction of Duauf. For the benefit of his son Pepi, this Duauf extols the advantages of being a scribe, contrasting the life of the professional writer with the hardships that have to be endured by the smith at his furnace, by the artisan wielding his chisel, and by the followers of numerous other highly undesirable callings, from stone masonry to gardening.

The uncertainties of life during the dark days which followed the collapse of the Old Kingdom are vividly portrayed in the Admonitions of an Egyptian Sage, a work in which the passing of the good old days is lamented, and the miseries of the present loudly proclaimed. In the absence of authority, there is robbery, murder, and famine throughout the land, and the poor have seized the opportunity to make themselves rich at the expense of their erstwhile masters, so that "jewels are hung about the necks of slave girls" and "those that once possessed beds lie on the ground, while he that slept on the ground now has a cushion."

With the restoration of law and order at the onset of the Middle Kingdom, the classic age of Egyptian literature begins. It is heralded, however, by the Instructions of Amenemhet, another series of fatherly admonitions which on this occasion reflect the uncertainties of the period just ended. After making his son Sesusri I co-regent, the Pharaoh Amenemhet withdrew from active participation in political affairs, explaining that he was weary of making efforts which had earned him nothing but ingratitude, and had even led to an attempt on his life. He counsels:

> *Be on thy guard against subordinates. Be not alone. Trust not a brother, know not a friend. If thou sleepest, do thou thyself guard thine heart, for in the day of adversity, a man hath no adherents.*

That the aged monarch had good reason for his fears was shown by his subsequent murder, an event which led to a masterpiece of story-telling entitled the Tale of Sinuhe. This Sinuhe was a court official whose duties concerned the royal harem (always a centre of jealousy and intrigue), and while the heir to the throne was away on a raiding expedition, Sinuhe overheard the news that Amenemhet had been assassinated. Although in no way implicated in the crime, he panicked and fled to the desert where, half dead from thirst, he was found by Bedouins. The Sheik of the tribe recognised him as an official of importance, and helped him on his way to Palestine, where a local prince welcomed him with a gift of land and the hand of his eldest daughter. After years of exile and many adventures, including a fight to the death in personal combat, Sinuhe at last returned to Egypt, where he was favourably received by the king, and so ended his days at home and in peace.

Other popular tales of the period include the Shipwrecked Sailor and King Kheuf and the Magicians. The last-named is a collective work containing a number of stories supposedly told to King Kheuf by his sons, the ingredients of the first of the series being a magician, an unfaithful wife, and a wax crocodile—in essence, saurian consumes paramour. The Shipwrecked Sailor, on the other hand, is a tale within a tale within a tale. It opens with a reference to a high-ranking Egyptian, returning empty-handed from a voyage made on behalf of the king, uncertain about the reception which awaits him, who is consoled by a companion's recital of the trials and tribulations which *he* endured on a previous voyage. His ship foundered in a great storm, and, as sole survivor, he was washed ashore on an island. Fortunately, the place was well provided with figs, vines, and other sources of nourishment, and, thankful to be alive, he made an offering to the gods. No sooner had he performed this pious obligation than there was a loud clap of thunder, and he was startled to find himself confronted by a bearded serpent, some fifty feet long. The creature, which by some happy chance could both understand and speak Middle Egyptian, proved to be friendly, and after asking the reason for the intruder's presence on the island, predicted that a rescue ship would soon arrive for him, and then proceeded to recount the story of *his* misfortunes, explaining how a falling star had crashed on the island, killing the entire ophidian population with the exception of himself. . . .

Altogether different from the foregoing is a poetic work entitled the Dispute of a Man with his Soul. In this philosophical epic, the Man, weary of life and contemplating suicide, argues for and against the proposal with his Soul. After seeming to approve the idea by suggesting the best way of carrying it out, the Soul at the last moment draws back, on the grounds that it has no immediate desire to find itself consigned to the Kingdom of the Dead. It suggests that the Man should take a more cheerful view of things, to which reply is made that conditions are such that life is no longer worth living—and so the argument goes on, inspired, it might well be, by the troubled times which followed the collapse of the Middle Kingdom and the arrival of the Hyksos invaders.

The subsequent emergence of the New Kingdom is told in the historic tale of King Apopi and Sekenere, and the story of the new empire's eventual decline is reflected in an account entitled the Voyage of Wenamon, in which an Egyptian envoy, seeking to purchase a consignment of cedar-wood abroad, is treated with scant respect by foreign officials.

The new era began when the authority of Apopi, the Hyksos king, was challenged by Sekenere, a prince of Thebes. The gallant Sekenere perished in the war which followed, but his son Amose continued the struggle and succeeded in expelling the invaders, and his reign marks the beginning of the 18th dynasty. A period of renewed power and prosperity followed, and before it came to an end, there began two closely associated revolutionary trends, the one literary, and the other religious. The Pharaoh Amenophis IV, otherwise Ikhnaton, attempted to establish a monotheistic religion in which only Aton, the sun, was worshipped. In so doing, he earned the undying hatred of the established hierarchy of Amon-Ra, and with the death of the would-be reformer, his heretical innovations were quickly swept away. But not every trace of the new faith was destroyed, for, inscribed on the walls of the tomb of Ikhnaton's father-in-law Ay was found a complete version of a stupendous Hymn to Aton. To its modern translators it appeared vaguely familiar, and it was then discovered that some unknown Hebrew writer, when compiling some of the so-called Psalms of David, had included Ikhnaton's hymn as the 104th of its many items!

CHAPTER III

THE KEY TO CUNEIFORM

I

Cuneiform writing, independently so-called by Engelbert Kampfer and others about the beginning of the 18th century, derives its name from the wedge-like shape of its characters. At first, however, the script was pictographic, and the various objects thus portrayed suggest that its originators lived in the marshlands at the head of what is to-day known as the Persian Gulf, where it chanced that an abundant supply of writing material was readily available in the form of clay.

Some time after 3000 B.C., the script was adapted to their language by the Semitic Accadians, and its use subsequently spread throughout the Near East, where it was variously employed by Anatolians and by Canaanites, by Hebrews and by Hittites. Of these interpretations, the simplified cuneiform of the Assyrians (whose language was a dialect of Accadian) consisted of about 600 signs, many of them ideographic, while the predominantly syllabic version of the Elamites contained, in its final form, fewer than 120 symbols. But in the hands of the Persians, the script was reduced to thirty-six near-alphabetic characters (consonants included the value of a short vowel), 4 ideograms, and a word divider—41 signs in all.

This achievement (*c.* 600 B.C.), without which the efforts of the modern decipherers of cuneiform writing would undoubtedly have been very considerably prolonged, was heralded by the arrival of groups of wandering Indo-Europeans at an inviting plateau which they named Iran, *i.e.*, homeland of the Ayrans. Among these migrants, made up of Bactrians and Margians, Drangians and Parthians, two tribes were prominent—the Medes (Mada), who occupied the western part of the tableland, and the Persians (Parsa), who settled to the south of the Medes.

For several centuries after their arrival, the newcomers were constantly menaced by (and at times subject to) the Assyrians, who in two campaigns under Ashurbanipal completely devastated the neighbouring kingdom of the Elamites. Incessant warfare, however, ultimately so weakened the supposedly invincible masters of Western Asia, that in the end they were not able to withstand a combined assault by the Median leader Cyaxares and Babopolasser of Babylon, and in 612 B.C. Nineveh, the famed Assyrian capital, was taken and destroyed. The victors shared the spoils, and a short-lived Median empire, thus brought into being, was centred at Ecbatana (modern Hamadan), with first Cyaxares, and later Astyages, at its head.

The Persians, meanwhile, had established a minor kingdom under Teispes, the first of a succession of rulers who derived their line from an eponymous ancestor called Achaemenes. By the middle of the 6th century B.C., the Achaemenid clan acknowledged the leadership of Cyrus II, who governed as a sub-king of Parsa under Median domination. But the ambitions of Cyrus the Great (as he was destined to become) did not allow him to continue in this secondary role, and within a few years of his accession, he instigated a revolt which not only resulted in his defeating the Medes, but which gained such momentum that he also succeeded in subduing the Lydians, and thereafter in engulfing the Babylonians. There was thus founded the first world empire, a domain which stretched from the Caucasus to the Indian Ocean, and from the Indus to the Mediterranean.

Throughout this vast area, three different tongues were officially recognised—the conqueror's own (now designated Old Persian); that of the Babylonians (Accadian); and Elamite (Susian)—and royal inscriptions were almost invariably presented in trilingual form, the three versions appearing side by side. Thus the Achaemenian kings, in addition to providing the investigators of cuneiform writing with a greatly simplified form of the script, also supplied equivalent texts in two other unknown languages and forms of writing.

What is in all probability the earliest known of these inscriptions was discovered at Pasargadae on the River Kur, among the ruins of buildings which Cyrus caused to be erected after his overthrow of Astyages the Mede. No town of any size appears to have occupied the site, but its structures included temples, a royal residence, and the burial place of the monarch. Originally, the grave stood in an open court, surrounded by colonnades, but these have long since disappeared, and all that now remains is the simple tomb structure itself, perched on a high substructure of six steps. Strabo recounts that when Aristobulous of Cassandreia entered the building on instructions from Alexander the Great, he found within a golden couch, a coffin of the same metal, and many garments lavishly decked with precious stones—items which, alas, no longer remain to confront the visitor to-day. Gone, too, is the inscription which the two Greeks saw above the entrance to the place:

> Stranger, I am Cyrus, the founder of the Persian Empire, the sovereign of Asia; envy me not, therefore, this sepulchre.

Cyrus was succeeded by his son, Cambyses, who in 525 B.C. defeated the Pharaoh Psamtik III at Pelusium, a victory which added Egypt to the Empire. Among the preparations of Cambyses for this campaign was the cold-blooded strangling of his younger brother Smerdis, lest during the king's absence abroad a rival claimant to the throne should emerge. The precise date of this precautionary deed is not known, for the murder was kept secret, and the people led to believe that the victim was confined to his quarters for reasons of state.

Retribution, as it happened, was not long delayed, and ironically enough, it was the covering-up of the crime which brought about the undoing of its author. No sooner was Cambyses safely in Egypt than the palace custodian, Patizithes the Magian, prevailed upon his own brother Gautama to impersonate Smerdis, and then raised a revolt in the dead man's name, secure in the knowledge that the king's brother was thought to be alive. Cambyses was thus caught in a trap of his own devising, for, in order to unmask the false Smerdis, he would be forced to reveal the death of the real one. Nevertheless, on receiving news of the uprising, he planned a hurried return, but died (by accident, according to one account, and by his own hand, if we are to believe another) before he could challenge the conspirators, whereupon Gautama assumed power.

But the triumph of the impostor was of brief duration, for among those who were aware of the true facts of the matter was Darius, the son of Hystaspes, an energetic member of a junior branch of the royal family. With the assistance of half a dozen loyal nobles, he surprised and killed the usurper and his brother, after which, according to Herodotus, the question of who among the seven should become king was left to the decision of their horses, it being agreed that the next morning they should go together to the outskirts of the city, and that the rider whose mount first neighed should have the kingdom. In the event, the winner owed his success to a trick of his groom, OEbares by name, who evoked the desired response from his master's animal with the somewhat unsporting assistance of the scent of the genitals of a mare. However all this may be, it was Darius who attained the throne—to be at once faced by a series of revolts throughout the kingdom, as one province after another sought to take advantage of the uncertainties of the moment. These widespread outbreaks Darius and his generals methodically suppressed, fighting (as he himself tells us) nineteen battles and defeating nine would-be rivals before the new ruler was able to convince his rebellious subjects that he was indeed master of the situation.

For the benefit of posterity, and no doubt as a warning to other potential trouble-makers, Darius commemorated his triumph over his enemies by recording the details on the side of a precipitous cliff at Behistun, high above the main caravan road from Ecbatana to Babylon. This, the most ambitious of the Achaemenian inscriptions, consists of hundreds of lines of cuneiform, chiselled on the rock face in Old Persian, Elamite, and Accadian. The account is illustrated by sculptured reliefs which depict Darius facing the discomfited rebels in the presence of Ahura-Mazda (Ormuzd), creator of the universe, and the supposed architect of Achaemenian greatness.

Darius also celebrated his victory by ordering construction work to be begun at a selected site near the junction of the rivers Kur and Polvar. Here, on the side of a hill overlooking the plain of Mervdasht, a huge rectangular platform was raised, some thirty acres in extent, supported on three sides by a strong fortified wall, and protected at the rear by a line of interconnected towers which ran over the crest of the mountain. And here, Darius and his successors established themselves in a series of magnificent edifices, among them the Tachara (Palace of Darius), the Apadama (Audience Hall, begun by Darius and completed by his son Xerxes), the Hadish (Palace of Xerxes), and a Hall with a roof supported by a hundred columns (the joint work of Xerxes and Artaxerxes I). Eventually, more than half of the platform area was occupied by these and associated establishments, a series of inscriptions on the walls of which proclaimed to the world the identity of the builders. It was these repetitive announcements which, at the beginning of the 19th century, were to assume an importance out of all proportion to their stereotyped contents.

The name which the Persians gave to this secluded retreat is not known, but the Greek writers called it Persepolis, and by Diodorus it was regarded as the capital of the Empire (the administrative centres of which, however, were in all probability Ecbatana, Susa, and Babylon). But as a place of residence it was so highly esteemed by the Achaemenidae that several of their number elected to prolong their stay indefinitely (three royal tombs were cut in the hillside at the rear of the platform), while other of the monarchs, including Darius and Xerxes, found a last resting place at nearby Naksh-i-Rustam.

Of the known world, only Europe remained beyond Persia's reach. But from the time of Darius I onwards, all attempts to remedy this omission were frustrated by the Greeks, until finally, in 334 B.C., during the reign of Darius III, Alexander the Great crossed the Hellespont and inflicted a defeat on the Persians at the Battle of Issus. Darius then essayed to come to terms, but Alexander demanded unconditional surrender, and after laying siege to Tyre, led an expedition to Egypt, where he was welcomed as a liberator. He then met and defeated another Persian force at Gaugamela, and subsequently encountered further strong resistance at Persepolis, where the palaces were looted and burned—by drunken revellers at a victory feast, according to one well-known account. As for the Persian king, he fled east to the remote province of Bactria, where he was assassinated by his cousin Bessus, who mistakenly thought to gain favour with Alexander thereby, and with his death, the Achaemenid dynasty came to an inglorious end.

It was replaced by that of the Seleucids (the Iranian equivalent of the Ptolemies), who were followed by the Arsacids (Parthian Period), by the Sassanids (Neo-Persian Empire), and eventually by the Arabs (Moslem Conquest), who overran the country about the middle of the 7th century A.D. Thereafter, the speech of the vanquished was submerged by that of the victors, and it was not until some 250 years later that the native tongue reappeared in a literary guise. But although Modern Persian is written in Arabic characters, it nevertheless provides a vital link, through Middle Persian (represented by Zend and Pehlevi, as preserved in certain religious works, and in a few Sassanian rock inscriptions) with the Old Persian language of the Achaemenids. To the would-be elucidators of the completely unknown cuneiform script, the potential value of this connection will be evident.

II

Like their early Christian counterparts, the proselytising Moslems had scant regard for cultures other than their own, as is shown by their wanton destruction of the famed Library of Alexandria in A.D. 642, after their conquest of Egypt. They made, indeed, no secret of their attitude, which was that if the Greek writings were in agreement with the Koran, they were clearly superfluous; and that if they were in *dis*agreement with the holy words of Allah, they were undoubtedly pernicious; and that in either case, they were fit only to be destroyed. In these sombre circumstances, it is hardly surprising that the Arabs appear to have taken little or no interest in the Achaemenian inscriptions, though the existence of some of these records was known to them. Ibn Haukal, about the end of the 10th century, expressed the opinion that the figures carved on the mountain-side at Behistun represented a schoolmaster, confronting a class of recalcitrant pupils, though the guess of a successor, made some 200 years later, was less inspired. This, the report of the Arab geographer Yakut, whose examination of the reliefs, if he troubled to examine them at all, can hardly have been undertaken at close quarters, declared that they showed the renowned Sassanian leader Khusru Parviz

(Chrosroes II), seated on his famous horse Shabdiz, in the presence of Queen Shirin.

No less fanciful were the tales which grew up about the remnants of the royal Persian citadels. The site of Persepolis was occupied by a city known to the Arabs as Istakhr, which in its day had achieved considerable importance as an administrative centre under the Sassanids. But with the founding of the Arab capital of Shiraz, some forty miles away, the usefulness of Istakhr gradually declined, and its Achaemenian remains were variously referred to as Chelel Minar (the Forty Minarets), as the Old Town (of Shiraz), or as Takht-i-Jamshid (the Palace of Jamshid), this last as a tribute to a legendary Persian ruler who was supposedly dethroned by an Arabian called Zohak, about 1000 B.C. The ruins were also linked with the name of King Solomon, the remains of the mother of whom, according to popular account, were housed in a tomb at a place called Murghab, some thirty miles to the north.

One of the first Europeans to visit these sites were Giosafat Barbaro, who arrived in Persia in 1472 as Venetian ambassador. In the course of his travels (an account of which was published some seventy years later), he examined both Takht-i-Jamshid and Murghab, and also Naksh-i-Rustam, where he observed among some rock carvings an outsize relief of a Sassanian king, which he took to be a representation of the biblical Samson. Some two centuries later another ambassador to Persia, an Augustine friar by the name of Antione de Gouvea, decided that the supposed ruins of the Palace of Jamshid (or Solomon) did in fact mark the site of Old Shiraz, as local rumour suggested. This identification was subsequently challenged by the official Spanish representative Don Garcia de Silva Figueroa, who conjectured that the ruins standing near the confluence of the rivers Kur and Polvar might well be the remnants of the famed city known to have been built by Darius the Great. An artist, who accompanied de Silva on his travels, copied some curious-looking signs which were thought to be some form of writing, though it was agreed that it was neither "Chaldean, nor Hebrew, nor Greeke, nor Aribike, nor of any other Nation which was ever found of old, or at this day to be extant."

Next on the scene was an Italian traveller, Pietro della Valle, the son of a wealthy Roman family, who conceived the then daring idea of making a protracted excursion to the East, as an antidote to the distressful effects of an unsuccessful affair of the heart, and as an alternative to suicide. He sailed for Constantinople from Venice in 1614, and after spending some time in Egypt, visited in turn Jerusalem, Damascus, Aleppo, and Bagdad, encountering at the last-named an unanticipated consolation in the shape of a Syrian maiden named Maani, whom he married. Despite the fact that Turkey and Persia happened to be at war, he then contrived to make his way from the country of one belligerent to that of the other, in due course paying a visit to various places of interest, including Takht-i-Jamshid. He, too, noticed groups of unfamiliar signs which he took to be some form of writing, portions of which he copied, though he was unable to decide whether the supposed script progressed from the right, or (as he inclined to believe) from the left.

Della Valle's visit was followed by that of Sir Thomas Herbert, who echoed the notion that the ruined site was that of Old Shiraz, and who recorded the existence there of "lynes of strange characters . . . so mysticall, so odly framed . . . consisting of Figures, obelisk, triangular and pyramidall, yet in such Simmetry and order as cannot well be called barbarous." It remained, however, for J. S. Mandeslo to make the interesting discovery, a few years later, that the mysterious characters showed signs of having been inlaid with gold.

In the second half of the 17th century, several examinations of the Achaemenid sites were made by the French traveller and author Jean Chardin, who had amassed a fortune trading in jewels in India, Armenia, and Turkey. On his eventual return to his native land, he found himself unwelcome there because of his Protestant inclinations, and in 1681, to escape this religious intolerance, he settled in London. Here, in a matter of months, he became court-jeweller, was elected a Fellow of the Royal Society, and was knighted by King Charles II. Sir John Chardin, in an account of his Persian discoveries, gave it as his considered opinion that the unfamiliar signs he had observed were a form of writing, and added that the inscriptions often occurred in groups of three. He moreover supposed (rightly) that the script ran from left to right, though he believed (wrongly) that it might also be read perpendicularly. This erroneous idea arose from the sight of a series of single-line inscriptions which adorned the tops and sides of door openings and windows, examination of which suggested that the individual signs might face in any direction. And further to add to the confusion of those who essayed to make some sense out of the inscription, there was at first no suspicion that three different languages were concerned—Elamite (ascending, on left); Old Persian (running horizontally at top, from left to right); and Accadian (descending, on right). It was as though an Oriental visitor to France, in complete ignorance of the existence of the Latin alphabet, and possessed of no knowledge of European tongues, were to happen upon a group of unfamiliar symbols, so arranged that it seemed to be immaterial whether they appeared as T, as ⊢, as ⊣, or presumably, as ⊥:

ALLER TOUT DROIT

GÅ RAKT FRAM

TODO SEGUIDO

Among later copyists of the inscriptions were the German traveller and physician, Engelbert Kampfer (who was the first to perceive that their fundamental unit was the wedge, and who named the writing accordingly); Samuel Flower (an enterprising agent of the East India Company, who introduced the useful practice of separating each sign by a dot); and Cornelias le Brun (who, by placing all three lines of a window inscription horizontally, one below the other, demonstrated that the two upright components were not intended to be read vertically). But it was not until the meticulous work undertaken by Carsten Niebuhr in 1765, that for the first time scholars had at their disposal copies of the inscriptions which were not only very nearly complete, but which also exhibited a standard of accuracy far greater than had hitherto been achieved.

Niebuhr's approach to Persia was by a decidedly roundabout route, an adventurous journey which began in 1761, when Frederic V of Denmark was planning to despatch a scientific expedition to Egypt, Arabia, and Syria. Five commissioners were appointed, to each of whom a particular aspect of the enquiry was assigned, and Niebuhr, as one of this select company, found himself in association with a naturalist, a philologist, an artist, and a surgeon. This oddly assorted group set out from Copenhagen, safely reached Constantinople, and thence journeyed, by way of Egypt, to the Yemen. From Jidda, the party went overland to Mokha, and eventually arrived at Sana, the capital, but not before two of its leaders had died. By the time Bombay was reached, two more deaths had occurred, and Niebuhr was left as the sole survivor. He then decided to make his way home by way of Persia and Mesopotamia, and so it came about that on 13 March, 1765, he found himself at Takht-i-Jamshid, where he remained busily at work copying the inscriptions for the next three weeks.

With the publication of his *Voyage en Arabie* (Amsterdam, 1776-80), students were for the first time provided with clear and complete copies of cuneiform inscriptions, and a scientific approach to the problem of their decipherment could at last be begun. Niebuhr drew attention to the fact that the inscriptions usually occurred in groups of three, such as those to be found on a series of tablets which he designated "B," "C," "D," and "E," "F," "G" (Fig. 4), and so on, ("A," the first of his copies, was unilingual); that the signs belonging to

Fig. 4. Niebuhr's "B" and "G" inscriptions.

each of the three groups were not the same; and that the three different systems invariably appeared in the same order.

In carefully distinguishing one symbol from another, Niebuhr further assisted his readers (as Samuel Flower had done before him) by separating the signs by means of a dot, though inexplicably enough, he failed to realise that a constantly recurring character in one of the scripts acted as a word divider. He did, however, draw attention to two similar versions of an inscription, in the first example of which the word ending the 3rd line appeared in the second example as the opening word of the 4th line, thus affording proof that the script read from left to right. And he also confirmed Le Brun's finding concerning the vertical components of the window inscriptions, by showing that when these were placed on their sides, the individual signs were at once seen to correspond with those already known from horizontal sources. Finally, Niebuhr pointed out that the characters which occurred in the first of the three columns were very much simpler than those to be found in the other two, and that they were considerably fewer in number. He appended a list containing forty-two of these signs, which it seemed to him were alphabetic, and the accuracy of his work may be judged from the fact that out of this total, only nine (including the word divider) were later found not to be true letters.

Although, strictly, Niebuhr was not himself a decipherer, it may be fairly claimed that he laid the foundations on which the work of subsequent investigators was based. Without his useful observations and suggestions, and the clear and accurate copies of the inscriptions he provided, the unravelment of cuneiform writing might well have been delayed for several decades.

III

The task of deciphering the wedge-shaped script offered a problem far more formidable than that presented by the Egyptian hieroglyphs, the investigators of which had the very great advantage of possessing a bilingual inscription, one of its versions couched in so familiar a form of writing and language as Greek. Cuneiform, on the other hand, offered no more than a confusing array of complex symbols, the apparent want of individuality among which was of itself sufficient to give rise to a sense of hopelessness among scholars, a feeling which may well have helped to engender the widespread and long sustained belief that the supposed script was not a form of writing at all.

Against this there was, of course, the evidence provided by

Greek and Roman sources, which afforded many, if on occasion somewhat contradictory, references to the writings of the inhabitants of Western Asia. Thus, whereas the characters of an inscription on the tomb of Sardanapalos (Ashurbanipal) at Nineveh were described by Strabo as Assyrian, the script was referred to by Athenaeus as Chaldean. But that the classical authors were agreed that cuneiform actually was a form of writing was not disputed. The issue was to what extent their statements about this and other matters could be relied upon, and here there was certainly excuse enough for doubt, as witness the assertion of Diodorus that the Behistun reliefs (consisting of fourteen figures, all of them unquestionably male) depicted Semiramis, an alleged daughter of the goddess Derceto, in the presence of 100 lance-bearers, and that the accompanying description of the scene was written in Syrian letters. Again, at a time when untold thousands of Babylonian tablet inscriptions still lay buried beneath the ruined cities of the Tigro-Euphrates valley, their very existence unsuspected, the notion that cuneiform was merely ornamentation found support in the circumstance that some examples of the Persian writing were to be found in such unlikely places as on the robes of sculptured figures, and even round the openings of doors and windows. Thus, from the onset, scholars could be divided into two main groups—those who, in the company of the distinguished Hebraist Dr. Thomas Hyde, suggested that the alleged script was meaningless, and those who were convinced that it was meaningful. Of the sharers of this conviction, however, some were holders of the opinion (expressed by Sir George Cornewall Lewis as late as 1862) that the problem of cuneiform decipherment, though real enough, was insuperable, and it was thus left to those who took a contrary view to set about the supposedly impossible task of solving it.

In the event, the investigators received considerable assistance from two recently published works—Anquetil-Duperron's *Zend-Avesta* (Paris, 1771), and Silvestre de Sacy's *Mémoires sur diverses antiquitès de Perse* (Paris, 1793). Duperron, who had been intended for an ecclesiastical career, developed a thirst for Oriental languages instead, and made his way to India in search of followers of the Persian religious leader Zarathushtra (the Greek Zoroaster), who had flourished about 660 B.C. At Surat, he encountered a Parsee community whose members were said to be the descendants of Persians who, some 1,200 years earlier, had exiled themselves rather than submit to Moslem domination, and who still practised the age-old rites associated with the reverence of fire as a manifestation of the divine Ahura-Mazda.

Duperron contrived to gain the confidence of the native priests, not to mention a working knowledge of the Zend and Pehlevi languages, and he was thus enabled to translate extracts from the liturgical *Venidad Sade* and other sacred writings, producing a rendering which, though it exhibited numerous defects, was at any rate better than no rendering at all. De Sacy's work, by contrast, concerned the Sassanian period of Persian history, and it gave translations (derived from accompanying Greek versions) of the short Pehlevi inscriptions to be seen at Naksh-i-Rustam. And as de Sacy showed, where these epigraphs appeared above the figure of a monarch, the reference was invariably to that ruler and to his father, and contained the phrase "King of kings."

The first serious attempt at cuneiform decipherment was made by O. G. Tychsen, a noted Rabbinic scholar, who was born in 1734 at Tondern, in Schleswig-Holstein, of parents of Norwegian descent. At the University of Halle, where he studied, he evinced a particular interest in Oriental languages, and in 1790, shortly after taking up the post of librarian and curator at the Museum of Rostock, he published a modest work on the Egyptian hieroglyphs. This was followed, a few years later, by his *De Cuneatis Inscriptionibus Persepolitanis Lucubratio* (Rostock, 1798). Tychsen accepted Niebuhr's view that the inscriptions were to be read from left to right, and that the triple groups contained writing of three different kinds. In addition, he suggested that the three scripts were probably representative of three different languages, and tentatively nominated Parthian, Median, and Bactrian. He also drew attention to a group of seven signs which was many times repeated:

〈〈⟩⟩ · ⟨⟨ · 𝍖 · 𝍦 · 𝍑 · 𝍓 · 𝍦

He noted, moreover, that this particular group was often followed by another, consisting of three or four signs:

𝍖 · ⟨⟨ · 𝍖 · 𝍢

He supposed that the first group might represent the name of a monarch, and that the second stood for *pius*, or some similar designation. But when he proceeded to assign arbitrary phonetic values to the component characters, and then sought to identify his transliterations by a reference to the words of various Aryan and Semitic tongues, he lost his way completely, despite the fact that several of his initial guesses happened to be correct. Among other things, he convinced himself that he had discovered a reference to one Aksak, whom he confidently assumed to be Arsaces I, founder of the Parthian kingdom. This ascription had the stultifying effect of committing him to a period of Persian history which was some three centuries too late.

The positive identification of the ruins at Takht-i-Jamshid and Murghab, meanwhile, was a matter of crucial concern to the decipherers, for upon the answer depended which royal names the inscriptions might be expected to contain. But throughout the greater part of the 18th century, one guess was to be regarded as almost as likely as another, and a heated controversy eventually developed between A. H. L. Heeren, who favoured Achaemenian authorship, and J. G. Herder, who did not. The issue was settled, at any rate to the complete satisfaction of one interested observer, in a paper by F. C. C. Münter which was read to members of the Royal Academy at Copenhagen in 1798. Münter's interest in the cuneiform inscriptions had been aroused by a sight of Niebuhr's *Voyage*, and he was subsequently in touch with Tychsen on the subject. As a result of his researches, he soon reached the conclusion that Tychsen was wrong in associating Takht-i-Jamshid with the Parthians, and that Heeren was right in ascribing it to the Achaemenians, and the evidence he adduced in support of this view did much to help resolve the doubts of his contemporaries. In short, the so-called Palace of Jamshid was in fact Persepolis, something of the history of which was known from Greek accounts, including the story of its looting by Alexander the Great—according to Plutarch, so great was the amount of treasure found there that 5,000 camels and 10,000 pairs of mules were required to carry it away.

As for the inscriptions, Münter supposed that these also belonged to the Achaemenian period, and that at least one of the languages of the triple group must in consequence bear a close relationship to Zend or Pehlevi, but there occurred to him the added possibility that one tongue only might be concerned. Understandably, he concentrated his attention on the simplest of the three scripts, and was quickly rewarded by the discovery that one of its signs, a diagonal wedge which occurred with the utmost frequency, was evidently intended to function as a word-divider. Having eliminated this particular symbol, he then undertook a statistical analysis of the contents of the inscriptions copied by Niebuhr, seeking those signs which appeared most often, in the expectation that these would prove to be vowels. Three signs stood out from among the rest, and of these, the first, which was present in almost every word, was represented 183 times, the second 146 times, and the third 107 times. They were:

Münter, of course, at first had no idea of their phonetic value. What he did was to compare the signs, which he supposed might represent *a, i,* or *u,* with the vowel forms of what he deemed to be related languages. As a result, he correctly matched the first of the three signs with the Zend character for *a,* failed to find anything resembling the second character, and was misled by a supposed likeness between the third sign and the Armenian symbol for *o.* All told, the outcome of his efforts was that he wrongly identified five vowels and half a dozen consonants, and assigned correct values to two signs—appropriately enough, *a* and *b.*

Münter also gave much attention to the often recurring group of seven signs which his predecessor had noted. From the fact that these particular signs were on occasion immediately followed by the same group, but with the addition of three or four other symbols, he concluded that the terminal characters were in all probability a grammatical inflexion. Tychsen, he was aware, had supposed them to signify *pius,* and considered that the preceding seven signs represented a proper name. Münter ultimately rejected this idea, in part because the group appeared with such frequency, but also because there was no likely royal name which contained the requisite number of letters in it. He supposed, instead, that the unknown word might have some titular significance, for example "king." But if this were the case, the double grouping of the signs almost certainly stood for the familiar phrase "King of kings," *in which event the word immediately preceding it must be the monarch's name.*

His reasoning, as it happened, was sound. But at this critical point, when he was about to make what might well have been a most useful discovery, he was led astray through no fault of his own. By a most unfortunate mischance, the inscription copy he was following contained one of Niebuhr's rare transcriptional errors, and to his disappointment, Münter found that what should have been the name of a king was represented by an impossibly short word of only two signs—the outcome of the inadvertent substitution of the mark of separation for a letter!

IV

After the exploratory moves made by Tychsen and Münter, the first decisive step towards the decipherment of cuneiform was taken by George Frederick Grotefend, at the time a twenty-seven-years-old Göttingen schoolmaster. Grotefend, who was born at Münden, Hanover, in 1775, had attended the University of Göttingen, where he studied philology. He later held a teaching post at the Gymnasium of Frankfurt-am-Main, and in 1821 became Rector of the Lyceum of Hanover. His published works include a Latin grammar and books on the rudiments of Umbrian and Oscan, but as he himself readily conceded (and as his critics never tired of pointing out), he possessed no particular knowledge of Oriental languages, and claimed no special qualifications for his self-imposed task.

Accounts of how Grotefend came to interest himself in the problem of cuneiform decipherment vary. The Persepolis inscriptions, alleged and supposed, were attracting an increasing amount of attention in philological circles, and according to one story, the young schoolmaster was persuaded to attempt their unravelment by the librarian Fiorillo, while according to another, the motive for his initial interest was the winning of a bet. But however this may be, he no doubt began by making a careful study of the accounts of Tychsen and Münter, and of such relevant works as those of Niebuhr, Duperron, and de Sacy. At all events, he adopted the view that the Persepolis inscriptions were Achaemenian, and concluded that in all probability they had served as models for the later Pehlevi epigraphs which de Sacy had translated. And if this were so, it would seem that Münter, despite the lack of success which had attended his efforts, had been right in his identification of the group of seven signs, twice repeated, and followed by a smaller group.

From the copies of the inscriptions at his disposal, Grotefend selected two of moderate length—the "B" and "G" of Niebuhr—and noted that the supposed phrase "King of kings" occurred in both. The shorter of the two forms, moreover, also appeared in the first line of the two inscriptions without the accompanying "of kings," it being followed by another word, the same in each case. Mindful of de Sacy's Pehlevi analogy, Grotefend surmised that the unknown word meant "great," thus providing him with a second provisional phrase, "King great," *i.e.*, "great King"—a title which, if his reasoning were correct, must be preceded by the royal name. But in this event, the two texts before him referred to different rulers, for the opening words were not the same, though each consisted of seven signs.

It was at this juncture that Grotefend perceived that the name which began inscription "B"—call him monarch Y— also appeared in the third line of inscription "G," though in a slightly extended form. The addition he supposed to be a case-ending which, inasmuch as it differed from the genitive plural presumably signified by the "of kings," he took to be indicative of the genitive singular. Encouragingly enough, the name was accompanied by another group of signs which (again relying on the Pehlevi model) he assumed to mean "son," the sense of the wording being that a monarch Z of inscription "G" was the son of monarch Y of inscription "B." Moreover, examination of the fourth line of inscription "B" revealed the existence of a third name, X, also in the genitive case, though unaccompanied by the designation "king," a name which must be that of the father of monarch Y.

It now seemed clear to Grotefend that he had happened upon the names of three members of the royal house of Achaemenes, whose relationship to one another was that of father, son and grandson. The next step was to identify those concerned, to choose, that is to say, appropriate names from a list of a dozen or so known rulers. As to this, the three in question could not be Cyrus, Cambyses, and Smerdis, for the two names in inscription "B" did not begin with the same letter, and Cambyses and Smerdis, moreover, were brothers, not father and son, a consideration which also excluded the trio Cambyses, Smerdis, and Darius. Similarly, Smerdis,

Darius, and Xerxes also failed to meet the precise kinship requirements. But Xerxes was the son of Darius, who was the son of Hystaspes, and the last-named, as Grotefend was aware, *was not referred to as a king by the Greek writers*. It thus appeared highly probable that Darius was the author of inscription "B," and Xerxes that of inscription "G," the two reading, in part:

Darius, Great King, King of kings . . . son of Hystaspes
Xerxes, Great King, King of kings . . . son of King Darius

The problem now was to ascertain the phonetic values of the characters concerned, *via* the three proper names. Although these were known only in their Greek form, Grotefend learned from Duperron's *Zend Avesta* that the Persian pronunciation of Hystaspes was Goshtasp, Gustasp, Kistasp, or Wistasp. Selecting the first of these versions, and disregarding the cuneiform case-ending, he allocated a letter or letters to each of the remaining seven signs, and then, in the light of the result, examined the group of characters which he supposed to represent Darius. Significantly, the *a* of Münter, which was common to both names, duly appeared in its proper place, and added confirmation was provided by the sign for *sh*, which also occurred in each of the two names:

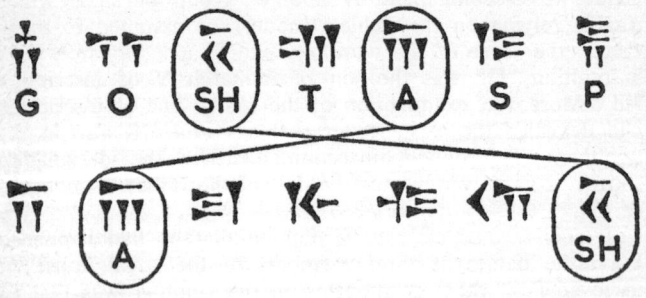

By adding five more letters, Grotefend obtained D A R H E U S H, and although it eventually transpired that the correct form was D A R Y A V U S H, he secured four correct values (D, A, R, and SH) despite this error.

Assuming the validity of his results thus far, he now knew the identity of no less than six of the seven characters composing the third name, in which the signs for *sh* and *a* were each twice repeated:

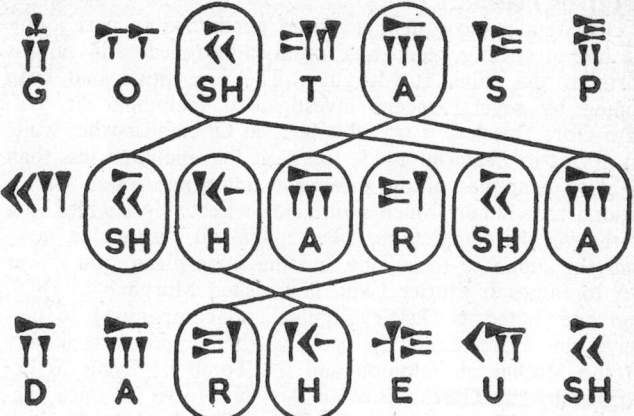

As for the missing value of the opening sign, Herodotus, in a discussion about the meaning of Persian names (a subject on which, as is now known, the Greek historian entertained a number of fanciful ideas, including the mistaken notion that Artaxerxes was a compound of Xerxes), mentions that Xerxes was derived from the Persian for "warrior," a word which Grotefend promptly equated with "king," inasmuch as the first two characters of the sign groups which he supposed to represent this title and the name Xerxes were the same. He next ascertained that the Greek letter *xi* transliterated the Old Persian *khsh*, and concluded that to the first sign of the two words there must be attributed the value *kh*. The Persian form of the name Xerxes thus emerged, somewhat disconcertingly, as KH-SH-H-A-R-SH-A, a result which, however, was seemingly upheld by Champollion's subsequent rendering of a hieroglyphic reference, "Xerxes the great King," discovered on the Vase of Caylus (the name should in fact be KH-SH-Y-A-R-SH-A).

In this highly ingenious manner, Grotefend obtained phonetic values for thirteen cuneiform signs, of which the discovery of one (the letter *a*) rightly belonged to Münter, while four others were later shown to be incorrect. Nevertheless, it was an outstanding achievement, news of which was first given in 1802. Full details were published by de Sacy in an article in Millin's *Magasin encyclopédique* in the following year, though in this account the description of the method of approach differs somewhat from that given by the discoverer himself.

Grotefend's subsequent activities concerned in part a single line of writing which was found to be repeated in various parts of the ruins at Murghab. The inscription had been copied by several recent investigators, including Sir William Gore Ouseley. It was this learned Orientalist who, while on a visit to Persia in 1811, found at Persepolis no less than eighteen examples of the famous window inscription which, though individually much mutilated, collectively enabled him to recover the complete text. Persepolis and Pasargadae, however, he supposed to be one and the same place, and it was left to James J. Morier (who first visited Murghab in 1809, and later acted as Ouseley's guide and companion) to perceive the close similarity between the supposed sepulchre of the Mother of Solomon and the Tomb of Cyrus as described by the Greek historian Arrian. Morier at once suggested that Murghab must be Pasargadae, but Ouseley was not to be persuaded: he was firmly convinced that Cyrus was buried at Fasa.

Grotefend, however, was quick to accept Morier's identification, and began to search for the name Cyrus in the short inscription aforementioned, from which he selected a likely-looking group of characters. His copy, however, contained one symbol too many, and when he substituted the sign values already in his possession, the group transliterated as Z-U-SCH-U-D-SH, a result which he ventured to modify (with justification, as it happened) in the light of the anticipated answer. The Z he changed to K, the SCH to SR, and the superfluous D to E, thereby obtaining K-U-SR-U-E-SCH, from which he finally extracted *Kurus*, in this manner almost exactly matching the correct rendering:

K U R U SH

By 1815, at least fourteen sign values had been correctly determined, no less than twelve of them by Grotefend. But thereafter, his efforts yielded little, and his early attempts at translation in particular were based on ill-founded guesswork. In the meantime, that his labours had any worth at all had been strenuously denied by many authorities from the onset, and so little was thought of the several papers which he presented to the Göttingen Academy that they were refused publication. Not until 1893, forty years after the death of their author, were the rejected MSS. unearthed by Wilhelm Meyer, and somewhat belatedly hailed as marking a turning-point in the long history of cuneiform decipherment.

V

It was in 1823 that the French Orientalist J. S. St. Martin drew attention to the fact that the inscription on the Vase of Caylus was a bilingual. But although he was highly critical of Grotefend's alphabet, for which he proposed to substitute one of his own, St. Martin can at most be credited with the discovery of two additional phonetic values. These he obtained by comparing the cuneiform version of Hystaspes with the Zend form *Vyschtaspo*, in preference to the *Goshtasp* used by Grotefend. As a result, he was able to assign the correct value *v* to the first character, and *y* to the second, thereby more closely approaching the right answer, which was *i*, the name in fact being Vishtaspa. But where his sign list elsewhere differed from that of his predecessor, he was in error.

In the meantime, as Grotefend himself had learned, it was one thing to identify a few well-known proper names, and quite another to transliterate groups of signs which were recognisable only in part, and yet a third to translate the unfamiliar (and often defective) words and phrases so produced. Thus he rendered the second paragraph of Niebuhr's unilingual "A" inscription, the twenty-five lines of which intimate that an adjacent stairway was constructed by command of Xerxes, as:

Xerxes the Monarch, the valiant King, the King of Kings, the King of all pure nations, the King of the pure, the pious, the most potent assembly, the son of Darius the King, the descendant of the Lord of the Universe, Jamsheed.

This reference to the legendary Jamshid (unhesitatingly identified by Sir Robert Ker Porter as Noah's eldest son,

Shem!) did not incline serious scholars to regard the effort as authoritative. Still less, it may be imagined, were they favourably impressed by Lichtenstein's attempt to make some sense out of Niebuhr's inscription "C":

> *The King, the Sovereign, Prince of all Princes, the Lord Saleh, Jinghis, son of Armerib, governor-general for the Emperor of China, Orkhan Saheb.*

But having regard for the fact that, in this instance, the hopeful translator directed his attention to the much more difficult Babylonian version (which, unwittingly, he appears to have read backwards), the outcome might well have been worse, even if it could hardly have been less accurate.

Elsewhere, however, there was a growing recognition of the importance of Zend to the investigators of Persian cuneiform, and studies which were to point the way to the next great advance were inaugurated by Rasmus Christian Rask, a distinguished Danish scholar and a pioneer in the field of comparative philology—his linguistic interests ranged from Zend, Pehlevi, and Sanskrit to Arabic, Hindustani, and Pali, not to mention Elu, Cingalese, and Icelandic—among others. It was Rask who demonstrated the incorrectness of the widely held view that the *Zend-Avesta* was of comparatively recent date—not earlier than the 3rd century A.D., according to some authorities.

After making a careful examination of Grotefend's results, Rask satisfied himself that the language of the 1st of the three columns of the Achaemenian inscriptions appeared to be closely related to Zend, though he was careful to add that it was not to be supposed from this that the two were identical. But he was able to show that the genitive plural

A N A M

which Grotefend had transliterated A-TSCH-A-O should, in fact, read A-N-A-M, a corrective simplification which added two more letters—*n* and *m*—to the list of those already known.

The need for a more reliable guide than Duperron's defective *Zend-Avesta* was supplied by Eugène Burnouf, who at the age of twenty-five had earned for himself a considerable reputation for Oriental scholarship. Six years later, in 1832, he was offered the chair of Sanskrit in the *Collège de France*, an appointment which led to there being brought to his notice a translation of the *Yasna* (a liturgical section of the *Avesta*) which had been made into Sanskrit by Persian scholars several centuries earlier. The outcome of this important find was the publication of his *Commentaire sur le Yaçna* (Paris, 1834), a work which proved of inestimable value to students of cuneiform.

Although, as the foremost Zend scholar of his day, it was in the role of a translator of Persian texts that Burnouf excelled, he also rendered valuable assistance in other ways. In his *Mémoire sur deux inscriptions cunéiformes trouvées près d'Hamadan* (Paris, 1836), he was able to make available additional trilingual material recovered from Van (Armenia) and Hamadan (Media), which had come into his possession after the murder of F. E. Schultz at Julamerk by Kurds in 1829. The Hamadan inscription, carved on the rock face of nearby Mount Elvand, was thought locally to refer to a treasure supposedly buried in the mountain. It consisted of two tablets, each inscribed with three versions of identical texts, with the exception that Darius announced himself as the author of one, and Xerxes acknowledged responsibility for the other. The triple Van inscription, which was also in the name of Xerxes, was in part a repetition of the Hamadan pair, but in addition it contained a final paragraph, the contents of which were new.

In common with other investigators, Burnouf was possessed of an incomplete version of the Old Persian syllabary which comprised phonetic values about the accuracy of which he was reasonably certain, and others which at best were to be regarded as doubtful. Thus armed, the procedure he adopted was to select some unknown sign, and then endeavour to assign to it a value not already allocated. Necessarily, the process was largely one of trial and error, but he relied upon his extensive knowledge of Zend to assist him in the recognition of any genuine word which might thereby be produced. One of his successes was the restoration of Münter's *a*, which Grotefend, for reasons of his own, had seen fit to alter to *v*—such emendatory tendencies were frequently displayed by the decipherers, who naturally preferred what they fondly believed to be the true worth of their own ideas, to the conflicting (and hence mistaken) notions of their wayward contemporaries.

In addition to the Van and Hamadan trilinguals, Burnouf also gave his attention to the inscription "I" of Niebuhr, as seemingly it contained many proper names. The reference was, in fact, to twenty-four Persian provinces, of which Burnouf contrived to identify sixteen, half of them correctly—Arabia, Babylon, Bactria, Cappadocia, Media, Persia, Sarangia, and Sogdiana. But even so, his success as a decipherer was by no means as great as he himself believed it to be. The list of signs which he compiled contained thirty-three values, and for twelve of these he claimed priority. Eight of the twelve, however, were later shown to be incorrect, while two others had already been determined, leaving him with the discovery of *k* and *z*.

Ironically enough, it was Christian Lassen, a close friend and collaborator of Burnouf, who achieved the outstanding results which were denied to his colleague. Lassen, a Norwegian, had studied at Heidelberg, and afterwards journeyed to England and then to France. It was while staying in Paris that he met Burnouf, whom he joined in the writing of a celebrated essay on Pali, the sacred language of the Buddhists of eastern India. In 1826, he left Paris for Bonn, where four years later he was offered a professorship at the University there. He kept in touch with Burnouf by letter, however, and among other matters of mutual interest, the two no doubt discussed the progress that was being made in cuneiform decipherment. It was nevertheless a coincidence that each publicised the result of his own investigations in the same year—Burnouf in his *Mémoire*, and Lassen under the title *Die altpersischen Keilinschriften* (Bonn, 1836).

Not surprisingly, the two publications were in many respects similar, even to the extent of the interest shown by their respective authors in the inscription "I" of Niebuhr. Lassen, for his part, had remembered the account given by Herodotus of how Darius had surveyed the Bosphorus, and had then set up two marble pillars inscribed with the names of all the nations represented in his fighting forces, and this recollection suggested to him that there might well be a similar collection of proper names to be found among the Persepolitan inscriptions. His attention, like that of Burnouf, was thus drawn to the catalogue of twenty-four Persian provinces, of which he identified no less than twenty—he failed only in the case of Arabia, Egypt, India, and Susa.

To Lassen must also go the credit for pointing out that a rigid application of Grotefend's sign values tended to produce unpronounceable words such as CPRD, THTGUS, and KTPTUK. This evident want of vowels suggested to him that some of the Persian signs must be syllabic rather than alphabetic, and he moreover announced the discovery that the sign for *a* was restricted in its use, in that it was employed only at the beginning of a word, or before a consonant or another vowel, and that otherwise it was included in the consonant sign. Even so, his transliterations were far from perfect, though his sign list contained twenty-three correct values—seven more than Burnouf's, and ten more than Grotefend's. If, as appears likely, he is entitled to be credited with the independent discovery of *k* and *z*, the identification of eight new values belongs to him, the other six being *d*, *g(a)*, *g(u)*, *i*, *m*, and *t*.

Collectively, the correct values of some three-quarters of all the signs of the writing of the 1st column had now been determined, and by 1845, less than half a dozen characters remained unidentified. That by this time the problem of the decipherment of the Old Persian cuneiform could be considered virtually solved, was demonstrated by the reasonably accurate translations which Lassen was able to prepare of all the Achaemenian inscriptions then available. Only one noteworthy item was missing from the collection, at once the least accessible and the most important: the record left by Darius the Great on the Rock of Behistun, with its 1,000 lines of writing containing ten times as many words as all the other material combined.

Even in modern times, the whereabouts of this extensive inscription and its accompanying reliefs had long been known. From the 17th century onwards, it had been seen and described by a succession of visitors to Persia, Ambrogio Bembo and Jean Otter among them, though at first its purport was far from being understood. Gardanne overstretched his imagination to the extent of seeing the figure of Ahura-Mazda as a cross, and below it the twelve apostles. Sir Robert Ker Porter, no less biblically minded, came to the conclusion that the sculpture was intended to portray the conquest of Israel by Shalmaneser V, and that the line of captives symbolised the ten tribes. A few years earlier, however, the more discerning J. M. Kinneir had rightly associated Behistun with Persepolis, and once this view gained acceptance, the hitherto inaccessible inscriptions acquired a new and important philological significance. And as it happened, the challenge presented by the problem of their transcription was met by the resourcefulness of a lone Englishman who, in the course of his professional duties, found himself stationed in the vicinity. Entirely on his own initiative, and at first acting alone and unaided, not only did he dedicate himself to the dangerous task of copying the writing, but, again working on his own, he also succeeded in deciphering it!

VI

Henry Creswicke Rawlinson was born at Chadlington Park, Oxfordshire, in 1810, and at school, though he evinced a considerable talent for Latin and Greek, he also excelled as an athlete, thanks to an exceptionally robust physique (he grew to be six feet tall). When he was sixteen, a nomination was secured for him with the East India Company, and he sailed for India in 1827. On board ship, he was fortunate enough to encounter Sir John Malcolm, a distinguished Orientalist and the newly appointed Governor of Bombay, who quickly succeeded in arousing in his young acquaintance an abiding interest in Persian affairs. As a result, on reaching his destination, Rawlinson studied not only Hindustani and Arabic, but also the language of Persia, to such good effect that in 1835 he was one of several officers chosen for a period of service in that land, and he found himself posted to Kermanshah in the capacity of military adviser to the brother of the Shah.

It was when he reached Hamadan, on his way to take up this appointment, that Rawlinson learned of the existence of the two Mount Elvand inscriptions, which he visited and copied. At the time, these trilinguals had still to be published by Burnouf, nor was Rawlinson familiar, as yet, with Grotefend's list of Old Persian sign values, though he was aware, without knowing the precise details of the achievement, that the names of three Achaemenian rulers had been identified. Thus in his subsequent investigation of the Hamadan inscription, he unwittingly duplicated the feat of his predecessor, in that, like Grotefend before him, he observed that except for certain well-defined groups of signs, the two sets of writing were identical. As for the differences, in the 12th line of one inscription, there occurred a word (call it y) for which there was substituted a different word (say z) in the other, while in the 19th line of the first inscription, yet a third word (x) was replaced in the second inscription by the aforementioned y:

	Inscription	
	1st	2nd
12th line	y	x
19th line	z	y

Precisely what was to be inferred from this? Using exactly the same reasoning employed by Grotefend more than thirty years earlier, Rawlinson came to the conclusion that the three groups of signs must represent proper names which, by their arrangement, were indicative of a genealogical succession of three consecutive generations of the Persian monarchy. In other words, that a King x was the father of a King y who was the father of a King z, and that the authors of the two inscriptions were father and son. From this point on, Rawlinson's wide knowledge of ancient Persian history left the outcome of the conundrum in no doubt, and the first three names he selected as being the most likely, in fact provided him with the correct answer. In this manner, he obtained the phonetic values of thirteen of the characters of the 1st column, which he assumed to be alphabetic.

At Kermanshah, meanwhile, he had learned of the extensive inscription to be found in the vicinity of Behistun, a mere twenty miles or so away. He was satisfied by this time that the writing on the Hamadan tablets contained no names other than the three he had identified, but recollected that Xerxes, in a speech to his uncle Artabanus (as dutifully recorded by Herodotus) had declared himself to be the child of Darius, the son of Hystaspes, the son of Arsames, the son of Ariaramnes, the son of Teispes, the son of Cyrus, the son of Cambyses, the son of Teispes, the son of Achaemenes. Might not a similar declaration be recorded at Behistun, the constituent names of which would enable him to identify additional characters?

As he approached his destination, Rawlinson could see the inscription from the highway, located some 300 feet above him on the almost sheer face of an isolated peak of rock which towered nearly 2,000 feet into the air. The climb, however, was well within his capabilities, and when he reached the memorial, he was impressed to find that it measured about 150 feet long by 100 feet high. Its base, conveniently enough, rested upon a narrow ledge upon which it was possible to stand upright, and Rawlinson was thus brought face to face with the main Persian text, which occupied five columns and consisted of more than 400 lines of writing. On his left were three more columns containing another 250 or so lines in the Elamite (Susian) character and language, while directly above him, and far beyond his reach, were the sculptured bas-reliefs which, down through the years, a succession of writers had so often, and so variously, described.

Of the fourteen figures, one was evidently a king, for he wore a crown and was accompanied by two armed attendants. In his left hand, the monarch grasped a bow, and his right hand was raised, as if in ackowledgement, to a divinity who hovered overhead, and who was shown graciously returning the salute. The king's left foot was planted on the body of a prostrate prisoner, whose arms were raised in an appeal for mercy, while nine other captives stood in line, their hands bound behind their backs, and a rope about their necks. Immediately above and below these figures were a series of short epigraphs, numbering 32 in all (11 Persian, 12 Elamite, 9 Accadian), and to the left of the sculptured panel, occupying two faces of an overhanging rock above the Elamite columns, were more than 100 lines of the Accadian version of the main inscription. The equivalent space on the right of the reliefs was occupied by four columns of supplementary texts.

This, then, was the famous Behistun inscription. Rawlinson afterwards estimated that the preliminary work alone must have required many months, and that it could not have been undertaken without the aid of an elaborate system of scaffolding erected for the purpose. Careful examination revealed that where flaws in the rock had been encountered, they had been made good by an embedding process which had entailed the use of molten lead. The lettering had then been engraved on the prepared surface, and treated with a coat of silicious varnish, despite which precaution, however, the writing was in places so badly weathered as to be illegible. Moreover, a portion of the first column of the supplementary texts (Elamite version) had been deliberately defaced by the sculptor, that room might be made for an additional figure— the last member of the line of roped victims, and evidently the unsuccessful author of a belated attempt at rebellion.

Rawlinson's immediate concern was the Persian section of the inscription, and much of the main body of this, once the comparative safety of the narrow ledge had been gained, was happily within his reach. And so, with an almost sheer drop of 300 feet at his back, and armed with notebook and pencil, he began to copy the writing. The task occupied most of his leisure hours for many months, and required the making of repeated journeys from Kermanshah to Behistun and back. But the work progressed steadily, and aided by the thirteen values he had secured from Mount Elvand, he was able to identify five groups of signs which occurred in the first paragraph of the Behistun inscription. One such group, consisting of five characters (of which he already knew four) was evidently a reference to the Arsames of the Greeks:

A R SH A

This name added *m* to his vocabulary, an acquisition which was of assistance in the identification of a collection of eight signs, of which he was now familiar with the first seven:

A R I Y A R M

Here, the last sign was evidently *n*, giving Ariaramnes. In a third group, all six of its characters were known to him, and these clearly read Persia:

P A R SA I YA

A fourth word contained nine signs, of which only the first was unknown to him, and he recognised the term Achaemenian:

KH A M N I SH I YA

The fifth group likewise offered no difficulty, as once again he was familiar with every sign but the first of what was evidently a reference to Teispes:

These five names yielded an additional five characters, and brought his total of correct identifications up to eighteen. Such was the extent of his progress, indeed, that when, towards the end of 1836, he at last managed to obtain information about the labours of Grotefend and St. Martin, it was at once apparent that neither of these investigators had anything to offer him, and that the results of their efforts had already been surpassed by his own.

Thereafter, one new name after another was identified by Rawlinson, providing him with a steady flow of additional sign values—*b* from Babirush (Babylon); *k* from Katpatuka (Cappadocia); *f* from Ufraata (Euphrates); and so on. By the autumn of 1837, not only had he succeeded in transcribing some 200 lines (about half) of the Persian text, but, assisted by his now extensive sign list, he had essayed a translation of the opening paragraphs. The results of these labours he transmitted to the Royal Asiatic Society in London, in the form of a paper which gave text, transliteration, and translation, and it is upon this document, and a supplement written two years later, that Rawlinson's claims as a decipherer of Old Persian cuneiform rest.

The paper was received in London early in 1838, where its arrival presented something of a problem, for the uniqueness of its contents made difficult an accurate assessment of its worth. On the advice of Edwin Norris, the Assistant Secretary of the Society, a copy of the communication was sent to Paris, where it excited great interest. Its author was at once made an Honorary Member of the French Asiatic Society, and steps were taken to ensure that he was fully informed about recent progress. In this way, Rawlinson was brought into touch with Burnouf, Lassen, and other European scholars, whose combined activities had already led to the recovery of almost the whole of the Old Persian syllabary. As for his own independent discovery of it, though it had entailed great daring and constituted a stupendous feat of in-

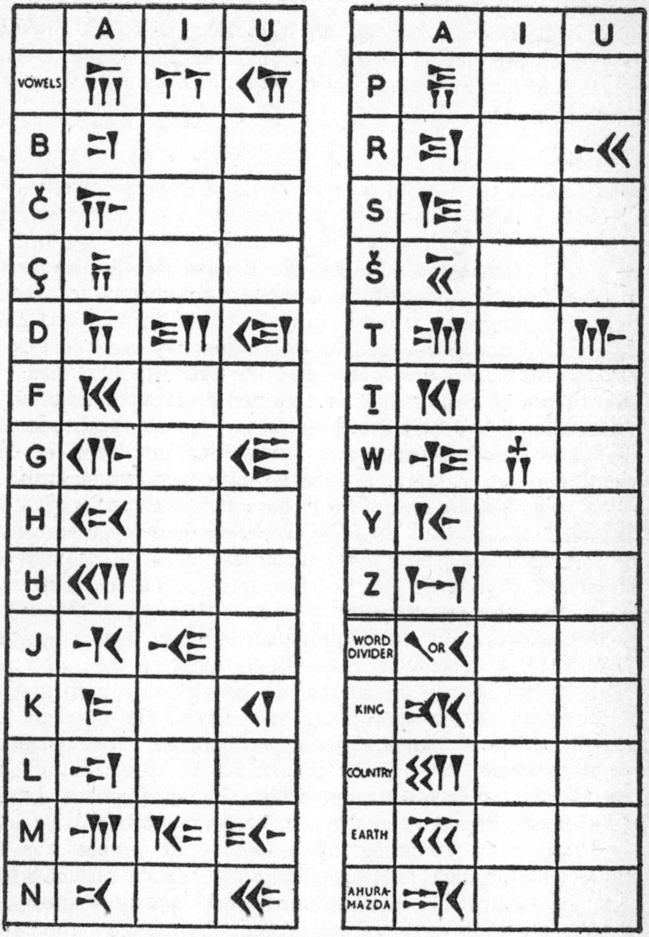

Fig. 5. Old Persian cuneiform syllabary.

dividual scholarship, it did not entitle its author to prior recognition in the matter of decipherment. But of the four remaining characters for which correct values had yet to be found, Rawlinson was able to identify two in 1838, and to share with Edward Hincks, an Irish clergyman, the discovery of a third during 1846, in which year the value of the fourth and last of the signs was determined by Adolf Holtzmann (Fig. 5).

VII

Once most of the Old Persian sign values were at their command, cuneiform scholars were able to give their undivided attention to the writing found in the 2nd and 3rd columns of the Achaemenian inscriptions. A careful search among this material soon revealed the existence of a succession of proper names in their expected positions, a discovery which established that the three texts were identical, and at the same time confirmed that the writing ran from left to right. The notion that the three versions were written in the same language, but in different characters, was no longer entertained, and as early as 1824 Grotefend had prepared a list of corresponding words in what he held to be three different languages, though he was not prepared to concede that any one of the three was Semitic.

Serious work on the Elamite version was begun by the Danish Sanscrit scholar Niels Louis Westergaard, who in 1843 visited Persia in search of inscriptions, particularly those which earlier transcribers had missed. He managed to obtain copies of two new items of importance, one from a porch at Persepolis, and the other from the tomb of Darius the Great at Naksh-i-Rustam. This last contained an extensive list of conquered lands, and Westergaard began his investigations by confining his attention to proper names (kings and provinces). His method, in the course of which he first ascertained the Elamite rendering, say, of Darius or Persia, and then analysed the contents of the sign group in the light of its Old Persian equivalent, was essentially one of identification and comparison. By this means, he obtained a list of sign values which enabled him to transliterate words which were unfamiliar to him, and thereafter to arrive at their meaning either by inference, or by reference to a trans-

PLATE 1. The Rosetta Stone, bilingual key to the Egyptian hieroglyphs. *(Photo: The British Museum)*

PLATE 2. Bushman paintings, Walk-y-a Cave, Southern Rhodesia.
(Photos: Glyn Edwards)

PLATE 3. Gathering and splitting papyrus for papermaking—a scene from the tomb of Puy-em-Re, Thebes.
(Photo: Egyptian Expedition of the Metropolitan Museum of Art, New York)

PLATE 4. Clay tablets, with pictographic inscriptions, from Jemdet Nasr, Mesopotamia. *(Photo: The British Museum)*

PLATE 5. Egyptian hieroglyphs, showing horizontal and vertical columns (see Fig. 2). *(Photo: The British Museum)*

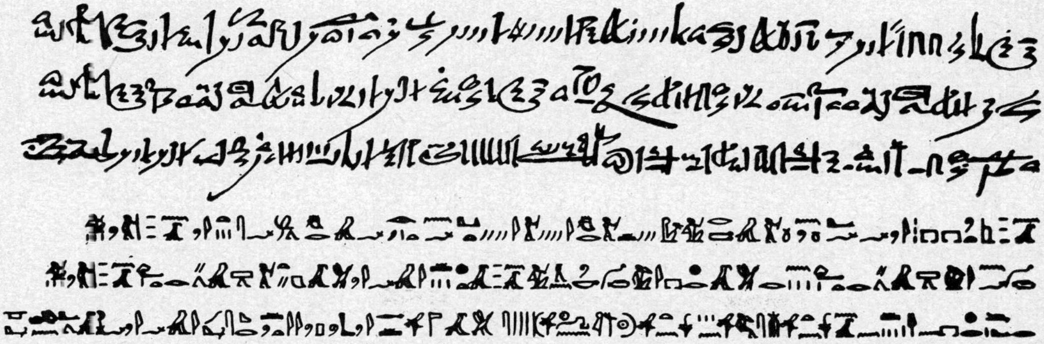

PLATE 6. Official hieratic of the 20th dynasty, with a hieroglyphic transcription in a modern hand—as with all handwriting, examples of hieratic differ, and before translating a text, Egyptologists transcribe it into hieroglyphs.

(Photo: Sir Alan Gardiner)

PLATE 7. (Above) Close-up of the cartouche of Amenemhet I, from the Lisht pyramid temple. (Photo: Egyptian Expedition of the Metropolitan Museum of Art, New York)

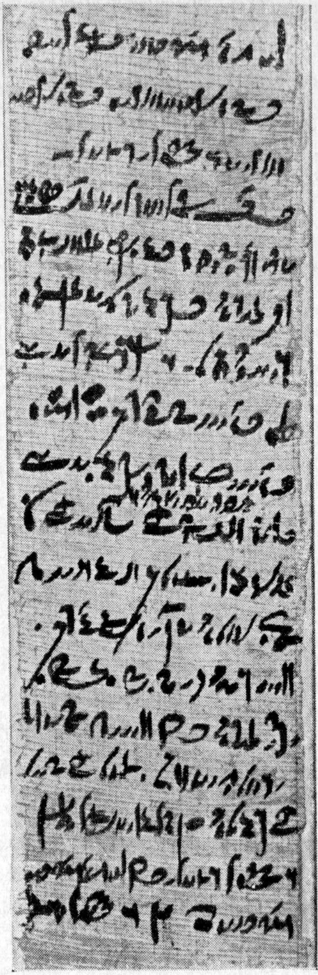

PLATE 8. (Right) Example of demotic writing.
(Photo: The British Museum)

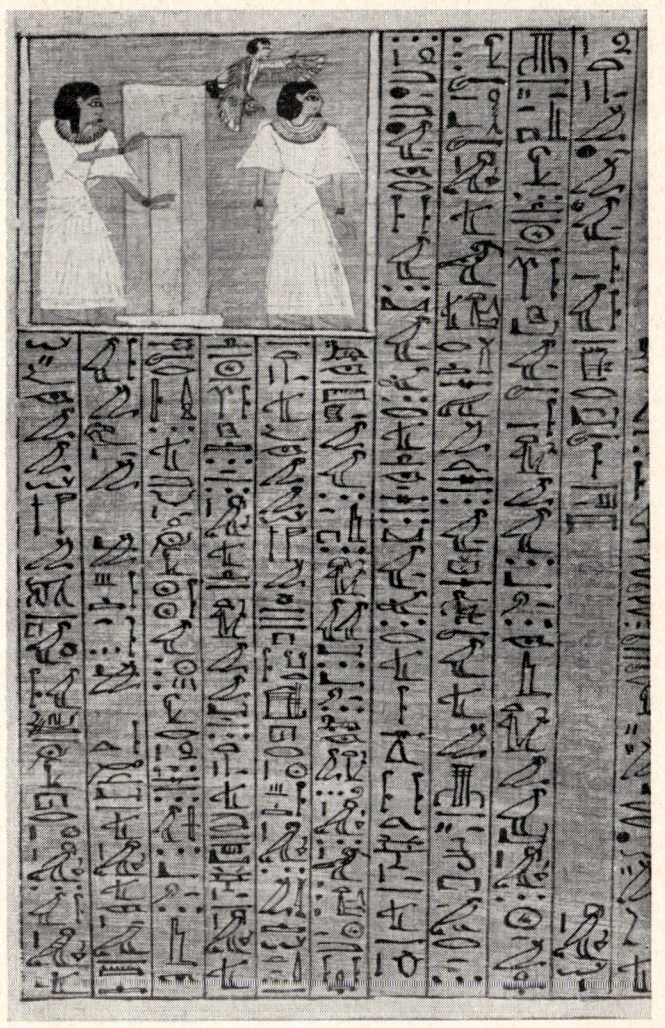

PLATE 9. Excerpt from the Egyptian so-called Book of the Dead.
(Photo: The British Museum)

PLATE 10. The ruins of Persepolis.

PLATE 11. Old Persian inscription from the Palace of Darius.
(Photos: The Oriental Institute, Chicago)

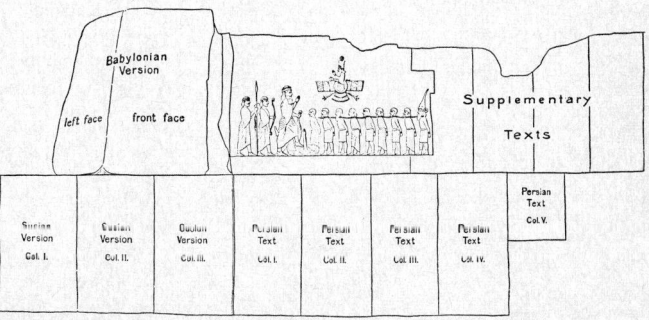

PLATE 12. General view of the sculptures and inscription of Darius the Great at Behistun, with *(below)* a key to the positions of the Old Persian, Elamite (Susian) and Babylonian versions of the trilingual. *(Photos: The British Museum)*

PLATE 13. Close-up of the Behistun relief, showing Darius facing the rebel leaders. *(Below)* A key to the Old Persian, Elamite and Babylonian Epigraphs.   *(Photos: The British Museum)*

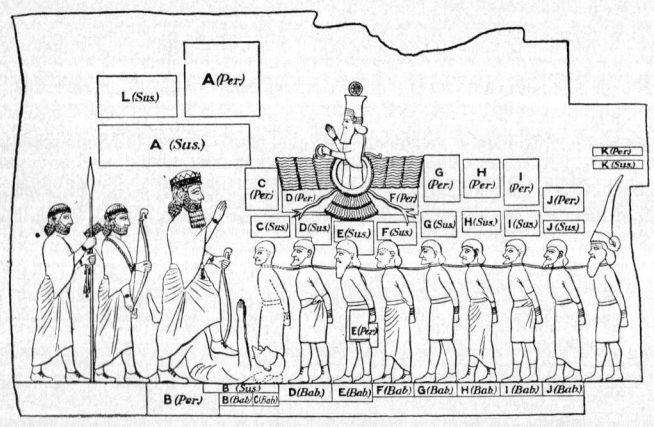

PLATE 14. (Left) Prism of Sennacherib, King of Assyria. It describes his expedition against Hezekiah of Judah in the summer of 701 B.C.
(*Photo: The Oriental Institute, Chicago*)

PLATE 15. (Right) One of the cuneiform tablets found at Tell el-Amarna, Egypt.
(*Photo: The British Museum*)

PLATE 16. (Left) Hittite hieroglyphs.

PLATE 17. (Right) Hittite cuneiform. This clay tablet from Boghaz-Keui contains magical rituals against pestilence. (Photos: The British Museum)

PLATE 18. The two sides of the avenue of inscribed slabs at Karatepe; *(above)* Hittite hieroglyphs; *(below)* Phoenician script. *(Photos: Max G. Scheler and H. T. Bossert)*

PLATE 19. *(Above)* Extracts from the account book of a merchant dealing in purple-dyed wool. *(Below)* The will of a citizen of Ugarit, appointing his wife heir to all his goods.

(Photos: The Cuneiform Texts of Ras Shamra-Ugarit)

PLATE 20. (Right) Cretan hieroglyphs.

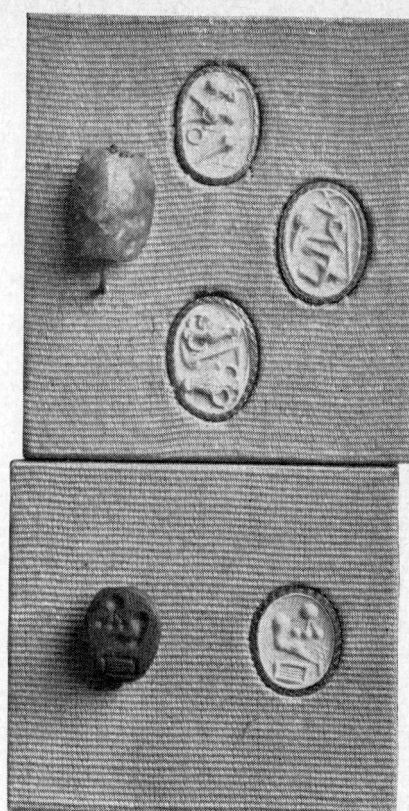

PLATE 21. (Below) Linear B tablets, palm-leaf type. *(Photos: The British Museum)*

PLATE 22. One of the page-form tablets recovered during excavations carried out at Pylos, on the Greek Mainland.

(Photo: C. W. Blegan)

lation of the 1st column. He concluded that the writing of the 2nd column was in part syllabic and in part alphabetic, and from a study of the relationship of vowels to consonants, he estimated that the number of characters exceeded 100, of which theoretical total he identified between 80 and 90.

At this time, the Elamite version of the Behistun inscription was not available, for, with the outbreak of the Afghan War in 1839, Rawlinson had been recalled to India. The Shah then arranged for the British Mission to be replaced by one from France, and King Louis Philippe sent as his representative Count de Sarcey, accompanied by a numerous staff which included Pascal Coste and Eugène Flandin, respectively an architect and an artist. But although Flandin paid several visits to Behistun with the intention of copying the inscripton there, and even succeeded in climbing up to the ledge at its base, he decided that the proposed task was far too risky an undertaking, and the idea was abandoned.

It was thus left for Rawlinson to continue the work which he had begun, and this he was able to do in 1844, when he revisited the site with two companions. With their assistance, he managed to obtain complete copies of the main Persian and Elamite texts, and also of all the epigraphs, though not before the difficulties and dangers associated with the enterprise had become evident enough. To reach the upper part of the Persian columns, a ladder was indispensable. But the supporting ledge, less than two feet in width, was so narrow in relation to the height of the inscription that steps of adequate length were unusable. On the other hand, after the ladder had been shortened so as to assist the angle of slope, it became necessary to stand on its topmost rung, without any support other than that which could be obtained by steadying the body against the vertical rock face with the left arm. Thus dizzily perched, and holding a notebook in one hand and a pencil in the other, Rawlinson unconcernedly copied the upper portions of the Persian text.

Reaching the three Elamite columns was an even more hazardous undertaking. The columns were located in a recess, at the far side of which was another supporting ledge, isolated by a sheer drop which could only be bridged at an angle. Rawlinson then discovered that by shortening his ladder to meet the demands of the Persian inscriptions, it had been left insufficiently long to extend over the chasm in such a way that it would lie flat and at the same time be fully supported. An attempt to overcome this difficulty was made by placing the ladder (which was of the wide Persian variety) on edge, with its upper side firmly lodged at either end, and its underside dangling in space. Rawlinson then began to cross by using his feet on the lower section, while clinging to the upper part with his hands. His weight, however, detached the lower part from the rungs, and it went hurtling into space, leaving him hanging by his arms in mid-air. That despite this mishap, which might easily have cost him his life, Rawlinson succeeded in copying the whole of the Elamite version of the inscription, speaks as eloquently of his determination as it does of his courage.

But during 1844 Westergaard had also been busy, and in his efforts to decipher the contents of the 2nd column, he was joined by Louis Caignart de Saulcy, and also by Hincks, who in 1846 read a paper "On the First and Second Kinds of Persepolitan Writing" to members of the Royal Irish Academy. And just when Rawlinson's own memoir on the subject was nearing completion, he received details of the efforts of his contemporaries, and realised that once again he had been anticipated in his results. At this, he forthwith placed all his Behistun material at the disposal of Norris, who by 1852 succeeded in deciphering almost the whole of it.

A. D. Mordtmann subsequently called the language Susian, as opposed to Westergaard, who, following St. Martin, had named it Median, and A. H. Sayce, who had proposed the term Amardian. It was eventually established that the writing, in its final form, comprised a system of some ninety-six syllabic signs (representing consonant-vowel and consonant-vowel-consonant combinations), together with about twenty ideograms and determinatives. Moreover, with evidence provided by inscriptions found at Susa, it was shown that the language was a development of that spoken by the people of Elam, and in 1897, Hüsing renamed it New Elamite. It has since been classified, somewhat vaguely, as Caucasian.

From 1842 onwards, meanwhile, excavations carried out by P. E. Botta and Henry Layard at the sites of ancient Assyrian cities in Mesopotamia began to yield a rich harvest of inscribed tablets, the writing of which appeared to bear a close resemblance to that found in the 3rd column of the Achaemenian inscriptions. Botta drew up a list of Assyrian signs, and although he could not read them, he contrived to assign the correct value (Shar) to the first syllable of the name of Sargon (Sharrukin), thereby enabling H. A. de Longperrier to identify the builder of the palace of Khorsabad.

These developments inevitably directed attention once again to Behistun, where it appeared that the key to the unilingual Assyrian tablet inscriptions was to be found. With this in mind, Rawlinson, in 1847, again returned to the scene of his earlier activities, on this occasion plentifully supplied with ropes, planks, ladders, and other essential equipment. The third and last of the main texts occupied two faces of an overhanging rock, immediately above the Elamite version. It was in an almost inaccessible position, and had he had to rely upon his equipment alone, he might well have failed in his task. He was fortunate, however, in securing the services of an agile Kurdish boy, who first squeezed himself up a chimney in the rock, then drove home a wooden peg, to which he fastened a rope, and afterwards tried to swing himself across the face of the cliff so as to reach a cleft on the opposite side. But he was foiled in this by the projection of the rock, and so, hanging on by fingers and toes, the boy inched his way across the almost bare wall of the precipice for a distance of 20 feet. He was then able to insert a second peg and attach the other end of the rope to it, whereafter, suspended in a makeshift painter's cradle, and working under Rawlinson's directions, he took paper casts of the entire text.

The inscription, much of it badly weathered, consisted of 112 lines of writing, to which Rawlinson gave his attention throughout 1848, and during the following year also. As the work progressed, the similarity of the unknown language to several well known Semitic dialects became increasingly evident, a fact which greatly assisted the task of elucidation. The sense of the writing was, of course, already known from the Persian version. But whereas the writing of the 1st column consisted of relatively few signs, it was clear that its 3rd column equivalent was composed of hundreds of different characters, some of which stood for a syllable, and others for an entire word. Moreover, it seemed that on occasion a given sign might represent several different syllables or words, and that, conversely, a number of signs were sometimes used to indicate the same word (principles of polyphony and homophony). Nevertheless, by 1850, Rawlinson had ascertained the values of about 150 characters, and aided by the Persian text, had determined the precise meanings of some 500 words.

Hincks, however, was the first to publish a list of identified characters, which included those representative of the vowels *a, e, i, u* (there was no Assyrian character for *o*). He showed, too, that many of the signs were syllabic, and drew attention to the existence of ideographs and determinatives. With this information at their disposal, it was possible for scholars to turn from the trilingual Achaemenian inscriptions to the unilingual tablets found in Babylonia and Assyria, and although it was recognised that the languages of the two countries were undoubtedly Semitic, and that both were closely related, it was also evident that the two systems were by no means identical. Worse, it transpired that two distinct methods of writing had existed in each region, thus multiplying by a factor of four the hundreds of signs which needed to be identified and understood. . . .

But, despite this formidable complication, the decipherers confidently claimed to be able to read the several forms of Mesopotamian writing, a claim which, however, left many sceptics unconvinced: among other things, they simply could not accept the suggestion that different signs were used to indicate the same word, or that a single sign could represent more than one word. Eventually the matter was put to a decisive test at the instigation of the mathematician William Henry Fox Talbot. He prevailed upon Edwin Norris, on behalf of the Royal Asiatic Society, to invite three or four well-known cuneiform scholars independently to translate an inscription on some newly found clay prisms of the Assyrian monarch Tiglath-pileser I, and to submit their results in sealed envelopes to an adjudicating committee. Fox Talbot himself attempted a translation, and the three others who were invited to do so were Jules Oppert, Edward Hincks, and, of course, Henry Rawlinson. The results, when examined, were found to be in reasonably close agreement on all essential points.

VIII

As the work of translating Babylonian and Assyrian documents went on, the conviction grew among those engaged in the task that the language of some of the texts was not Semitic. The matter was brought to a head in 1855, when Rawlinson, after examining a tablet sent to him from

Larsa by the archaeologist W. Kennet Loftus, announced that the writing was in an unknown tongue. Hincks, in the following year, recognised that the language was agglutinative, but all attempts to discover its affinities were (and still remain) unsuccessful, perhaps with good reason, for it is in all probability the oldest known language in the world.

The prospects of decipherment, which at first appeared far from promising, suddenly and unexpectedly improved. In Mesopotamia, Henry Layard, after digging among the ruins of Calah, transferred his attention to the so-called mound of Kouyunjik. This was, in fact, the remains of the famous Assyrian capital of Nineveh, and the excavator was rewarded by the discovery of a priceless find in the shape of the library of King Ashurbanipal, amounting in all to more than 20,000 clay tablets. When a consignment of this material was later examined by Rawlinson and Norris at the British Museum, it was found to contain a number of lexicons and phrasebooks, evidently compiled with a view to helping Semitic students of the unknown tongue. And as may be imagined, the discovery of these interlinear translations was also of the utmost assistance to modern scholars, whose difficulties vanished in so far as the characters and phonetic values of the writing was concerned. The fact that the language itself seemingly stood alone, however, greatly hampered attempts to gain an understanding of its grammatical structure, and even now the interpretation of unilingual texts continues to be attended by some uncertainty, though the general meaning can usually be made out clearly enough.

There remained the question of ownership. As to this, a possible answer was provided by a consideration of the fact that the appearance of so complicated a mode of writing as cuneiform could hardly have coincided with the emergence of the Babylonian Empire. It thus seemed that its invention and development must be attributed to another age, if not to another people—*perhaps a people of non-Semitic stock*. Might it not have been the case that a comparatively highly civilised community had been overwhelmed by Semitic tribes, whose members thereafter absorbed much of the alien culture, even to the extent of preserving a knowledge of the language? As for the identity of this hypothetical and long-vanished people, a clue was provided by a reference in an inscription to a ruler who styled himself "King of Sumer and Accad," in the light of which Rawlinson suggested the name Accadian for these early inhabitants of Mesopotamia.

Oppert, however, argued that they were more properly to be regarded as Sumerian, a view which ultimately prevailed, and the term Accadian is now applied to their Semitic conquerors and to the language thereof, as spoken by their successors the Babylonians. As for the later conquerors of Babylonia, while the majority of their royal inscriptions were written in classical Accadian, they actually spoke (and sometimes wrote in) a closely related dialect which has since been designated Assyrian.

It was many years, however, before the truth of the Sumerian hypothesis could be demonstrated beyond all doubt, for, as its authors quickly discovered, it was far easier to postulate a pre-Babylonian, non-Semitic cultural source than it was to provide convincing evidence of its one-time existence. The problem was aggravated by the continued failure of the search for cognate languages, and some scholars went so far as to deny the reality of both the Sumerians and their unique mode of speech. A leading exponent of this view was an able Semiticist by the name of Joseph Halévy. Himself a Hebrew, Halévy was obsessed by the notion that the Babylonians, to whom he traced the ancestry of the Jewish people, were the ultimate source of the civilisation of Western Asia, and he strenuously argued against the proposed transference of the credit for much of this advancement to the non-Semitic Sumerians. The Sumero-Assyrian phrase-books he sought to explain away by advancing the theory that the Sumerian language, alleged and supposed, was merely a system of secret writing which had been invented by the local priesthood for the mystification of their lay customers, and the plausibility of this ingenious thesis, in the absence of the evidence necessary to refute it, led to an argument which was as profitless as it was prolonged. Moreover, in the midst of this disputation about language, another controversy arose over the manner in which cuneiform writing had evolved. Jules Oppert held that the signs had originally been pictographs, whereas the German scholar Friedrich Delitzsch maintained that the script had been developed from a comparatively small number of basic characters, various combinations of which had given rise to the hundreds of different signs.

Both of these acute differences of opinion were eventually resolved by the discovery of Sumerian texts which not only antedated the earliest Babylonian records, but which also provided indisputable evidence of the pictorial origin of the cuneiform writing. Primitive examples of the script, as found on some hundreds of clay tablets unearthed at Warka (ancient Uruk) during the years 1928-31, were found to consist of clearly recognisable drawings of objects. In as much as each symbol seemingly represented a complete word, this embryonic writing was capable of being read in almost any language, and it was other considerations which pointed to the Sumerians as the probable authors of it.

Something of the history of the Sumerians had by this time been gleaned from various archaeological discoveries, and it appeared that by the 4th millennium B.C. they were already in occupation of the territory which lies between the Tigris and Euphrates rivers at the head of the Persian Gulf, to the north of which was the Land of Accad, the abode of a Semitic people. Of the race or the original home of the intruders, nothing is known with any certainty. The suggestion has been made that by the construction of their tall, pyramidal ziggurats, the newcomers sought to reproduce on a flat alluvial plain some of the features of a mountainous domain, a theory which B. Hrozný supported with philological evidence by drawing attention to the fact that the Sumerian word for east (*im-kur-ra*) would appear to indicate the existence of mountains in that direction, from the vicinity of which their remote forebears possibly came. On the other hand, Berossos, a native priest (3rd century B.C.) and the Manetho of Babylonia, tells of a legendary race of monsters, half fish and half man, which emerged from the waters of the Persian Gulf and settled along the coast, bringing with them a knowledge of agriculture, writing, and metal-working.

At all events, the Sumerians founded a number of city-states, notable among which were those of the Adab, Eridu, Lagash, Larsa, Uruk, and Ur. These communities were frequently engaged in internecine struggles, and from time to time one or other of them would dominate the remainder. There were also wars with foreign neighbours, which on occasion resulted in total defeat. Thus, about 2450 B.C., the whole of the region was subdued by the Semitic conqueror Sargon of Accad, whose extensive realm also came to include Elam and Assyria. Under his grandson, Naram-Sin, however, the empire was overrun by barbaric hordes known as the Gutium. These invaders were ultimately driven out, whereafter the Sumerians gained a fleeting independence, and there flourished the illustrious 3rd dynasty of Ur under Ur-

Nammu ("King of Sumer and Accad") and his successors. But eventually, Ur suffered destruction at the hands of the Elamites, who were in turn defeated by the Amorites (Westerners), the Semitic founders of the 1st dynasty of Babylon, whose 6th king, the famous Hammurabi, subdued the whole of Mesopotamia, by which time (*c.* 1900 B.C.) the Sumerians had lost their national identity.

Their system of writing, meanwhile, had been completely transformed. With the gradual elimination of curved lines, the original pictures had become increasingly stylised, and hence less easily recognisable. The process was hastened when the angle of the lower edge of the reed stylus with which the signs were traced became broader, thus causing the impression made by the point of the instrument to assume its characteristic, wedge-like shape. Another fundamental change concerned the direction of the writing. Originally, the characters were arranged in vertical columns which read downwards, and which progressed from right to left. But it was eventually discovered that the script could be followed more readily by tilting the tablet to the left, so that the eye could traverse it horizontally, and the mode of writing was altered accordingly. In effect, the characters were turned through an angle of 90 degrees, and henceforth read from left to right (Fig. 6).

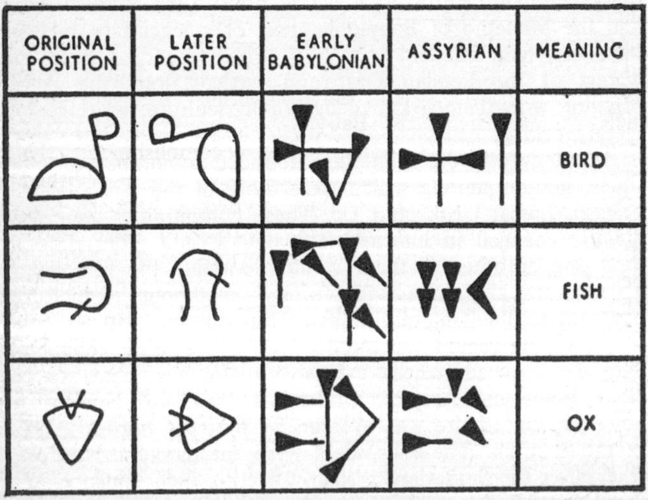

ORIGINAL POSITION	LATER POSITION	EARLY BABYLONIAN	ASSYRIAN	MEANING
				BIRD
				FISH
				OX

Fig. 6. Development of cuneiform writing (after A. Poebel).

The conversion to phonetic writing was assisted by the predominantly mono-syllabic nature of Sumerian root words, to such an extent that by the time of the 3rd dynasty of Ur, the number of signs had been progressively reduced from about 2,000 to less than a third of this number. Individual signs, however, were combined to form innumerable composite characters—*e.g.*, the symbols for "water" and "heaven" together signified "rain":

WATER   HEAVEN   WATER OF HEAVEN

In the course of adapting the Sumerian script to their language, the Semitic Accadians and their successors gave new values to many of the existing symbols—the Assyrians, for instance, adopted the composite character indicative of "water of heaven," but used it ideographically to indicate their own word for rain (*zunnu*). They also appropriated many others signs to represent syllables which variously consisted of a vowel preceded by a consonant (*di, nu*); a vowel followed by a consonant (*ab, uz*); or a vowel which was both preceded and followed by a consonant (*gal, pap*).

Even after the complete subjugation of the Sumerians, their language continued to be employed for learned and sacred purposes, much as Latin remained in use in Europe and elsewhere after the collapse of the Roman empire. Nor was the art of writing the only Sumerian achievement to which the Accadians, the Babylonians, and the Assyrians became heir. Among their many other accomplishments, the Sumerians evolved an elaborate legal code; they established recognised banking practices; they devised a standard system of weights and measures; they introduced wage stabilisation and price control; they undertook vast irrigation schemes; they laid the foundations of a highly distinctive architecture; they studied astronomy and mathematics, dividing the day into twenty-four hours and the circle into 360 degrees; and they produced a literature devoted to narratives about the creation of order out of chaos, the innate sinfulness of man, and an attempt by the high gods to sweep him off the face of the earth by means of a flood to end all floods—epic tales which were given to the world by their Semitic successors, including the Hebrews, who claimed them as their own.

IX

Up to the middle of the 19th century, the existence of the Old Empire of the Babylonians, let alone that of their Sumerian predecessors, was unknown. Historically, the early period of Mesopotamian civilisation was a blank, and knowledge of the region and its inhabitants prior to the arrival on the scene of Alexander the Great, was restricted to extracts from the no longer extant works of Berossos, to some mutually contradictory accounts given by Herodotus and Ctesias, and to sundry references about the Assyrians and the Chaldeans (Neo-Babylonians) in the Old Testament. Nor did the first results of cuneiform decipherment give any hint of the far-reaching discoveries which were to follow. The Persian inscriptions, when at last they could be read, were found to consist for the most part of statements to the effect that Darius (or Xerxes) was a veritable King of kings; that he was the son of Hystaspes (or of Darius); and that he was responsible for the building of this palace (or that stairway). The extensive memorial at Behistun, it is true, was more informative, in that it provided or confirmed historical details which were hitherto unknown or in doubt. On the other hand, the Elamite and Accadian versions of all these inscriptions merely repeated what had already been said.

It was at this juncture that the excavational activities of Botta, Layard, and others began to bring to light an ever-increasing number of unilingual inscriptions, most of which were written in the character and language of the 3rd of the Persian columns. Not only did these cuneiform texts appear on the walls of palaces and temples, but they were discovered on bricks and on foundation stones, on boundary markers and on gate sockets, on prisms and on cylinders. And there were also recovered, at first in their hundreds, and then in their tens of thousands, the ubiquitous baked clay tablets, upon which were recorded a seemingly endless array of mortgage deeds, marriage contracts, promissory-notes, itemised accounts, legal codes, official communications, royal correspondence, not to mention a superabundance of myths, spells, omens, rituals, hymns, lamentations, liturgies, prayers, and the like.

It was a careful examination of this material which finally

established that Assyrian culture was essentially Babylonian, and that the Babylonians and the Accadians, in turn, were heavily indebted to the Sumerians. Although the Assyrians, as the contents of their libraries showed, were great collectors of the literary works of their predecessors, their own contribution amounted to little more than official records of their kings and their conquests. The story thus unfolded is one of continuous slaughter and destruction, of cities besieged, taken, and consigned to the flames, and of whole populations impaled on stakes, or blinded, dismembered, and left to die in heaps. It all makes grim and horrifying reading, even in a century which has witnessed the liquidation of the Kulaks, wholesale exterminations of the Jews, and the annihilation of entire cities by atom bombs.

So-called *limmu* lists, found among the Assyrian records, reflected the custom of naming each year after some high dignitary, beginning as a rule with the king, and of recording the outstanding events which took place during his period of office. In addition to providing information about the order of Assyrian monarchs and the lengths of their reigns, these lists have on occasion afforded clues of vital chronological import, as happened in the case of the following entry opposite the name of Pur-Sagail, Governor of Gozan:

Revolt in the city of Ashur. In (the month of) Sivan there was an eclipse of the sun.

This passing reference to an astronomical phenomenon enabled the event in question to be identified as a total obscuration of the sun, visible at Nineveh and lasting 2 hours 43 minutes, which occurred on 15 June, 763 B.C., with the result that the purely relative sequence of dates associated with it could then be fixed in terms of an absolute chronology. A similar feat was attempted by F. X. Kugler with the aid of the so-called Venus tablets of Ammi-zaduga, 10th king of the 1st dynasty of Babylon. These tablets, which concern astrological omens, were based upon observations of the planet after which they were named, but their usefulness is conditioned by the fact that the various astronomical phenomena involved repeat themselves approximately every 275 years, thus leaving the investigator with a choice of possible dates.

In pursuance of their astrological beliefs, the Babylonians were assiduous observers of the heavens, and at a date unspecified and unknown, their star-gazing led to the discovery of the Saros, a period of 223 lunar months, at the end of which the moon returns almost exactly to its original position in regard to the sun and its own nodes and perigee. Which is to say, it was found that the conditions which make for solar and lunar eclipses re-occur at intervals of eighteen years (more precisely, some 6,585 days), and the ancient soothsayers were thereby enabled to predict the occurrence of these celestial events, an accomplishment which no doubt did much to enhance their reputations in the more dubious realm of astrology. As to this, such was the importance attached to oracularities that no monarch thought of engaging in war, or of setting out on a journey, or of disposing of an unwanted wife, without first being assured of a favourable outcome, any more than one of his subjects considered starting up in business, or of moving to a new address, or of cheating his best friend, without first ascertaining the attitude of the high gods to the proposal. Nor were the planets the sole source of advance information. For those trained to observe it, the future was also to be seen in the entrails of animals, in the flight of birds, and in the patterns which formed when oil was poured on the surface of water.

The department of divination, it goes without saying, was strictly an ecclesiastical one, and an unquestioning belief in the efficacy of the process was no doubt regarded as a cardinal article of faith. But as the records show, even in those days there were sceptics who were not prepared blindly to accept the doctrine of divine revelation on the mere word of those whose business it was to dispense and profit by it. More, this theological pretension was challenged on ethical grounds, and against it was raised the very real problem of human misery and inequality. Why, it was asked, if the high gods were just, all-seeing and all-powerful, and hence in full control of terrestrial events, were evil-doers allowed to prosper at the expense of the righteous, who were so often called upon to endure hardship and suffering? To this cry from the heart, which has continued to echo down through the ages, there was, alas, no convincing response, and even in these days of monotheistic enlightenment, there is a lingering suspicion that the question remains unanswered and unanswerable.

Just as the astrological activities of the Babylonians led to useful discoveries in astronomy, so by their interest in animal interiors they acquired an extensive knowledge of anatomy, and thereby earned for themselves a considerable reputation for surgical skill. The Babylonian physician who resorted to the knife, indeed, could not afford to make mistakes. The law, not content with invoking the death penalty for quackery, prescribed that a doctor's hands should be cut off if, after he had opened a wound with a metal scalpel, the patient subsequently died. With these and other penalties hanging over his head, the wonder is that the medical practitioner was not legislated out of existence, though much relieving of human ills was attempted by means of massage and poulticing, and by a judicious administering of herbal remedies and mineral preparations. Textbooks exist which list measures appropriate in the case of afflictions of the head, teeth, and eyes, and of snake bites and scorpion stings, treatments which were combined with powerful exorcisms designed to oust the causative demon or demons.

The accounts recording these and other achievements of the ancient peoples of Mesopotamia attracted the attention of a much wider audience in modern times when George Smith, a member of the staff of the British Museum, announced in 1872 that, while examining material recovered by Hormuzd Rassam, Layard's assistant and successor, he had come upon a fragmentary reference to a Babylonian account of the Deluge. Such was the extent of the popular interest which this statement aroused that the *Daily Telegraph* advanced the sum of 1,000 guineas to enable Smith to visit Nineveh in search of the remainder of the story, and much of the missing material was, in fact, recovered. Other copies and versions came to light later, and it transpired that the Deluge reference was but part of an epic story which told of events in the life of Gilgamesh, the semi-divine, semi-human son of the mother goddess Nin-Sun, and that the narrative, which in its final form occupied twelve tablets, each recounting an adventure in which the hero of the story was in some way concerned, was evidently a composite tale made up of what had originally been a series of disconnected myths and legends.

The story opens with Gilgamesh as the 5th and not very popular King of Erech, who has ordered that all the young men of his domain shall undertake the construction of a protective wall round the city. The people eventually call upon the goddess Aruru to turn the king away from his oppressive purpose, and she responds by prevailing upon a hunter named Enkidu to visit Erech. The king and the new arrival become friends, and succeeding tablets describe a number of adventures they have together. In the 6th account, Gilgamesh is wooed by Ishtar, the goddess of love, but the intended victim, who is well aware that if he succumbs to the lady's charms, it will mean his end, ignores her blandishments. The slighted goddess then calls upon her father Anu to avenge her, and he answers her appeal by sending a ferocious bull to attack Gilgamesh who, aided by Enkidu, manages to dispose of the creature.

In the 7th tablet, Enkidu contracts a dread disease from which, in the 8th instalment, he dies. The next two portions of the story describe the wanderings of Gilgamesh in search of one Ut-Napishtim, who is regarded with favour by the high gods, and from whom Gilgamesh hopes to learn how to escape the fate which has overtaken his friend. In the course of his journeyings, he encounters lions and scorpion-men, not to mention the goddess Sabitu, guardian of the Sea of the Dead. At first she is unfriendly towards him, but is eventually persuaded to permit him to make a voyage which at last brings him to Ut-Napishtim. In the 11th (Deluge) tablet, Ut-Napishtim reveals the remarkable manner in which he, the favoured one of the gods, escaped the wrath from on high. He then informs his listener of the existence of a magic weed which will restore his youth. Gilgamesh obtains some of the life-giving plant, but, before he can derive any benefit from it, it is snatched from him by a demon in the guise of a serpent. And in the 12th and last episode, a disconsolate Gilgamesh is vouchsafed a sight of the departed Enkidu, from whom he receives a not very encouraging impression of the shadowy existence which awaits him in the Land of No Return.

The story told to Gilgamesh by Ut-Napishtim, as given in the 11th of the twelve accounts, describes how the high gods, gathered together in the city of Shurippak, decide to eliminate mankind by means of a great flood. The intention was that the extermination should be complete, but Ea (otherwise Enki), the god of the deep, ostensibly addressing himself to a reed hut, by this subterfuge warns Ut-Napishtim of the impending disaster, and instructs him to avoid the danger by building a ship, six stories high, each containing nine compartments. Ut-Napishtim hastily sets to work, making the vessel watertight by smearing it with pitch, inside and out. He then herds his family on board, accompanied by a representative selection of animal life, and awaits events. A tremendous storm then breaks upon the world and, after six days of unprecedented flooding, only Ut-Napishtim and his companions remain alive. On the seventh day, the tempest abates, and as the waters gradually recede, land is seen. On the eighth day the vessel drifts on to the mountain of Nisir, and there lodges. But a dove, later let loose, can find no resting place, and comes back to the ship. So does a swallow, sent off the next day. Finally, a raven is despatched and, when it does not return, the voyagers cautiously emerge, and give thanks for their deliverance.

Other similarities between Sumero-Babylonian legends and the Old Testament record have also been found. Ashurbanipal's library contained seven clay tablets on which were inscribed a Creation Epic known as "When in the height . . ." from the first two opening words of the text. The poem, amounting to some 994 lines in all, concerns the origin of the universe, and describes the coming forth of the gods from chaos. The forces of disorder, represented by Apsu and the she-dragon Tiamat, are overthrown in battle by Marduk, ably assisted by Ea and the seven winds. After killing Tiamat, the triumphant Marduk cuts the monstrous body into two, and fashions the heavens out of one portion, and the earth out of the other. Then he arranges the stars in their courses, and finally creates man out of an admixture of blood and clay. Significantly, the Hebrew word (*tehom*) for the watery chaos out of which order was brought is another form of the Babylonian name for Tiamat. . . .

As for the events which followed the creation of man, the very name Eden is Babylonian (*edinu*, "plain"), while that its supposed location was in Mesopotamia is confirmed by the Hebraic reference to the great river with its four branches, one of them named Euphrates, and another Hiddekel, *i.e.*, Idigat, or Tigris. Account, too, must be taken of the discovery of a Sumerian cylinder inscription which reveals the existence of an early woman-from-rib story, and relates how Enki and Ninhursag, as the occupants of an earthly paradise, were surrounded by no less than eight forbidden fruits, and of how their fall from grace was occasioned, not by the low cunning of a serpent, but by the wiles of a fox.

Nor are these correspondences confined to the Book of Genesis. At the beginning of the present century, the de Morgan expedition to Susa discovered (in three pieces) a black diorite stele covered with some 3,600 lines of cuneiform writing. Examination revealed that the monument had originally been set up in the great temple of Marduk at Babylon, and that it had been carried off to the Elamite capital by a raiding party. On it were written the Sumero-Babylonian laws as codified by the great Hammurabi, a compilation which, with its stipulations about marriage and divorce, hire purchase and property rights, slander and adultery, not only afforded a most informative glimpse of Babylonian affairs, but also revealed itself, by a series of parallels so extraordinary that much of the phrasing was repeated word for word, as the undoubted fount of Mosaic Law!

All this need occasion no surprise, when it is recollected that the Old Testament record incorporates a wealth of oral material which, over a period of more than 1,000 years, was gradually put into written form by a succession of Hebrew editors and redactors, some of whom were undoubtedly in close contact with the peoples of Egypt and Babylonia during the years of the Sojourn and the Captivity. As for those who still subscribe to the belief that the sacred writings of the Hebrews are original, inspired, and inerrant, the existence of these extensive borrowings, though hardly capable of refutation, should prove to be less of an embarrassment than the list of Neo-Babylonian and Persian monarchs to be found in the Book of Daniel, a reference which the secular records incontestably show to be incomplete, muddled, and in part fictitious.

CHAPTER IV

SOME SUBSIDIARY SYSTEMS

I

An unexpected outcome of archaeological research during the 19th century was the discovery that over a period of several hundred years, there had flourished in northern Syria and Asia Minor (Anatolia) a powerful and hitherto unknown empire which, in its day, had rivalled those of Egypt and Babylonia. Its founders, it appeared, were the descendants of migrants who made their way into Armenia and Cappadocia prior to 2000 B.C., and these forerunners, identified as the Luvians, were closely related (so their language suggests) to a more powerful tribal group which later followed and absorbed them. As for the people of Hatti, the indigenous inhabitants of the region thus occupied, they were completely subdued by the newcomers, upon whom, however, they contrived to exert a marked influence, linguistically and otherwise.

What is now termed the Old Kingdom of the empire established by the intruders is associated with the name of Labarnash (or Tabarnash), c. 1650 B.C., a leader whose grandson, Mursilis I, transferred the capital to the site of Hattushash, the chief Hatti city (now Boghaz Keui—Gorge Village), and in all probability the Pteria of Herodotus. By the capture of Aleppo, Mursilis extended his sphere of interest to northern Syria, and as a result of a daring raid upon Babylon, he also brought about the downfall of the famed dynasty of Hammurabi. His subsequent assassination by a brother-in-law was followed by a period of unrest throughout the kingdom, but order was eventually restored by one Telepinush, who prevailed upon the nobles to introduce legislation governing the succession to the throne. Regarding the happenings of the next century and a half, however, little is known, except that during this period the Old Kingdom disintegrated, and that for a time the people of Hatti (as the Babylonian and Assyrian accounts refer to them) seem to have come under the rule of the neighbouring kingdom of Mitanni, and to have paid tribute to Tutmosis III of Egypt.

The New Empire was inaugurated by Tudkhaliash II (c. 1430 B.C.), though its growth was at first retarded by the presence of the Mitanni in the east, and by Egyptian occupation of Syria in the south, and his successors had to face a series of internal uprisings in one district after another. It was not until the energetic Shubbiluliu attained the throne that the situation was brought under control by strong measures at home, and by artful action abroad. Among his neighbours were the Amorites, whose territory was sandwiched between the kingdom of Mitanni and the city-states of Phoenicia, both of which areas were at that time loyal to Amenophis III of Egypt. Shubbiluliu prevailed upon the Amorite leader Abdashirta to make a diversionary attack upon the Phoenicians, while he led an army across the Euphrates against the Mitanni. Thereafter, the unsuspecting Amorites, having served their purpose, were set upon by Shubbiluliu in turn, who thus added their recent Phoenician conquests to his own, and so became the most powerful monarch in Western Asia.

Considerable light has been thrown on this dramatic chain of events by Egyptian records, wherein there are references to the people of a country called *Ht* (the usual English rendering of which is Kheta), with whom the Egyptians had come into contact as a result of the expansionist activities of Tutmosis I, a Pharaoh who penetrated far beyond the traditional confines of the Nile valley, and actually reached the banks of the Euphrates. This incursion was consolidated by Tutmosis III, who in nineteen years fought no less than seventeen campaigns, in the course of which he conquered Palestine (Battle of Megiddo, 1479 B.C.), Phoenicia, and Syria.

The story of how these territorial gains were later thrown

away was revealed by the discovery of the Tell el-Amarna Letters, an accumulation of official correspondence which was accidentally unearthed by an Egyptian peasant woman in 1887. The documents, in the form of several hundred clay tablets, were inscribed in cuneiform, and written, for the most part, in Accadian, the diplomatic language of the period. They proved to be a series of highly informative administrative and other exchanges which had passed between Amenophis III and Amenophis IV (Ikhnaton), and various vassals and independent foreign rulers, including those of Babylonia, Assyria, and Mitanni. And they showed that whereas Amenophis III, by maintaining friendly relations with Tushratta, King of Mitanni (to whom he was related by marriage), had managed to retain control over the Asiatic possessions bequeathed to him by his predecessors, his son Ikhnaton, the religious reformer, by a policy of studied disinterest and neglect, had let these hard-won acquisitions slip from his country's grasp. In the course of a few disastrous years, not only were Egypt's dependencies relinquished one after another with hardly a move being made to save them, but Artatama, the brother of the King of Mitanni, encouraged no doubt by this evident lack of leadership, joined an anti-Egyptian group and entered into an intrigue with Shubbiluliu, a move which led to the murder of Tushratta and to the loss of Mitanni independence.

In the years which followed, the Pharaohs Seti I and Rameses II fought valiantly but in vain to retrieve the lost empire in its entirety—in the end, Palestine and southern Phoenicia were all that could be recovered. The struggle eventually led to the indecisive Battle of Kadesh, and though Rameses publicly declared the outcome to be a great Egyptian victory, privately he appears to have appraised the situation somewhat more realistically. At all events, after spending a disheartening three years putting down a number of uprisings which subsequently took place in Palestine, he eventually signed a treaty of peace and alliance with the enemy, the essence of which was that the Pharaoh, as the winner, received yet another foreign bride to add to his already impressive collection of wives, while the King of the Hatti, as the loser, was consoled by his being allowed to retain sovereignty over Syria. But, from this point on, the power of the Hatti Empire began to wane, and Anatolia was eventually overwhelmed by an irruption of Thracians, Phrygians, and other (Aegean) Peoples of the Sea. Assyrian records, however, continue to refer to Syria as the Land of the Hatti, whose eastern capital at Carchemish remained in being until it was captured by Sargon II in 717 B.C., whereafter the empire and its people disappeared from the pages of history.

While much of this information was being pieced together from the newly deciphered inscriptions found in neighbouring lands, additional evidence which pointed to the one-time existence of a powerful kingdom in Asia Minor and Syria was being collected from this region of Western Asia itself. In 1812, J. L. Burckhardt, an intrepid Swiss traveller who risked his life exploring Arab lands in the guise of a devout follower of Mohammed (in those days, his only guarantee of safe conduct), found himself in the Syrian town of Hama (ancient Hamath). And here, set in the wall of a house in the bazaar, he noticed a stone covered with what appeared to be a form of hieroglyphic writing, though the signs bore little resemblance to the familiar Egyptian characters. Burckhardt duly reported the discovery in an account of his journeyings which he published some years afterwards (*Travels in Syria and the Holy Land*, London, 1822), but half a century passed before the matter claimed any attention. Eventually, J. A. Johnson and S. Jessup, two American visitors to Hama, observed several more of these inscribed blocks, similarly embedded in the walls of buildings. The hostility of the natives, however, prevented the making of accurate copies, a problem which resolved itself when William Wright, a missionary stationed at Damascus, arrived on the scene in the company of the Turkish Governor of Syria. This high official, in the face of considerable public unrest, ordered the removal of the stones to Constantinople, though not before Wright had obtained casts of the markings, one set of which he despatched to the British Museum.

Other examples of the strange writing, meanwhile, often in association with rock carvings, or in the vicinity of the remains of ancient cities, had been noted in widely separated parts of Asia Minor—at Boghaz Keui by C. Texier and W. Hamilton, at Ivriz by E. J. Davis, and at Bor, Euyuk, Bulharmaden, Sipylos, and elsewhere by other observers—and in 1874, Wright ventured to ascribe the writing to the Hittim (Hittites) mentioned in Hebraic records, a suggestion which was taken up by A. H. Sayce, who subsequently announced the discovery of what he believed to be a long-forgotten empire.

In the somewhat uncertain light of Old Testament references, however, the proposed identification was not without its difficulties. While on the one hand it was here indicated that Syria was the homeland of the Hittites, on the other they were listed, together with the Horites and the Perizzites, the Amorites and the Jebusites, as just another of the luckless tribal groups which had the misfortune to reside in the coveted Land of Canaan. Moreover, preconceived ideas about racial affinities were also destined to be upset. As the "Sons of Heth" who dwelt in Hebron in Abrahamic times, the Semitic background of the Hittites had long been taken for granted, and indeed the very names of individuals mentioned in the Hebraic accounts—Ahumelech, Ephron, Uriah—seemingly provided confirmation of this assumption.

Among the Tell el-Amarna Letters, however, were two documents addressed to Tarchundaraus, King of Arzawa (a domain on the Mediterranean seaboard), written in an unknown language. And significantly enough, this same tongue was later encountered in a few fragments of text which were discovered in the vicinity of Boghaz Keui. This linguistic evidence was studied by the Norwegian scholar J. A. Knudzton, who announced in 1902 that in the course of his examination, he believed he had found Indo-European characteristics—a suggestion which was greeted by so many expressions of incredulity and disbelief on the part of leading philologists that its author, much abashed, was constrained to withdraw it.

The importance and implications of the fragment of text found at Boghaz Keui, however, did not go unrecognised, and Hugo Winckler contrived to secure a concession to dig there on behalf of the German Oriental Society. Excavations were carried out in 1906-7, and again in 1911-12, as a result of which more than 10,000 cuneiform tablets were recovered, the majority of them written in the unknown language of the Arzawa letters, which was thus revealed to be the official tongue of the Hittites, while other of the documents, couched in Accadian, left no doubt that Boghaz Keui had been the capital city of the empire, and that the Kheta of the Egyptians, the Hatti of the Babylonians, and the Hittim of the Hebrews, were one and the same people. It was also clear that the Hittites had made use of two different scripts (cuneiform for their daily needs, and hieroglyphic for monumental purposes), and at least two different languages (Accadian and Hittite). As regards these, the situation was that the cuneiform writing (evidently acquired directly or indirectly from the Babylonians) could be read and understood in Accadian, and read without being understood in Hittite, while the hieroglyphic script (seemingly an independent invention, inspired by its Egyptian counterpart) was neither readable nor intelligible. In these circumstances, it was obvious that any immediate prospect of decipherment lay with Hittite cuneiform.

With the death of Winckler in 1913, the study of the Boghaz Keui texts was entrusted to a group of Assyriologists, and sensational results were almost at once achieved by the Czech scholar Bedřich Hrozný, who, between 1914 and 1916 not only deciphered the language, but also showed that it was essentially Indo-European, as Knudzton had earlier supposed.

At the onset, in the absence of bilinguals, Hrozný had to contend with a collection of syllabic and ideographic signs which he could read (since the script was of the familiar Mesopotamian variety), but which he could not understand. Apart from the occurrence of proper names in the writing, he was assisted to some extent by the fact that the Hittite scribes often had resort to Babylonian word signs, just as a writer in English might find it convenient to make use of such Latin expressions as *in situ*, or *vice versa*. The meaning (though not necessarily the Hittite pronunciation) of odd words could thus be made out, and the process was assisted by the fact that these substitute words were irregularly placed, so that a comparison of duplicate texts on occasion provided added information.

One such word sign which Hrozný seized upon was the ideogram NINDA, meaning "bread." It occurred in a sentence which transliterated as:

Nu NINDA-an ezzateni, vadar-ma ekuteni.

From evidence provided by other examples, there was reason to suppose that the ending *-an* of *NINDA-an* was the termination which denoted the Accusative Singular, while the word "bread" might well be expected to be accompanied by the equivalent of the expression "to eat." This meaning was accordingly ascribed to the *ezza-* of *ezzateni*, the ending of which, from occurrences elsewhere noted, suggested the phrase "you eat, you will eat." Furthermore, as the words *vadar-ma ekuteni* had as their counterpart *NINDA-an ezzateni*, it appeared likely that *vadar*, as the equivalent of "bread," referred to a drink of some kind—at which juncture the word "water" at once presented itself for consideration. But in this event, *ekuteni* must signify "you will drink," so that the complete sentence seemingly read:

Now you will eat bread, then you will drink water.

Given the correctness of this interpretation, the affinity of the Hittite tongue with well-known languages was clearly evident:

Hittite	German	English
Nu	Nun	Now
Ezzateni	Essen	Eat
Vadar	Wasser	Water

Moreover, once this all-important relationship had been established, it was relatively easy to detect other close resemblances to familiar Indo-European forms:

Hittite	Latin	English
Uk	Ego	I
Kwis	Quis	Who
Kwiskwis	Quisquis	Whoever

This, then, was the basis of Hrozný's decipherment of the language of the Hittite cuneiform writing, and of his contention that, by its structure and its vocabulary, it revealed itself to be essentially Indo-European. But in his initial enthusiasm, the investigator tended to claim rather more than was justified by the facts, for, as it later transpired, though it was without doubt basically Indo-European, the language of the cuneiform texts had been influenced very considerably by a number of alien tongues. As a result of the changes thus brought about, philologists found themselves unable to accept many of the meanings which Hrozný had assigned to Hittite words on the strength of a similarity to their supposed Indo-European equivalents, and not a few authorities, rushing no less incautiously from one extreme to the other, rejected his findings in their entirety. Fundamentally, however, Hrozný's solution was sound, as was confirmed by further research during the next decade and, by 1925, most of the leading cuneiform scholars had acknowledged the fact. Since then, a reasonably satisfactory understanding of the language has been gained, and in 1936 E. H.

Sturtevant was able to publish a glossary which listed more than 3,000 Hittite words and their meanings.

With this knowledge had come an appreciation of the complicated nature of the Hittite racial affinities, for, as early as 1919, Emil Forrer had announced that no fewer than eight different tongues were to be found among the Boghaz Keui tablets. Of these, however, only Hittite and Accadian appeared to have enjoyed an official status, for these languages largely predominated. But some tablets were inscribed in the Hurrian tongue of the people of Mitanni, and in the Aryan language spoken by their rulers, while yet others were written in Sumerian (seemingly studied, but not spoken); in Luvian (a close relative of Hittite); in Palaic (also of Indo-European origin); and in Hattian, the language of the aboriginal inhabitants. To this collection, moreover, a ninth now needed to be added, for despite hopes to the contrary, it had become evident that the language of the Hittite hieroglyphs, though it was related to that of the Hittite cuneiform, was not identical with it.

Attempts to decipher the Hittite picture writing, meanwhile, had been going on ever since the recovery of the Hamath stones in 1872, though with little success. A preliminary examination showed that the lines of script were intended to be read boustrophedon fashion, in that they progressed alternately from right to left, and from left to right. It also appeared that the first line of an inscription might start at either end, though it was observed that the opening word was usually to be found on the right. The direction of writing, however, was at no time in doubt, as heads and similar portrayals invariably faced towards the beginning of the line. But the characters were unusual in that in an early monumental form, they were elaborately carved in raised relief, whereas in a simplified cursive style, later developed, the signs were incised (Fig. 7).

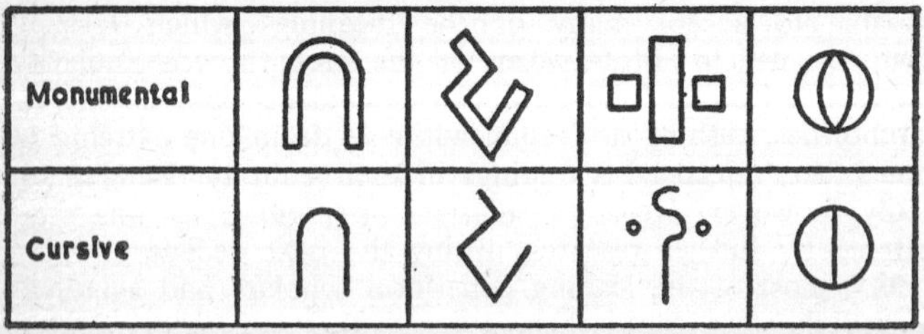

Fig. 7. Hittite hieroglyphs—monumental and cursive forms.

A possible clue to the meaning of a few of the signs was provided by A. D. Mordtmann in 1863, when he published a description of a silver boss or seal, said to have been acquired by a dealer in Smyrna. It was a coin-shaped object, in the centre of which was shown standing a figure holding a stave, surrounded by miniature pictographs, the whole encircled by a marginal area containing cuneiform signs. Prior to the appearance of Mordtmann's account, the seal had been offered for sale to the British Museum, where it had been subjected to a critical examination by Henry Rawlinson and Samuel Birch, both of whom came to the conclusion that it was a fake—Birch supposing that it was a copy, cast from a stone original, and Rawlinson concluding that it was an out-and-out forgery. In the face of these unfavourable opinions, the Museum declined to buy, though the opportunity was taken to have a number of wax impressions made. In 1880, however, A. H. Sayce, after careful study, became convinced that the centre figures were Hittite hieroglyphs, and that they were surrounded by their cuneiform equivalent—that the seal, in other words, was a bilingual. But whatever the merits of this, the much disputed Tarkondemos Boss, it could at best afford little help to the decipherers, if only because the supposed hieroglyphic counterpart of its ten cuneiform signs amounted to no more than six symbols—out of a total of more than 200.

Although many of the hieroglyphs were easily recognisable, in that they clearly depicted parts of the human body, the heads of animals, articles of furniture, and so on, this was no great aid when it came to determining how the symbols were to be read, and inevitably guesswork largely prevailed. At all events, out of a dozen or more attempted decipherments, no two were in agreement, and R. S. Thompson, in proclaiming the result of a study of some new texts recovered from Carchemish in 1911, almost as a matter of course began by explaining how little his findings had in common with those of other investigators, including A. H. Sayce, R. Rusch, P. Jensen, C. R. Conder, and A. Gleye! Eventually, even some of the would-be decipherers began to realise that little or no progress was being made, and in 1924 Jensen expressed the belief that in the absence of an extensive bilingual key, the prospect seemed hopeless.

What was required, it was evident, was a new approach by fresh minds, unencumbered by preconceived ideas, a need which was in due course met by the efforts of five scholars

122 LOST LANGUAGES

of diverse nationality—H. T. Bossert (German); P. Meriggi (Italian); B. Hrozný (Czech); F. Forrer (Swiss); and I. J. Gelb (American). At first working independently, these five have succeeded in reaching a considerable measure of agreement concerning the phonetic values of many of the signs, and an instructive insight into some of the methods which were employed is provided by I. J. Gelb's *Hittite Hieroglyphs*, I, II, III (Chicago, 1931, 1935, 1942). From the combined works of his predecessors, published during the previous fifty years, Gelb found himself able to accept the reading of barely a dozen signs, attributable to Sayce, F. E. Peiser, Jensen, A. E. Cowley, and Carl Frank. Among these signs, whose meanings were hardly in doubt, were:

| WORD DIVIDER | IDEOGRAM MARK | KING | CITY | LAND OR COUNTRY |

Although he was inclined to accept the genuineness of the Tarkondemos Boss, and also that of several other bilingual seals, Gelb, like others before him, found a much more useful source of information in the geographic names which appeared on the monuments. In as much as the presence of these names was indicated by the appropriate determinative (single or double mountain peak), there was no difficulty in detecting them, though their correct identification was, of course, another matter. The precise whereabouts of Carchemish, for example, long famous as an important Hittite centre on the Euphrates, was unknown until George Smith recognised that it was the modern Jerablus. Again, although it was reasonable to suppose that if a certain place name frequently appeared in a group of inscriptions, the reference would in all probability be to the particular location concerned, this did not help very much unless something of the history of the site was known from outside sources—*e.g.*, a reference to it by name in Assyrian or Greek accounts.

In the event, five sites fulfilled the necessary conditions, respectively those of Haleb, Hamath, Tunni, Gurgam, and Carchemish. Of these, Carchemish (first read by Jensen as long ago as 1894) was the most important, for its name-group occurred with great frequency and offered as many as fourteen variant spellings, of which the following may be taken as a typical example:

SOME SUBSIDIARY SYSTEMS 123

KARKA   (KA)   ME   SA   WA   SI   (CITY)

Gelb noted that the first sign was regularly followed by a symbol (*ka*) which, from the fact that it was, however, omitted on two occasions, he deduced must serve as a phonetic complement. But, if this were so, the first sign was thus shown to be ideographic. This first sign, moreover, was known to occur only in this one place name, and in the name of a god which was also exclusive to Carchemish, the inference being that the name of the city incorporated the name of a patron deity. With the assistance of the Assyrian rendering of Carchemish (Karkameš), the Hittite form emerged as Karka(ka)-me-sa-wa-si-(city).

In all, the phonetic values of a score of syllable-signs were established by this means. But it soon became evident that the method had its limitations, and to supplement the information obtained in this way, Gelb essayed the onerous task of making a complete concordance of all the words (as indicated by the word divider) and groups of words which appeared in the inscriptions, a task which entailed a prior listing of each individual sign and its variants. Thereafter, working on the assumption that the Hittite hieroglyphs, as a form of writing, were broadly divisible into two categories —ideograms and phonograms—he endeavoured to distinguish the one from the other. In this, he was assisted by his word list, for examination showed that certain signs appeared only at the beginning of words, never as a grammatical ending. Hence it seemed that in a word consisting, say, of five signs, the first and second, and perhaps also the third, of these symbols could be regarded as ideographic, whereas the fourth and fifth characters *must represent phonetic values whose function was to assist the reading of the preceding signs.*

As a result of pursuing this reasoning, Gelb reached the important conclusion that the Hittite hieroglyphic writing contained rather less than sixty phonetic signs, a number too large for it to be alphabetic, and yet insufficient for it to be syllabic. But if the writing were not alphabetic, it *must* be syllabic—a paradox to which a possible answer was provided by the special case of the Japanese and Cypriot syllabaries, in which the number of signs (respectively forty-seven and fifty-six) was much reduced by virtue of the fact that, at any rate in writing, these systems made no distinction between voiced and voiceless consonants, and were restricted to the use of signs expressing either a vowel alone, or a consonant plus a vowel. Gelb thus concluded that in the Hittite hieroglyphs, there were no signs beginning with a vowel, *e.g., ap,* and no closed syllables, *e.g., pam*; and that there were only syllables ending in a vowel, *e.g., pa,* while closed syllables could be written only by using two syllables, each ending in a vowel, *e.g., pam=pa* and *me.*

In all, he was able to assign values to about fifty of the syllabic signs, more than half of which he regarded as reasonably certain (Fig. 8). And his results, generally, have been justified by the findings of the other investigators, who have, of course, made their own particular contributions—the ascribing (by all four) of the value *wa* to the commonest of all the signs; the identifying of the letter *u* by Bossert and Meriggi, from its occurrence in the name of a king of Hamath, U(ra)-ḫi-li-na-sa; the recognition of the letter *i* by Meriggi and Hrozný; the identification of the relative pronoun and other forms by Forrer; and so on. Inevitably, there were some items about which the investigators agreed to differ—a sign which Hrozný and Gelb were sure represented the letter *e,* Bossert and Meriggi preferred to read as *ra*. Even so, by 1949, as the result of a long-sustained process of comparing and criticising one another's findings, the five Hittologists had succeeded in establishing an agreed list of phonetic values. But while very considerable progress in the decipherment of the writing had thus been made, the problem of the language remained. Thus, notwithstanding the fact that the inscriptions could be read in part, they still remained largely unintelligible—at which juncture the finding of an extensive and long awaited bilingual was announced!

The initial discovery had been made in 1946, when Bossert, exploring among the foothills of the Taurus mountains in the company of Halet Çambel, happened upon the fortified hilltop posts of Domuztepe and Karatepe, located on either side of the Jeyhan River (the ancient Pyramos). Operations began in 1947, and although some attention was given to the lower and smaller ruin of Domuztepe, the main excavations were carried out at Karatepe, which was approached

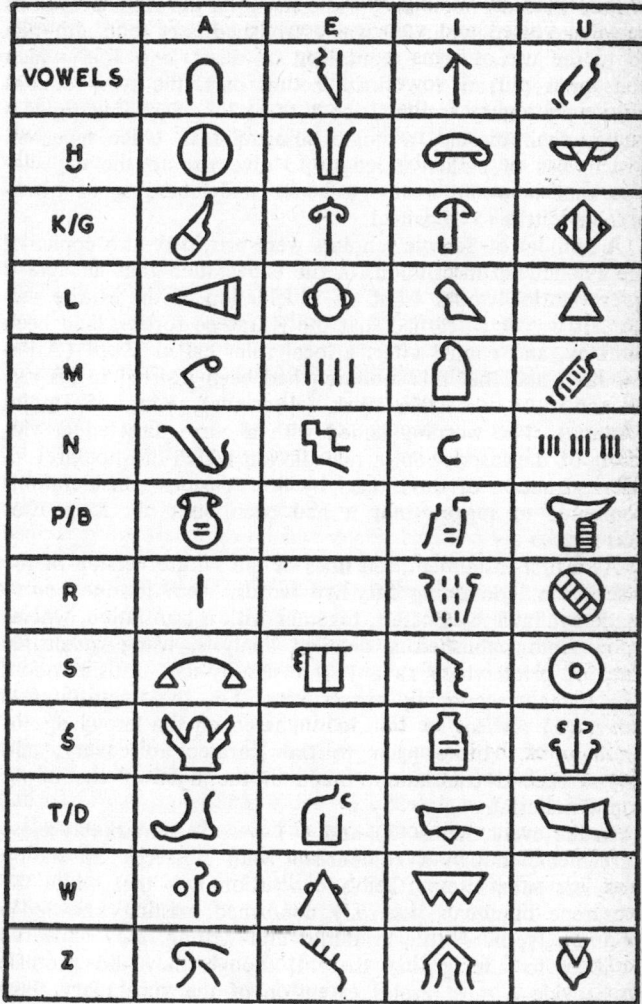

Fig. 8. Hittite hieroglyphic syllabary (after I. J. Gelb).

by two T-shaped entrances, flanked by inscribed and sculptured slabs. And in each case, the left-hand inscriptions were written in Old Phoenician, while those on the right proved to be Hittite hieroglyphic! It was established later that, although the Semitic rendering contained at least one line which was omitted from its Hittite counterpart, the two versions were very nearly identical, so that at long last investigators had at their disposal a single bilingual text, twice repeated, which was of sufficient length to give rise to the expectation that it would enable a better understanding of hieroglyphic Hittite to be gained.

A number of Semitic scholars were provided with copies of the Phoenician inscription, in the expectation that an agreed interpretation would assist the elucidation of the Hittite section. It was thus learned that the Karatepe fortress had been built by, and named after, a local ruler called 'Zwtd (Asitavandas), and that this monarch had been assisted in his rise to power by a certain 'Wrk (Avarikus), King of Dnnjm (Adana). The wording ended with a curse directed at violators of the inscription, a malediction which did not prevent the destruction of the citadel by fire. Various considerations combined to suggest that it had been built not long after 700 B.C.

As a first instalment, ten lines of the Hittite version of the inscription, containing fifty-five words, were in due course made available by Bossert, together with a translation, whereupon Gelb published a detailed analysis, using quadruple lines of print which gave (1) a sign-by-sign transliteration; (2) the corresponding transcription, *i.e.*, the linguistic features; (3) an English translation based on the knowledge of hieroglyphic Hittite prior to the Karatepe discovery; and (4) a second translation, made in the light of the newly found material.

In the event, items (3) and (4) were in remarkably close agreement, though a comparison with Bossert's translation was less satisfactory. Gelb's conclusion was that while the Karatepe bilinguals generally confirmed existing knowledge of hieroglyphic Hittite grammar and writing, they appeared unlikely to add greatly thereto, though they did promise to provide a most useful extension of the vocabulary. But, as M. J. Mellink has remarked, the full impact of these epigraphic discoveries remains to be seen.

Much has been learned, meanwhile, from the Hittite cuneiform records. Most of this material was recovered from the ruins of Boghaz Keui, and was thus manifestly earlier than 1200 B.C., at about which time the destruction of the city took place. In certain instances, more precise dates can be assigned to tablets by virtue of their contents. Thus, among some correspondence was found a letter relating to a request which had been received from Rameses II (1292-1225 B.C.), calling for a shipment of the highly prized wonder metal iron, the secret of the production of which was at that time a Hittite monopoly.

The documents (following J. B. Pritchard) may be conveniently classified as Historical, Invocational, Mythological, Ritualistic, and Legalistic. The historical material includes the Hittite version of the famous treaty between Hattushilish III and Rameses II of Egypt, the details of which were already known from inscriptions carved on the walls of the Temple of Amon at Karnak. Since Accadian, as the Tell el-Amarna Letters revealed, was the *lingua franca* of the period, it was evident that the Egyptian version, with its reference to a silver tablet sent by Hattushilish to Rameses, who had "made his frontier where he wished in every land," was a translation. And from the cuneiform original it was clear that the Egyptian account had been subtly edited to make it appear that it was the Pharaoh who had granted peace, though in other respects the two copies of the treaty were substantially the same, it being agreed that aggression was to be renounced, and replaced by a defensive alliance.

Another treaty, made between Shubbiluliu and Mattiwaza of Mitanni, also provided information of historic interest, in that it described the manner in which the King of the Hatti had crossed the Euphrates and conquered one Mitanni province after another. Equally informative was an account given in the Annals of the conqueror, subsequently compiled by his son Mursilis, from which it was learned that when in the country of Karkamis (Carchemish), Shubbiluliu had sent some of his forces to the district of Amqa (in the vicinity of Lebanon), a raid which caused Egypt much concern, as that country was then without a king, the Pharaoh having recently died. No doubt after mature consideration, the bereaved queen (whose name is given as Dakhamun) sent an envoy to Shubbiluliu, requesting the hand of one of his sons in marriage. At first, the Hittite king was inclined to regard this unprecedented offer as a trick, and he played for time. The queen, however, reproached him for his distrust, whereupon Shubbiluliu hesitated no longer.

The sequel to this story (not, alas, a happy ending) came to light through a passing reference in another text. Among various Hittite prayers—including a Daily Prayer for the king, and a Prayer to be Spoken in an Emergency—was found the so-called Plague Prayer of Mursilis. In this petition, Mursilis asks forgiveness from on high for various transgressions, including the aforementioned attack which his father had made on the Egyptian territory of Amqa. This raid, it appears, had resulted in the taking of some prisoners, and by way of retribution (or so it seemed to Mursilis) the gods had caused these captives to carry a dread pestilence with them into the land of the Hatti, whose people had been sorely troubled thereby for the past twenty years. And in the course of this tale of woe, it is revealed that although Shubbililiu, acting in good faith, had earlier answered the Egyptian queen's request for a husband by sending her one of his sons, the youth had been waylaid *en route* and treacherously done to death, presumably on the orders of a rival Egyptian aspirant to the throne.

The culprit is not named, but the late husband of the widowed queen is referred to in the Annals as Bibhururiyas (a parallel text gives the variant Nibhururiyas). Modern scholars at first considered that this Bibhururiyas might be Ikhnaton himself, but he has since been identified, with some probability, as one of this Pharaoh's sons-in-law. Ikhnaton was the father of six daughters, but he left no male heir to succeed him, and after his death the throne was occupied briefly and in turn by two youthful successors, the second of whom was the well-known Tutankhamon. And it was his consort, Ikhnaton's third daughter Enkhosnepaaton, it is now believed, who wrote offering herself and the crown of Egypt to a son of Shubbiluliu. As for the plotter who did not stop at murder to foil the queen's intention of marrying a foreign prince, it may well be that he revealed his identity by occupying the throne himself. At all events, the next ruler of Egypt was the priest Ay, a close associate of Ikhnaton.

Among numerous (if badly preserved) mythological texts found at Boghaz Keui are copies of the Gilgamesh legend, written in several languages, including Accadian and Hittite. A series of local epics, which also deal with the activities of the gods, concern The Moon That Fell From Heaven, and The Song of Ullikummis. A typical example, entitled Kingship in Heaven, tells of the olden days when Alalus ruled aloft. During the ninth year of his reign, his leadership was contested by a powerful deity who rejoiced in what, to Anglo-Saxon ears, was the somewhat improbable name of Anus. In the ensuing struggle for power, Alalus was vanquished, and sought refuge in the dark earth below. Anus then ruled in his place, until his authority was challenged in turn by one Kumarbis. Recognising the superiority of his opponent, Anus attempted to flee to safety, as Alalus had done before him. But Kumarbis caught him by his feet, dragged him from the sky, and then, in the euphemistic words of the chronicler, "bit his knees." Having thus deprived the unfortunate Anus of his manhood, Kumarbis added insult to injury by swallowing the evidence, whereupon the victim of this outrageous assault solemnly gave warning of dire consequences to follow. As a result of this action, Anus declared, there had been implanted within Kumarbis a heavy burden in the shape of three gods-to-be—the mighty Storm-god, his attendant Tasisus, and the river Aranzahas (Tigris). . . . Hereafter, the text is much broken, but it appears that the Storm-god duly developed within, and made good his escape from, his unwilling host, whom he afterwards defeated in battle. Thus the Storm-god assumed the kingship of heaven, and became the chief Hittite deity.

Among various rituals which the texts enumerate are those designed to counteract Sorcery and Impotence, the one which concerns this last affliction being an involved procedure which calls for such comestibles as loaves, figs, grapes, chaff, and grain, and the use of the fleece of an unblemished sheep, not to mention the services of a virgin and a eunuch. There are also rituals against Pestilence and Domestic Quarrel, and for the Erection of a New Palace. The Removal of a Threat Implied by an Evil Omen is likewise dealt with at some length, the essence of the procedure being the bringing of a healthy prisoner of war to a sanctuary, where a priest anoints him with the oil of kingship. After various ceremonies have been enacted, the officiating cleric then declares "This man is the king . . ." (and, addressing himself to the powers of evil) "pursue ye this substitute." The prisoner is then released, and sent back to his own country, his relief at this unexpected good fortune no doubt heavily overshadowed by the impending doom which has been wished upon him.

Rules and regulations governing the duly accredited representatives of the high gods on earth, range from edicts about cleanliness to precautions against fire. Seemingly, the accidental burning down of temples had occurred with such alarming frequency in the past that a nominal penalty was no longer considered to provide sufficient insurance against it. Hence the warning that in the event of any trouble of this kind, all those in the temple at the time, together with their families, would suffer death. There were also revealing references to the fate of offerings to the gods, in that the temple attendant was reminded that whatever silver or gold was entrusted to him, he was merely the caretaker. Similarly, when oxen were driven into the presence of a god as food, it was strictly against the regulations for a priest to select a fattened specimen, and to substitute therefor a lean animal of his own. . . .

Other directives are addressed to Commanders of the Guard and to members of the Palace Staff, the instructions to the last-named being designed to "ensure the king's purity." There is a warning against carelessness in the preparation of the royal meals (the king's god, if not the king himself, will always be watching), and water carriers in particular are called upon to strain the contents of their pitchers—an occasion is cited on which the royal eye detected a hair in the drink, a discovery which the culprit, one Zuliyas, did not long survive. Also under penalty of death, shoemakers are enjoined to use only oxhides taken from the palace kitchen, while all personnel, from cooks to bakers, and from cup-bearers to table-men, must swear an oath of loyalty to the king every month.

To the populace as a whole there applied a body of laws which had evidently been inspired by the earlier Code of Hammurabi. The collection is represented by two tablets (a third seems to be missing) known as "If anyone . . ." from the opening phrase of many of its items. In the time-honoured manner, a distinction is made between the free man and the slave, and monetary compensation payable to the latter is usually half that due to the former. Thus the recognised penalty for biting the nose of a slave is 15 silver shekels (the price of a horse in pasture), whereas the injured person, if a free man, received double this sum. Similarly, the mutilation of a man's ear entailed a penalty of 6 or 12 shekels, according to the status of the victim. Inexplicably enough, a bitten nose appears to have been adjudged a greater hurt than the loss of teeth (by knocking out) or of an eye: such relatively minor injuries cost the aggressor no more than 10 or 20 shekels respectively. In the same way, penalties imposed upon offenders varied in accordance with their rank. A free man who killed a snake while pronouncing another man's name was liable to a fine of 1 silver mina (50 shekels), whereas a slave who committed this grave offence forfeited his life. Other enactments relate to a series of probable and improbable family situations, and to relationships between the sexes. But the greatest cause for concern, judging by the amount of legislation concerning it, was the high incidence of stealing. Of the 200 odd items listed on the two tablets, no less than a quarter relate to theft of one kind or another. The comprehensive nature of the regulations may be gathered from the ruling that if a dog devours a consignment of lard, and the owner of the lard finds him out, he is legally entitled to kill the animal, and to recover from the stomach thereof his missing cooking fat. . . .

II

From the head of the Persian Gulf, extending in a wide arc along the Tigro-Euphrates valley as far as Carchemish, and thereafter curving seawards and following the Mediterranean coastline in the direction of Egypt, is a great semicircle of cultivable land which J. H. Breasted, contrasting it with the barren mountains and deserts which border it on either side, aptly termed the Fertile Crescent. And from about 3500 B.C. onwards, it is believed, there poured into this uberous region from the inhospitalities of the Arabian peninsula, a succession of people who were linguistically, if not racially, closely related—the Semites.

Among the first of these migrants were the forerunners of the Accadians and the Babylonians, and at intervals of about 1,000 years they were followed by the Amorites (from whose ranks the Canaanites emerged), by the Aramaeans (of which family the Hebrews were a branch), and by the Nabataeans. Inevitably, the latecomers tended to encroach upon the territorial acquisitions of those who had preceded them, and so it came to pass that the Nabataeans dispossessed the Edomites (who had earlier ousted the Horites), while the Israelites forcibly occupied much of the Land of Canaan (by all accounts, on the somewhat dubious grounds that it had been promised to them, apparently without reference to the existing inhabitants). Ultimately, those surviving Canaanites who were not absorbed by the interlopers retained only a narrow strip of country along the Mediterranean seaboard (now shared by Lebanon and Syria), which was subsequently called Phoenicia by the Greeks.

The boundaries of this region were not precisely defined, and down through the centuries its coastal length varied from 150 to 200 miles, according to the vagaries of the prevailing political situation. In this confined and fluctuating area, the Canaanites soon outgrew the available agricultural resources, and to avoid starvation they were forced to harvest the sea as well as the land. Fortunately, the mountains of Lebanon were well stocked with cedar, and this wealth of timber provided ample material for boat-building. Moreover, from these same mountain heights, the distant outline of Cyprus could be seen, and visitations to the island led to the establishment of a colony there.

Thus committed to a seafaring existence, the Phoenicians undertook the exploration of other adjacent lands, and bartered goods with the local inhabitants. And from simple traders, they developed into manufacturers, one of their most celebrated products being a handsome purple dye, extracted from molluscs, and used to colour the woven goods which they made from wool provided by neighbouring shepherd tribes. Thereafter, in their role of manufacturers and merchants, they built up a great commercial empire, and their goods and services became known throughout the Mediterranean area. Eventually, greatly daring, Phoenician sailors ventured beyond the Pillars of Hercules (Straits of Gibraltar), and so encountered the enormous waves of the Atlantic, and beheld the inexplicable phenomenon of the tides. In the new world thus opened up to them, they founded Gades (Cadiz) in Spain, and visited the Scilly Isles (if not Cornwall, as some authorities suppose) to obtain supplies of tin. But their greatest maritime achievement was undertaken at the instigation of the 26th dynasty Pharaoh Necho (*c* 609-593 B.C.), who is said to have re-dug an ancient canal connecting the Nile with the Red Sea. From this point of departure, the Phoenicians sailed in a southerly direction, hugging the coast and landing to plant and reap a crop each autumn. In the third year of their unprecedented journey, they at last saw ahead of them the familiar Pillars of Hercules, and so reached Egypt once again after having circumnavigated the African continent. Herodotus subsequently expressed his disbelief in the accomplishment, on the grounds that the voyagers claimed that, in the course of their journeyings, they beheld the sun on their right-hand side—a supposedly incredible detail which would hardly have been invented, and which thus confirms both the account and the feat.

No less important were the cultural activities which the peregrinations of the Phoenicians engendered. In the foreign lands where their trading posts were established, it may be supposed that local inhabitants were employed in the capacity of agents, and that, as such, they were initiated into the mysteries of reading and writing, and the keeping of accounts. It was in some such manner, no doubt, rather than by way of the legendary Cadmus, that the Greeks received the Semitic script, if not in the form of a consonantal alphabet (as has long been held), then in the guise of a syllabary without vowels (as Gelb maintains).

Until the second decade of the present century, the earliest known example of this writing was that found on the Moabite Stone, the thirty-four-line inscription of which commemorates the successful revolt of King Mesha against Ahab of Israel (c. 869-850 B.C.). Other inscriptions, *e.g.*, that on the Ahiram sarcophagus, have since been found which take the so-called alphabetic writing back several hundred years, and which suggest that from about 1550 B.C. the Canaanites were busily experimenting with half a dozen different kinds of writing, including cuneiform. Prior to 1930, however, little in the way of historical or other records attributable to the Canaanites could be found, and the conclusion was reluctantly reached that the missing documents must have been written on perishable materials such as papyrus or parchment, and that these had long ceased to exist. This supposed loss was particularly lamented by those biblical scholars who, mindful of the Babylonian and Egyptian parallels to be found in the older portions of the Old Testament, had entertained hopes that, following the Conquest, some of the later books, *e.g.*, those of Job, Ezekiel, and Isaiah, might afford evidence of Canaanite influence upon the Hebrews, and that a study of the source of such borrowings might possibly provide explanations of certain obscure and difficult scriptural passages.

In the meantime, early references to Phoenicia were to be found in foreign accounts, notably those of Egypt. The so-called Palermo Stone (part of an ancient stele, set up in

5th dynasty times) records that the Pharaoh Snefru (*c.* 2650 B.C.) despatched an expedition by sea to a port on the Lebanese coast, where his representatives acquired 40 shiploads of cedar logs for boat-building and other purposes. From then on, he and his successors maintained a proprietary interest in the area until, with the advent of Tutmosis III, almost the whole of Phoenicia was conquered and claimed by Egypt. Thereafter, the territory remained subject to the Pharaohs for nearly four centuries, until it was lost to the empire by indifference at home, and by diplomatic intrigues abroad, as the Tell el-Amarna Letters disclosed.

This famous and informative correspondence also revealed that by 1400 B.C. the Phoenician coastline, from Mount Carmel northwards, was dotted with city-states possessed of towns and harbours of considerable importance—Acco, Tyre, Sidon, Berytus, Byblos, Simyra, Arvad, and Ugarit. With one exception, the sites of all these once famous ports were soon identified. Acco, the modern Acre, finds mention in the conquest lists of Tutmosis III, while in the Amarna Letters its local ruler is accused by Burraburiash II, King of Babylon, of plundering his caravans. As a stepping-stone to the rich Plain of Esdraelon, and southern Galilee, the town was of strategic importance, and was one of the objectives assigned by the Hebrew high command to the tribe of Asher (who failed to take it).

The fabulous Tyre, now known by its Arabic name of Sur (rock), was built upon an island adjacent to the mainland, a location which made it difficult to besiege—it held out against Nebuchadrezzar for no less than thirteen years (585-573 B.C.). Its reputation for near-impregnability, however, was later shattered by Alexander the Great while *en route* for Egypt after defeating the Persians at the Battle of Issus. He solved the problem of military assault by laboriously constructing a causeway from shore to island, and took the citadel by storm in seven months, whereafter 8,000 Tyrians paid for their temerity with their lives, and 30,000 others were sold into slavery.

The equally famous Sidon, hailed as the mother of Tyre, achieved such renown in Homeric times that it gave its name to the whole of Phoenicia, whose people came to be known as Sidonians. The Saida of to-day, it is one of the most ancient of the coastal cities, and even in the 1st century A.D. its reputation for venerableness was such that Josephus ascribed the founding of it to a grandson of Noah. Its long and stormy history was terminated for a time as the result of a revolt against Artaxerxes, an abortive uprising in the course of which the entire town was set ablaze, and 40,000 of its citizens roasted alive in their homes, whereafter the disgruntled Persian leader consoled himself by disposing of the smouldering rubble heap for the price of the melted gold and silver it contained.

As for the remainder of the ancient ports mentioned in the Egyptian records, Berytus was identifiable as the modern Beirut, Byblos was the present-day Jebail, Simyra had become known as Sumra, and Arvad or Aradus (like Tyre, once an island city) was now Ruad. Only Ugarit and its site remained unknown and undiscovered, and despite much effort on the part of archaeologists and others, all attempts to determine its whereabouts failed. And when the mystery was eventually solved, it was by accident, not by design.

A few miles to the north of Latakia (ancient Laodicea), opposite Cyprus on the Syrian coast, is Minet el-Beida, the White Harbour of the Greeks. In this vicinity, on 25 April, 1928, while engaged in ploughing a field, a native encountered a flagstone, the lifting of which disclosed a subterranean passage. The passage led to a burial chamber, which the discoverer proceeded to rifle in the immemorial manner. But word of the find reached the alert ears of the local Governor, who passed on the news to the Bureau of Antiquities in Beirut. As a result, the site was visited by C. Virolleaud, who found some rubbish in the tomb, but little else. But when, in due course, a plan of the sepulchre was placed before René Dussaud in Paris, he at once observed a close resemblance between it and the vaulted tombs of Mycenae, while among the rubbish aforementioned he found remnants of Aegean pottery belonging to the 2nd millennium B.C. In view of this evidence of overseas influence, which pointed to the existence of an ancient seaport in the vicinity, the *Institut de France* despatched an archaeological expedition to the area, headed by C. F. A. Schaeffer, with Georges Chenet as his co-worker and companion.

The work of excavation was begun almost exactly a year after the making of the initial discovery, at first in the vicinity of what proved to be a necropolis, and then at the nearby mound of Ras Shamra (Fennel Head), a 60-foot-high hill overgrown with the aromatic plant from which it took its name. And it was this extensive accumulation of manmade debris which proved to be the site of the ancient city to which the necropolis and harbour of Minet el-Beida belonged —the long-lost Ugarit.

The cosmopolitan associations of this Canaanite city were shown by the varied nature of the finds. It was clear, moreover, that these influences had at times been at variance with one another. Pieces of a great sphinx, made of green stone, bore a hieroglyphic inscription which showed that the carving was a gift to the city temple from Amenophis III. But this and other Egyptian statues had been deliberately broken, no doubt at the instigation of the invading Amorite leader Abdashirta, or by the followers of the scheming Shubbiluliu, whose purpose in Phoenicia Abdashirta served. At all events, a statue of the Hittite deity Teshub was also unearthed.

From this and other evidence, something of the history of the site was gradually pieced together. The lowest level of the mound showed signs of occupation during the Neolithic period (5th millennium B.C.). Between 3000 and 2000 B.C., signs of ethnic changes marked the arrival of the Canaanites, who subsequently established strong ties with Egypt. From about 1750-1550 B.C. this association was interrupted by the Hyksos invasion of the Nile valley, but was afterwards continued until the Amarna period. As a result of Hittite incursions, the King of Ugarit then, perforce, acknowledged the suzerainty of Shubbiluliu (as copies of his correspondence with this powerful monarch show). Later, the city came under Egyptian control once more, and so remained until it was invaded by Achaeans from Mycenae. The final blow fell towards the end of the 12th century, when the region was overrun by the Assyrians under Tiglath-pileser I, in the course of which campaign Ugarit was so effectively destroyed that it ceased to exist.

It was this abandonment of the site which helped preserve for posterity the most important find of all—portions of the missing Canaanite literature, unexpectedly in the guise of clay tablets inscribed in cuneiform. The first of these priceless records was discovered during the second month of the excavations (May, 1929), and led to the finding of a room, divided by three pillars, which had evidently served as a library. Examination of the documents brought another surprise. Although some were in the familiar Accadian script, the majority proved to be in an unknown writing which appeared to consist of no more than twenty-seven (a number later increased to thirty) cuneiform characters, apparently alphabetic!

More of these unusual tablets came to light later. The originals, meanwhile, numbering about fifty, many of them fragmentary, were published with commendable promptness by Virolleaud, who at once interested himself in the question of their decipherment, as did Hans Bauer of the University of Halle, and the French scholar P. Dhorme, then at the *École Biblique,* in Jerusalem. All three were highly trained Semiticists (an important prerequisite, as will be seen), while both Bauer and Dhorme possessed a considerable knowledge of ciphers (Dhorme had been decorated by the French Government for some outstanding work in this field during the First World War).

In as much as neither the language nor the writing was at first known, the problem appeared much more difficult than it actually was. The fact that cuneiform characters had been used suggested that the inventors of the script must have been influenced by the conventional Accadian writing. But here, apart from the fact that both scripts progressed from left to right, the similarity ended. It was as though some of the familiar Roman letters of to-day had been adopted for use in a novel alphabet, in which the accepted phonetic values had been changed about, to which rearrangement, moreover, some new symbols had been added. On the other hand, the fewness of the signs suggested that the writing must be alphabetic, or at any rate phonetic—and it is a cardinal principle of the theory of decipherment that such a writing must admit of interpretation *if the underlying language can be determined.*

What, then, was the language? In pondering this all-important question, the decipherers independently came to the conclusion that the most likely answer, having regard for geographical and other circumstances, was that it must be Semitic, in all probability a Canaanite (Phoenician) dialect. This basic assumption was supported by a number of considerations, *e.g.*, by a noticeable tendency towards triliterality (individual words, most conveniently, were separated on some of the tablets by vertical strokes); by what appeared to be certain grammatical characteristics; and by the discovery of a Hebrew word, *grzn* (*garzen*) on an axe.

On a similar bronze tool, Virolleaud came across half a dozen characters which he took to be the name of the owner or manufacturer (in fact, the symbols stood for the title *rb khnm*, as Dhorme later showed). The same six characters also occurred at the beginning of one of the tablets, where they were preceded by three vertical strokes. Virolleaud boldly assumed that the text was in the form of a letter or similar communication, addressed to the person bearing the name (title) he had elsewhere discerned, and that the three strokes represented the preposition "To," *i.e.*, the opening words of the missive read "To rb khnm." He accordingly identified the three vertical strokes in terms of the Semitic *lamed*, "to," and gave the sign in question the value "l." He then compiled a list of all the words he could find containing this symbol, and searched among them for possible Semitic equivalents, in particular for common expressions and titles. He quickly happened upon the three-letter word:

M L K

which suggested the Hebrew *mlk* (king), a meaning seemingly confirmed by a similar word of four letters, evidently the plural:

M L K M

Another word containing the tell-tale letter "l" proved to be the name of the god Baal:

B ʽ L

and yet others were identified as spellings of the numbers "three" and "thirty." Virolleaud had by now secured the letters *l, m, k, b, a, š,* and *t* (from B'lt), at which point he came upon a tablet which appeared to be an itemised account, containing a column of figures. He was able to distinguish the words *ḥmš* (five), *šš* (six), *sbʽ* (seven), *šmn* (eight), *ʽsrh* (ten), *ḥmš ʽsrh* (fifteen), and *šmn ʽsrh* (eighteen), and, after this, decipherment was virtually automatic—*g* was given by *Dgn* (Dagon), and confirmed by *gpn* (vine); *z* was obtained from *zt* (olive), and additional proof as to its correctness furnished by *arz* (cedar), *zmr* (sing), and *ʽz* (strength). Similarly, *ṭ* was revealed by *ḥṭ* (sceptre), *ṭb* (good), and *špṭ* (judge), *ṡ* by *kṡe* (throne), and so on.

Dhorme and Bauer, meanwhile, were working along similar

lines, though for a time the last-named was puzzled by the use, on a dozen or more occasions, of -*s* as a suffix, until he finally tumbled to the fact that it was intended as an abbreviation for the word "sheep." He had begun by determining the relative frequencies of the various signs, and had then essayed to identify certain suffixes, prefixes, and monosyllabic words, assisted by a knowledge of their probable Western Semitic equivalents, and by the fact that in this tongue the letters *k*, *m*, and *w* belonged to all three categories. In this manner, he arrived at the following alternative values for several of the unknown characters, here numbered from 1-4:

$$1 \text{ or } 2 = w$$
$$2 \text{ or } 1 = m$$
$$3 \text{ or } 4 = n$$
$$4 \text{ or } 3 = t$$

Thereafter, employing the probable-word technique, Bauer searched for and found the word "king," thus verifying that $2 = m$, and hence that $1 = w$. He was also successful in recognising the written numbers "three" and "four," and, the names of leading deities, among them El, Baal, and Astarte, and in the event, it was he who first published a preliminary decipherment. The account appeared in the *Vossichen Zeitung* for 4 June, 1930, and the American scholar W. F. Albright, who chanced to be in Jerusalem in the summer of that year, presented a copy of the report to Dhorme, who at once perceived that he was mistaken in two of his values. Following Virolleaud in a search for words containing the letter "1," he had duly identified Baal, and thus armed with the consonant "b," had elsewhere read *bn* as *bt*, and *vice versa*. This confusing of "n" with "t," and of "t" with "n," as may be imagined, adversely affected his prospects of identifying Semitic words, in that a phrase such as "Not now, but next month" transliterated as "Ton tow, tub texn motnh." Once this simple, but most misleading, error was corrected, Dhorme was able to make a rapid advance which increased the number of correctly identified symbols to twenty. Bauer, in turn, acknowledged this step forward, and by October had increased the total to twenty-five, whereafter Virolleaud rounded off the achievement. Thus, between them, the three scholars solved the problem of the Ugaritic language and writing in a matter of a few months (the essentials of Bauer's investigations were completed in precisely one week!)—one of the quickest cases of decipherment on record.

Some twenty years after this achievement, added confirmation was provided by the contents of a small tablet, unearthed in the course of subsequent excavations at Ras Shamra. This document gave a complete ABC of the cuneiform script, which was here shown to consist of thirty signs, in which listing the twenty-two conventional Phoenician characters were shown in their correct order, interspersed with additional consonants, some of which were known to have disappeared from the West Semitic speech during the 12th century B.C. or thereabouts (Fig. 9). The identity of the site of Ras Shamra, meanwhile, which Emil Forrer, not long after Schaeffer's arrival there, had suggested might be Ugarit, was established by references contained in other tablets, one of which gave the name of a local ruler as *Ngmd* (vocalised as Niqmadda), among whose titles was that of *Mlk Ugrt*—King of Ugarit.

Other texts, such as schoolboy slates on which the same word had been written a number of times, indicated that a school for scribes had existed in the vicinity of a temple dedicated to Baal. One of the teachers, a priest called Rabana, had compiled a dictionary as an aid to his pupils, and had written his name in the margin. It was evident, too, that several foreign languages had been taught at this theological college, including Sumerian (for learned and ecclesiastical purposes) and Accadian.

Legal documents among the finds were represented by a warrant ordering the arrest of some absconding miscreant, and by the will of a more worthy citizen, who had left all his worldly possessions (including his servants of both sexes) to his wife Bidawa, whom his two sons, Jaatlinu and Jaanhama, were called upon to obey at all times, under threat of eviction from the family home, and the payment of a fine of 500 silver shekels to the king. Other illuminating sidelights on the life of the times were provided by the contents of a manual for the treatment of horses, including those animals which displayed a tendency to neigh or bite too much, and a tabulation headed *Ganba* (Price), which revealed the established bargaining procedure at the local bazaar. This list gave not only the Great Price (with which the negotiations began) and the Small Price (with which the haggling came to an end), but also the Gross Price, the Net Price, the Fixed Price, the Good Price, the Beautiful Price, and the City Price.

The contents of the majority of the tablets, however, were

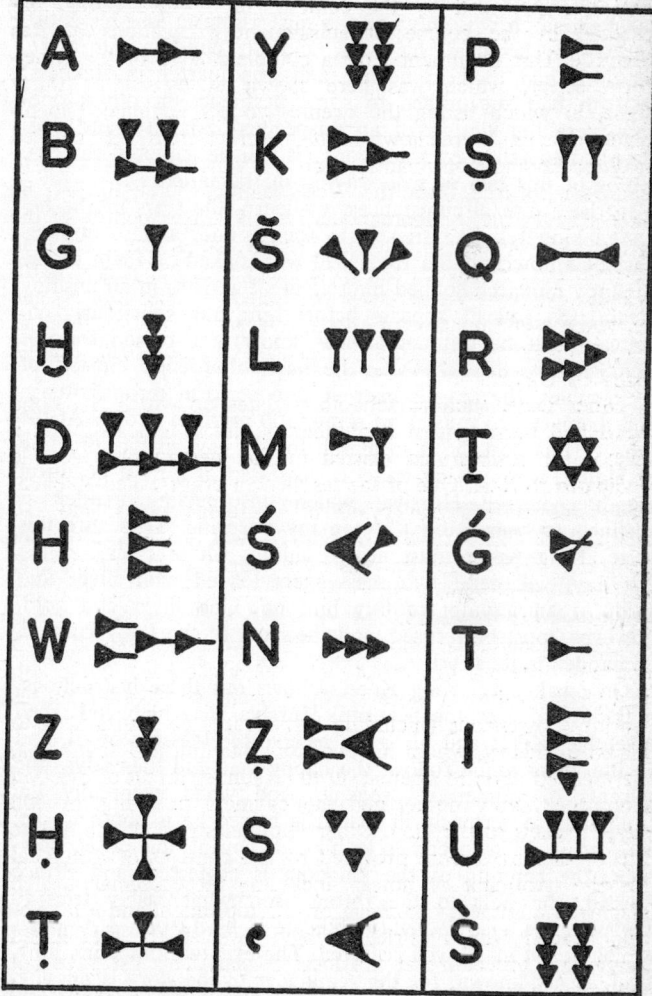

Fig. 9. Ugaritic syllabary (after C. H. Gordon).

of a mythological and religious character, a representative example of which is the Legend of Keret. The account opens with Keret, one of the early kings of Sidon, pictured as a tragic monarch who has had the misfortune to lose his entire family—his brothers, his wife, and his children. Of these, one-third had died in health, and one-quarter in sickness; one-fifth had succumbed to some pestilence or other; one-sixth were the victims of an unspecified calamity; and one-seventh had fallen by the sword (it will be gathered that the author of this tale of woe was no mathematician).

In these dire circumstances, we learn, the tears of the bereaved king fell like shekels to the ground, and so copious was their flow that the royal bed was soaked by them as the unhappy monarch sobbed himself to sleep. But, in an ensuing dream, the god El appears before him, and solicitously enquires (as if he did not already know) the reason for this lachrymatory display. After he has unburdened himself of his troubles, the king is instructed to perform certain rituals, and thereafter to muster an army, 300 myriads strong. At the head of this host, he is to march for six days in the direction of Udum, whose King Pabel is possessed of a most beautiful daughter named Hurriya, which unsuspecting maiden is destined to bear King Keret many offspring. To secure this prize, King Keret must attack Udum, whose ruler, on the 7th day, will send two messengers loaded with silver and gold, in an attempt to buy him off. The silver and gold, however, must be refused, and the hand of the Lady Hurriya demanded in its stead.

On awakening, King Keret follows out these instructions, and duly obtains the beautiful Hurriya. The high gods then assemble, Keret and his bride receive the blessing of El, and in the years which follow, the happy pair find themselves the parents of numerous progeny. And when eventually the king falls so seriously ill that it is feared he is about to die, it is again El who comes to his aid. During this crisis, however, the running of the kingdom is neglected, and Prince Yassib, the heir to the throne, somewhat rashly tries to persuade his aged father to abdicate in his favour, a proposal which is not at all well received. The eventual outcome, however, is not known, for the remainder of the story is missing.

The precise linguistic affiliations of the ancient Semitic tongue in which this and similar accounts are written has been the subject of some difference of opinion among scholars. According to Albrecht Goetze and his followers, Ugaritic is to be regarded as a distinct language, related to Accadian on the one hand, and to Canaanite on the other. In the view of Albright and others, however, both Ugaritic and Hebrew are West Semitic dialects to which the term Canaanite may, with due caution, be applied. At all events, a comparison of Ugaritic literature and the sacred writings of the Hebrews reveals extraordinary, and perhaps otherwise inexplicable, resemblances in language, style, and ideological content.

Like their Hebraic counterparts, many of the Ugaritic texts are poetic in form, and make extensive use of the device known as parallelism, which entails a reiteration of similar or antithetic thought, *e.g.*,

> *The heavens rain oil*
> *The wadies run with honey.*

Both literatures, in unmistakably identical terms, make mention of a monster called Leviathan, slain by the god Baal in the one account, and by Yahweh in the other. The Ugaritic version, moreover, gives the information, previously unknown, that the creature was endowed with seven heads. There are likewise references to a number of Canaanite sacrificial practices which duly reappear in the Old Testament record, where they are described in the same technical terms used in the Ugaritic rituals—the Peace Offering, the Trespass Offering, the Wave Offering, the Offering Without Blemish, the Bread of the Gods. Similarly, many familiar and hitherto supposedly Hebraic expressions are encountered in their earlier Ugaritic guise—"The hind longing for the springs of water" (Ps. 41:2); "The river of God" (Ps. 65:9); "The dew of heaven, and the fat of the earth" (Gn. 27:39); while other phrases, though less literal in their employment, show evident signs of adaptation: "He who rides upon the clouds" ("Behold Yahweh rides upon a swift cloud"—Is. 19:1); "I will divide the sea" ("To Him which divided the Red Sea in sunder"—Ps. 136:13); and "I know that Aleyn, the son of Baal, liveth" ("I know that my Redeemer liveth"—Jb. 19:25).

In the face of these and many other correspondences, some of them no less startling (there are Ugaritic references to a Holy of Holies in the temple, to a popular hero called Daniel, who "decides the cause of the widow, and judges the case of the orphan," and to Baal who, as a Son of God (*bn elm*) is put to death, later to rise again), the conclusion is inescapable that many of the religious beliefs and practices of the Canaanites were adopted by the Hebrews, and so found their way into the Old Testament.

Although, like that of the ancestors of the Hebrews themselves, the religion of the Canaanites was undoubtedly polytheistic, it has been suggested that by the time of the Conquest, their beliefs had begun to evince monotheistic leanings, in that its two principal deities were El and his son Baal. On a stele found at Ras Shamra, El is pictured as a bearded old man, seated on a throne, and in the act of receiving an offering from the King of Ugarit. He is referred to as the "Father of years" (*cf.* the "Everlasting Father" of Isaiah, and the "Ancient of days" of Daniel), and is revealed as a remote and transcendental overlord, as the possessor, that is to say, of the very attributes with which the Israelites came to invest their own deity, originally conceived as a tribal moon-god whose abode was a tent. Certainly it would appear to be highly significant that El is the name by which Yahweh is called in Genesis (often in the plural of majesty, Elohim).

It is at all events clear that much of the supposedly lost Canaanite literature is, in fact, preserved in the sacred writings of their Hebrew conquerors, though the precise extent of the borrowing has yet to be determined. In the meantime, the discovery of isolated examples of the Ugaritic script at Beth Shamesh, and also at Mount Tabor, in Galilee, suggest that other extensive accumulations of these revealing documents may well await discovery in localities far beyond the confines of Ras Shamra.

III

What was long held to be the oldest written record found on the Greek mainland was an inscription on a dipylon vase from Athens. But the find, dated about 750 B.C., could hardly be considered of great historical significance, for this long lost message from the past merely stated:

Whoever of the dancers makes merry most gracefully, let him receive this.

Until comparatively recently, the beginnings of Greek history were associated with the ending of the Bronze Age *c.* 1100 B.C., an event heralded by the arrival in the Aegean area of a supposedly new race (the Greeks) in the guise of the iron-possessing Dorians. But in fact, as is now recognised, by the time this particular Hellenic contingent appeared on the scene, the land had already been Greek for nearly 1,000 years. Even so, prior to 1870, the Homeric epics relating to this earlier period were regarded as fictitious, and the well-known historian George Grote voiced the sentiments of the time when he declared that in the eyes of modern enquiry the Trojan War was a legend, and nothing more—a view no sooner expressed than it had to be modified as a result of the archaeological activities of Heinrich Schliemann.

Contrary to all expectations, Schliemann succeeded in locating the site of the supposedly fabulous citadel of Troy, and after carrying out extensive excavations there, identified nine superimposed layers, the sixth of which he regarded as Homeric. And having thus confounded the experts, he then gave his attention to the Greek mainland, where once again his unconventional ideas produced startling results. According to an ancient tradition, echoed by the Greek geographer Pausanias (2nd century A.D.), the ruined stronghold of Mycenae contained the grave of Agamemnon, and other of the returned warriors from the siege of Troy who had been treacherously slain by Aegysthus and Clytemnestra. So at Mycenae Schliemann began to dig—and quickly silenced his critics (who looked upon the enterprise as a waste of time and effort) by locating the so-called royal burial circle, containing a series of shaft graves, cut in the solid rock to a depth of 25 feet. All told, the remains of nineteen persons—men, women, and children—were recovered, together with numerous weapons and gold ornaments. There was thus revealed evidence which pointed to the existence of a Mycenaean civilisation extending as far back as the middle of the 2nd millennium B.C. and beyond, though there was as yet nothing to suggest that its precursors were Greek.

To these discoveries there were soon added those of Arthur Evans in Crete. Together with the Greek Archipelago and the mainland, this island constitutes one of the three main geographic regions of the Aegean area, and the interest of Evans in its archaeological possibilities was first roused in 1886. He was then Keeper of the Ashmolean Museum in Oxford, in which capacity he received from Greville Chester a Cretan seal-stone, engraved with unfamiliar hieroglyphic markings. With the intention of following up this clue, which he believed might lead to the discovery of written records belonging to the early inhabitants of the region, Evans journeyed to Greece in 1893, and in the following year, after making a tentative exploration of Crete, he purchased a part of a ruined site at Knossos. The remainder of the area was acquired by him in 1900, in which year the task of excavation was begun, and almost at once a large collection of clay tablets was discovered. These documents, however, were inscribed, not with the hieroglyphs found on the seal-stone, but with an altogether different script. In all, three kinds of writing were revealed—that which had first attracted attention, and two cursive scripts, one seemingly a modification of the other, which the discoverer designated Linear A and Linear B. In all three instances, neither the language nor the writing was known, a state of affairs which was destined to persist for the next fifty years.

Evans, meanwhile, became increasingly absorbed in the immense task of excavating and reconstituting the Knossos ruins. The main structure, evidently the remains of a palace, occupied about five acres, and comprised a veritable maze of rooms, halls, and corridors, in parts several storeys high, and grouped about a central courtyard. And here, in the shape of amenities which included bathrooms replete with hot water supplies and a forerunner of the modern flush closet, was found evidence of a civilisation of an unexpectedly high order, which the excavator, in deference to Minos, a legendary ruler of this island domain, termed Minoan.

Neolithic remains at the site were found in the shape of an underlying deposit, some 36 feet thick. This Stone Age occupation, which must have lasted many thousands of years, seemingly came to an end about 4000 B.C., and, as a matter of convenience, the succeeding Bronze Age was divided into three main periods, distinguished as Early, Middle, and Late Minoan (EM, MM, LM). Each of these periods was further subdivided into three phases, numbered I-III, and representative of initial rise, subsequent maturity, and eventual decline. Absolute dating was achieved by way of Cretan art (in particular, ceramic art) and Egyptian synchronisms, *e.g.*, a style of pottery characteristic of LM I, exported from the island to Egypt, was found in the Nile valley among other remains belonging to the 18th dynasty (1580-1350 B.C.).

It was estimated that the great palace dated from the MM I period (2100-1900 B.C.). During MM II, the structure appeared to have been destroyed, whereafter it was redesigned and rebuilt, and then once again badly damaged. A final reconstruction was undertaken in LM I, and this handiwork survived until LM II. The place was then laid waste and deserted, though there were indications of a tentative reoccupation during LM III, whereafter the ruins were left to moulder and decay, their maze of corridors and underground drains in due course giving rise to the Greek legend of the Cretan labyrinth and the dreaded Minotaur, half human, half bull, which supposedly inhabited it.

The end of the Cretan civilisation appeared to be as inexplicable as its beginnings. According to Thucydides, Minos was a Greek, though Herodotus declared otherwise, while, if Homer was to be believed, as many as five different peoples had lived on the island at one time or another. Modern opinions were equally at variance. W. Dörpfeld, who had assisted Schliemann at Troy, inclined to the view that both Cretan and Mycenaean art were essentially Phoenician. Eduard Meyer, an expert in ancient history, was content to exclude Asia Minor as its source, while Evans was convinced that the island culture, which he conceded might have been African in origin, had developed indigenously in its Aegean surroundings. So highly did he rate Cretan achievements, indeed, that he ended, in the face of mounting evidence to the contrary, by contending that the Mycenaeans were Minoan invaders, and that the mainland civilisation was the result of Cretan colonisation. This view he maintained right up to the time of his death in 1941, and such was the weight of his authority that it long delayed a true appreciation of Aegean affairs during the Bronze Age.

Stratigraphical evidence on the mainland, however, led to a recognition of Early, Middle, and Late Helladic periods, roughly corresponding to, but distinct from, their Minoan counterparts, and by 1930 not a few archaeologists had reached the conclusion that the arrival of the first Greeks in Greece coincided with the beginning of the Middle Bronze Age, *c.* 1900 B.C., and that their coming anticipated by some eight centuries the Dorian so-called invasion. Seemingly, the newcomers had mingled with the Early Helladic inhabitants of the area, a people who were not Indo-European, and who had introduced non-Greek place and other names ending in *-nthos, -assos, -ttos,* and *-ene, e.g.,* Korinthos, Parnassos, Hymettos, Mykene.

Thus, in direct opposition to Evans and his views, there

arose a school of thought which held that the mainland civilisation, though it may well have been influenced by that of Crete, was largely independent of it. As for the evidence, cultural and otherwise, which Evans regarded as proof of Cretan conquest and occupation of the mainland, it was suggested that this should in fact be interpreted the other way about, in that it was indicative of mainland control of Knossos!

The piquancy of the situation was increased by the discovery of hundreds of Linear B tablets on the mainland at Pylos and Mycenae. Like their Cretan counterparts, these documents conformed to one or other of two main types, in that they were either rectangular (page-form), or long and narrow, often with rounded ends (palm-leaf style). And it was evident, too, that after the clay had been roughly shaped and inscribed, and the tablets dried (not baked) and filed in wooden boxes, their preservation had been accidentally ensured by the subsequent firing they received when the buildings in which they were stored were burned to the ground, either unintentionally, or as the result of enemy attack. Even then, luck continued to play a part—at Pylos, for example, it was frequently observed that tablets which happened to have fallen face downwards were often badly damaged by microscopic rootlets, whereas others which had chanced to land right side up were in a much better state.

It was now apparent that the Linear B material was far more widely distributed on the mainland than it was on Crete itself, where (unlike the Linear A records) it was restricted to Knossos. But the significance of this peculiar distribution of what were held to be Minoan documents remained open to more than one interpretation, and Evans and his supporters doggedly adopted the view that it merely confirmed Cretan domination of the mainland. In these contentious circumstances, the question of the decipherment of the Linear B script became one of crucial importance, for it was clear that the information thus obtained would decide the issue.

But in this vital matter, little or no progress had as yet been made—and it was largely Evans himself who was to blame, for scholars had been given scant opportunity to study the relevant documents. His *Scripta Minoa* (London, 1909), when it appeared, was mainly devoted to the hieroglyphic and Linear A material, and of the all-important Linear B script, only fourteen tablets were included. Some twenty-five years later, Evans gave another 120 of these tablets to the world, in the fourth volume of his monumental *The Palace of Minos* (London, 1935). But the bulk of the material, amounting to some 3,000 tablets, still remained unpublished at the time of the death of their negligent finder. A large and disorderly accumulation of notes then received attention from his erstwhile associate, Sir J. L. Myers, and details of the missing documents, more than 50 years after their discovery, at last appeared in *Scripta Minoa II* (London, 1952), by which time they were merely of academic interest in so far as the question of their decipherment was concerned.

Early investigators thus had little enough to go on. From the onset, it had been perceived by Evans that the tablets were evidently inventories, in which a decimal system of counting was used. The nature of the contents appeared to be indicated by a series of ideograms, some of which were clearly intended to represent persons, animals, and various commodities of one kind and another. These pictorial symbols, moreover, were accompanied by groups of two or more other signs, of which there were about ninety in all—too numerous to be alphabetic, and hence regarded as syllabic.

J. Sundwall, an indefatigable student of the script from 1914 onwards, employed the method of internal comparison, stressed the need to identify the objects depicted ideographically, and called for an analysis of the measurements employed, while A. E. Cowley drew attention to the fact that the totals shown on the tablets were invariably introduced by one or other of two pairs of signs. Generally, it was assumed that the Linear A script was an earlier form of Linear B, and that both expressed the same language, though attempts by various investigators to identify it with Hebrew, Finnish, Hittite, Egyptian, and even Sumerian, were unsuccessful. Another approach, made independently of the inscriptions, sought to ascertain the probable characteristics of the language spoken by the Bronze Age inhabitants of the Aegean area, with particular reference to the non-Greek place names aforementioned a false and bifurcated trail which led on the one hand to Anatolia, and on the other to Etruria.

It was at this unprogressive stage that C. W. Blegan, in 1939, located the site of an extensive Mycenaean palace at Epano Englianos, in the vicinity of Pylos—and almost at once stumbled upon an archive room from which several hundred clay tablets were recovered. In view of the prevailing uncertainties of the international situation, the documents were cleaned, photographed, and hidden in a place of safety. A few of the records, sufficient to give an indication of their nature, were published forthwith, and from the evidence thus provided, it was apparent that the writing was identical with that on the Linear B tablets which Evans had found at Knossos. As it was by this time widely believed that the Mycenaean civilisation was Greek, the find raised questions of considerable importance to holders of the Minoan point of view, but any doubts were resolved, at any rate for the moment, by the assumption that the mainland records were an importation, not a native product.

The task of editing the new material was entrusted to Emmett L. Bennett, of the University of Cincinnati, and his labours culminated (after a delay caused by the war) in the publication of *The Pylos Tablets* (Princeton, 1951), wherein the texts were grouped according to their ideogram context. At the same time, a careful examination of the tablets was undertaken by Alice E. Kober, of Brooklyn, the results of whose penetrating studies appeared in a series of articles published from 1943 onwards until her untimely death in 1950. Both contributions were of fundamental importance, and the work of Kober demonstrated, among other things, not merely that the language of the tablets exhibited grammatical inflexions (as was, of course, not unexpected), but that certain regular sign variations were analogous to changes which were to be observed in another inflected language—Latin:

ser-vu-s	a-mi-cu-s	bo-nu-s
ser-vu-m	a-mi-cu-m	b-onu-m
ser-vi	a-mi-ci	bo-ni
ser-vo	a-mi-co	bo-no

Given the syllabic nature of the Linear B symbols, might it not be the case that, like the ablative endings *-vo, -co, -no* above, the equivalent sign endings also shared the same vowel, but different consonants? And, conversely, that other pairs shared the same consonant, but different vowels—as did *vo/vu, co/cu, no/nu*?

The outcome of this reasoning was a tabulation cautiously described by Kober as "the beginning of a tentative phonetic pattern" (afterwards more familiarly referred to by the decipherers as "the grid"), in which the syllabic signs were groups in accordance with their supposed vowel and possible consonant content, the arrangement being such that the scheme could be extended in either direction, as required (Fig. 10).

| | | V1 | V2 | V3 |
		o	u	?
C1	v	vo	vu	v?
C2	c	co	cu	c?
C3	n	no	nu	n?
C4	?	?o	?u	??
C5	?	?o	?u	??
C6	?	?o	?u	??

Fig. 10. Linear B—the start of the grid.

As utilised by the decoders, the grid assumed the form of a board bristling with orderly rows of nails, on which labels bearing the various syllabic signs could be hung and moved about as the situation developed. The method was particularly valuable in that it precluded random attempts at vocalisation, since any alteration to an already assumed syllabic value had immediate repercussions on all other signs sharing the same horizontal and vertical columns.

In London, meanwhile, an event of decisive importance had occurred in 1936. In that year, at an exhibition to commemorate the jubilee of the British School of Athens, Sir Arthur Evans gave a talk on Minoan affairs, and among his audience was a schoolboy named Michael Ventris. The lecturer's account of the undeciphered writing of the Knossos tablets so captured the imagination of this young listener that he decided to devote himself to the solving of the problem. Subsequently, although Ventris made architecture his career, his leisure moments were given to this self-imposed task.

From the onset, Ventris inclined to favour the supposed Etruscan affinities of the unknown language of the tablets, and published what he himself afterwards described as an adolescent article on this aspect of the problem. But in 1950, encouraged by the availability of additional Pylos material, and spurred on by the activities of Sundwall, Bennett, Kober, and other investigators, he undertook a new series of analytical studies, listing the phonetic signs according to the frequency of their occurrence, and noting in addition those which were predominantly initial or final, or which tended to occur in pairs, or which were at no time found in association with one another. Consideration was also given to the various sign groups, and a functional classification attempted. On a purely comparative basis, four categories were tentatively distinguished:

1. Personal names
2. Place names, and names of buildings
3. Names of trades and occupations
4. A general vocabulary

In January, 1951, in order to test the validity of these and other findings, Ventris began an exchange of notes and ideas with a score of scholars who shared his interest in the problem, among them Bedřich Hrozný, who by this time had succeeded in convincing himself (but not his colleagues) that he had at last solved the riddle (he professed to have detected similarities in the Cretan writing, not only to Egyptian and hieroglyphic Hittite, but also to Proto-Indic, Sumero-Babylonian, Greco-Latin, and Cyprian!).

The eighth of the Ventris communications concerned the outcome of his statistical investigation. In this note, he suggested that the frequent initial use of three of the signs in all probability indicated that they were representative of simple vowels, one of which appeared to have the value *i,* and another the value *a*—this last an identification already suspected by several of the investigators, including Kober. That the value of the third sign might be *e* was suggested by the number of times it was found among groups of signs thought to be men's names, and in this event, a fourth sign, also regarded as a likely vowel, could be assigned the value *o.* Though the identification of consonants was a much more difficult feat, by February, 1952, the contents of the grid had been considerably extended, thanks to a few slender clues and much judicious guesswork.

It was at this stage of the investigations that *Scripta Minoa II* at long last appeared, and while for the most part the Knossos material tended to confirm the existing structure of the grid, there seemed to be some inconsistency between the spelling variations exhibited by certain words. In an attempt to eradicate this, Ventris gave consideration to the

SOME SUBSIDIARY SYSTEMS 153

syllabic value *jo* for one of the signs concerned, a value which he had earlier had occasion to reject. And among other things, the amendment had a marked effect upon triple groups of signs earlier listed by Kober as appearing in alternative (inflected) forms. From them, by incorporating *ja* and *jo* values, in association with the third vowel provisionally identified as *i*, and by inserting numbers where unknown consonants occurred, Ventris obtained a series of skeletal words which, by their very appearance, suggested the substitution of various consonants for the numbers. It was as though, to the incomplete words listed hereunder on the left, the values 1=D, 2=H, 3=L, 4=N, 5=R, and 6=S offered themselves as likely to reveal the familiar place names shown on the right:

I^1-AH-O	ID-AH-O
^{6}A-^{2}A-^{5}A	SA-HA-RA
BO-^{6}T-O^4	BO-ST-ON
^{4}A-P^3-E^6	NA-PL-ES
PA-^{5}I-^{6}	PA-RI-S

But what the astonished Ventris obtained, however, were the names of five of the leading towns of Crete—Amnisos, Knossos, Tylissos, Phaistos, and Lyktos! More arresting still, this identification of six of the consonants automatically endowed no less than 31 of the grid signs with fixed phonetic values, and these, when applied to the contents of some of the tablets, seemingly gave the word "coriander" and the phrase "fitted with reigns" *in Greek!*

This momentous discovery was announced in a note (the twentieth of the series) which Ventris despatched to his fellow decipherers in June, 1952, though it was qualified by the suggestion that the supposed Greek words were probably a mirage. But no sooner was the report on its way than Ventris realised, after applying the newly derived phonetic values to the contents of other tablets, that, unbelievable though it appeared, there was no escaping the conclusion that the language of the Linear B tablets was indeed an archaic form of Greek.

Much, of course, remained to be done before the worth of this revolutionary thesis could be established. To this end, Myers put Ventris in touch with John Chadwick, of Cambridge, who had also been working on the problem, and whose cryptographic talents and extensive knowledge of Greek dialects promised to be particularly useful. The immediate outcome of this collaboration was the publication of a joint paper, "Evidence for Greek Dialect in the Mycenaean Archives" (*Journal of Hellenic Studies*, Vol. LXXIII, 1953), in which a table of sign values was given (Fig. 11), many interpretations were proposed, and the language of the Linear B records was identified as a Greek dialect akin to Arcado-Cyprian.

The reception accorded the Ventris discovery by leading archaeologists and philologists combined encouragement with some reservations. In 1952, Blegen had resumed work at Pylos, and had recovered several hundred more tablets from the site, and others soon afterwards came to light at Mycenae and elsewhere on the mainland. Would the contents of this additional material confirm the proposed solution? As it happened, it was one of the records from Pylos which, most convincingly, provided the answer. As yet unseen by Ventris, this document was examined by Blegen early in 1953. He reported that judging by its ideographic content, it evidently concerned pots, some with three legs, others with three or four handles, yet others with no handles. And in terms of the proposed phonetic values, the accompanying sign groups transliterated as *ti-ri-po* (tripod); *ti-ri-o-we-e* (with three handles); *qe-to-ro-we* (with four handles); and *a-no-we* (without handles). "All this," wrote Blegen, "seems too good to be true. Is coincidence excluded?"

The fact, now generally recognised, that the language of the Linear B tablets is an early form of Greek, raises the question of how the script came to be adapted to it. As to this, the adoption and extension of the Minoan signary was no doubt an outcome of mainland control of Knossos during the island's LM II period, the beginning of which, according to Evans, was attended by the emergence of a "new dynasty of aggressive character." At all events, what must now be termed the *Mycenaean* Linear B script was unquestionably derived from an earlier Minoan version, most likely that designated Linear A, which can in turn be traced back to the Cretan hieroglyphic writing. And this, though Egyptian in character, is apparently an independent system.

In their comprehensive *Documents in Mycenaean Greek* (Cambridge, 1956), Ventris and Chadwick themselves introduce a note of caution concerning the extent of the decipherment of the Linear B script. There remains, for example, the problem presented by many of the ideograms. Bennett has

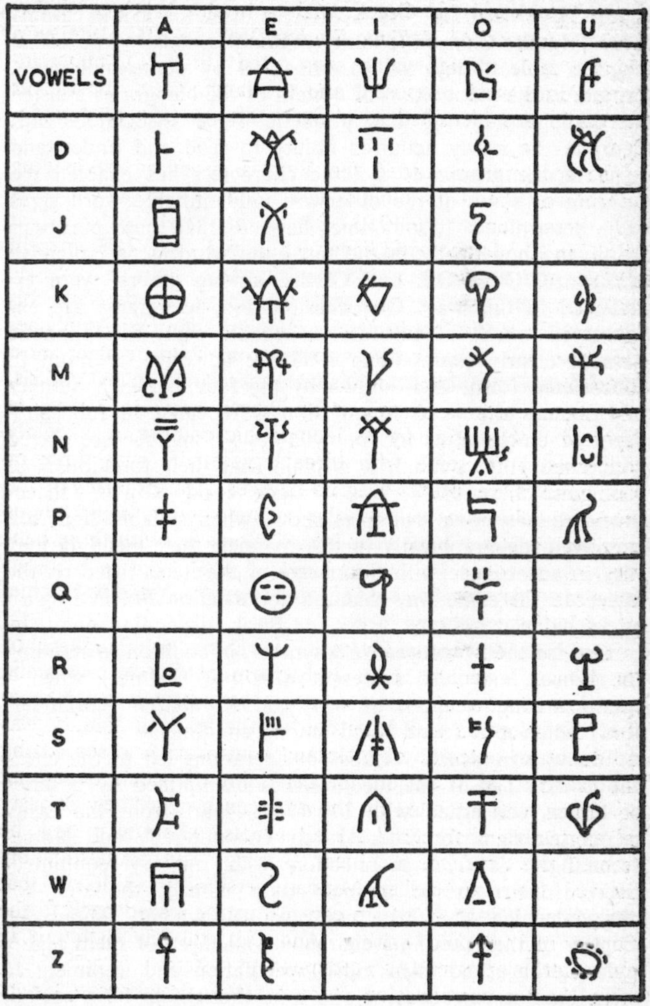

Fig. 11. Mycenaean syllabary (after Ventris and Chadwick).

listed (Fig. 12) considerably more than 100 of these word signs (and there may well be others, yet to be encountered), and except where they are clearly pictorial (as in the case of Men, Tripods, Chariots), their meaning is usually impossible to guess unless they are accompanied by contextual clues. But just as the recognition of certain of the ideograms assisted the decipherment of the phonetic signs associated with them, so the newly acquired ability to read and understand many of the groups of syllabic characters has enabled the meaning of some of the otherwise unidentifiable word signs to be determined. It sometimes happens that these meanings are given phonetically in the text—the word signs indicative of Bronze, Olive Oil, and Cloths, among others, were established in this way. On occasion, too, ideograms are encountered which incorporate a syllabic sign, the phonetic element clearly representing a Greek adjective or noun in abbreviated form, as is shown by the fact that in a number of instances the word in question is repeated in full. Similarly, when the signs for the syllables *Wi* and *Ko* are placed within the Hide symbol, it is plain that their function is to distinguish between *Wrinos* (oxhide) and *Kōwos* (sheepskin). But as other examples show, when syllabic signs are employed ideographically in this manner, their meaning may vary in accordance with the nature of the items listed on the tablet. In the same way that the abbreviation *Bk.* in English might be read as Bank, Bark, or Book, depending upon the context, so the Mycenaean *Ko* symbol, in addition to standing for *Kōwos*, may also represent *Koruthos* (helmet) when it occurs among weapons of war, and *Koriandna* (coriander-seed) when it is found listed among condiments.

The way in which various considerations led to the elucidation of other of the ideograms is exemplified by a series of tablets concerned with livestock. Apart from the easily recognised signs for Deer (rarely encountered) and Horses (seemingly listed in connection with military equipment only), four domestic animals were named, the sign for one of which, the Pig, was also self-evident. About the identity of the remaining characters, all three of them highly stylised, there had been much speculation and argument in the past. But what was at one time thought to be a variant of the Horse is now regarded as a representation of the Ox, so that by a process of elimination, the investigators were left with two symbols which could not be other than those of Sheep and Goats. The problem was thus reduced to the ques-

LIST OF IDEOGRAPHIC SIGNS

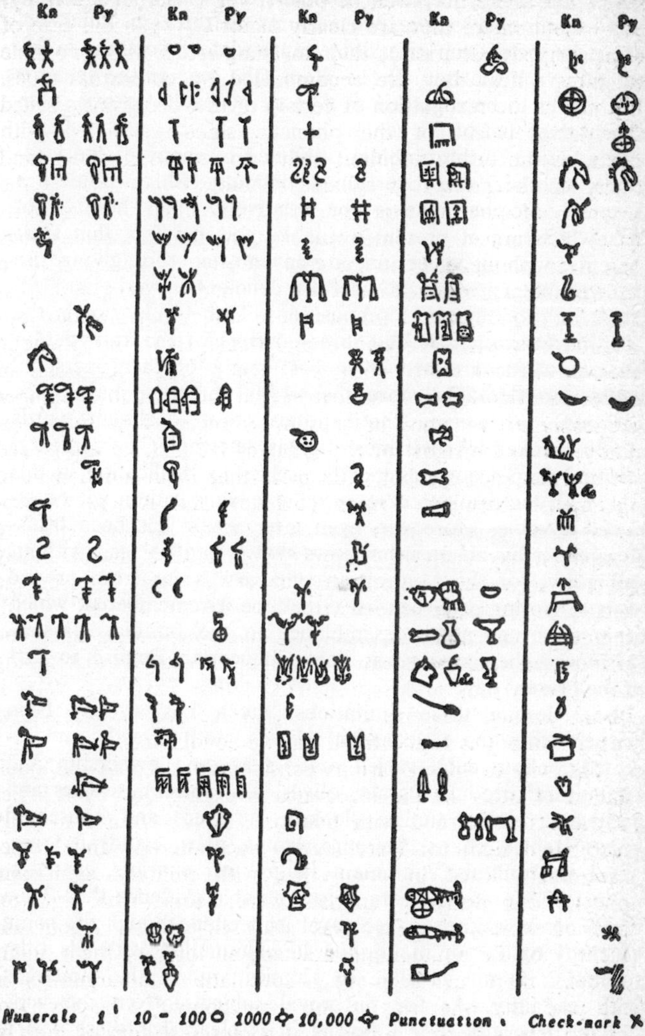

Fig. 12. Linear B—list of ideograms as encountered at Knossos (Kn) and Pylos (Py) (Emmett L. Bennett).

tion of deciding which was which, and it appears to have been satisfactorily resolved by according the value Sheep, as the commoner of the two animals, to the sign which occurs most often—on occasion, appropriately enough, in association with the symbol for Wool (the hair of the sheep is presumably to be regarded as a more probable textorial constituent than that of the goat).

In addition to the problem presented by many of the ideograms, another, and overriding, difficulty which hinders a complete decipherment is the relatively small number of texts which are at present available, and the fact that their contents, without exception, are inventorial, thus giving rise to a vocabulary which is woefully deficient in verbs and adverbs, in pronouns and prepositions. Unhelpful, too, is the fact that between half and three-quarters of the known Mycenaean words are proper names, many of them personal names (considerably more than 1,000 of these have been recorded), for, whereas the identification of vocabulary words can be checked by their meaning (as determined by context), personal names do not lend themselves to verification in this way, with the result that some syllabic signs cannot yet be assigned a value. Moreover, even after a text has been transliterated, it by no means follows that it can be read without ambiguity, for the Mycenaean syllabary is far from precise in its rendering of Greek—a Greek, be it remembered, which bears about as much resemblance to the familiar classical version of the language as does Chaucerian English to that of the present day.

But, despite these limitations, much has already been learned from the Mycenaean records, both directly and indirectly, about such varied matters as land ownership and agricultural produce (grain, olives, figs, spices), textiles and garments (cloths, tunics, cloaks), furniture and household goods (tables, chairs, firetongs, lamps, pans, cauldrons) and naval and military equipment (ships, war chariots, corselets, helmets). Moreover, there is indisputable evidence that Pylos and Knossos acknowledged royal leadership, though the name of the king is not mentioned in conjunction with his title, so that it is not possible to identify any of the monarchs with certainty. As for the royal subjects, from the wide variety of trades they followed, it is clear that there was a considerable differentiation of labour—there are references to shepherds and goatherds, wood-cutters and huntsmen, carpenters and masons, metal-workers and bow-makers, spinners and weavers, bath attendants and serving women. Other callings include those of physician, herald, and messenger, while the customary army of priests and priestesses was available to attend the wants of a no less inevitable galaxy of gods and goddesses. Subject always to the proviso that the identification of personal names rests on superficial resemblances, these divinities appear to include such well-known representatives of classical Greek mythology as Zeus, Hera, Athena, and Poseidon, not to mention possible references to Hermes and Dionysus. The tablets also mention persons who bear the names of more than 50 of the characters found in Homer, among them Castor, Theseus, Hector, and Achilles, but, in the complete absence of monumental inscriptions, there have been no identifications of an historic nature. The apparent limiting of Mycenaean writing to commodity tablets and clay sealings (apart from a few inscriptions found on jars at Tiryns, Thebes, and elsewhere) thus raises the question of the extent of early Greek literacy, and S. Dow inclines to the view that the use of the Linear B script was confined to a few specialists. Against this, it has been argued that some of the records seemingly belonged to private citizens, and that the existence of inscribed jars indicates that persons other than professional scribes knew how to read and write. It has also been surmised that from their outlines, it would appear that the characters of the Linear A and B scripts were primarily designed for writing in ink on papyrus or its equivalent, rather than for scratching on clay tablets, and that as these latter documents were in all probability periodically pulped or otherwise discarded, the flames which accidentally led to their preservation may have simultaneously destroyed what were intended to be more permanent records.

However this may be, the fact remains that after the destruction of Pylos and other centres of culture at the close of the Bronze Age, there is a blank of some three and a half centuries among the records, and that Greek writing, when it eventually reappears, does so not in a Minoan, but in a Phoenician, guise—a different script entirely. Must we believe, then, that with the arrival of the Dorians, and the wholesale destruction which attended their coming, the art of writing was so completely lost that it was never regained in its original form? Or are we to suppose, as A. J. Wace has hopefully suggested, that the Greeks were much too intelligent a people to forget how to write, and that the onset of the Iron Age must have been marked by a period of transition, during which the use of the Linear B script was continued until the manifest advantages of the Phoenician system led to a gradual abandonment of the one, and the eventual adoption of the other? Wace even envisages the possibility of finding documents giving a muster roll of ships anticipating the Homeric Catalogue and Agamemnon's battle order, and echoes the wistful speculation of Blegan that in some palace or other there may be preserved the archives of a political bureau or of a foreign office. . . .

Fig. 13. Part of the Ahiram inscription from Byblos (after R. Dussaud).

CHAPTER V

AMONG THE UNDECIPHERED

I

At the second International Congress of Classical Studies, recently held at Copenhagen, I. J. Gelb described the achievement of the late Michael Ventris in solving the problem of the Linear B script as "the most successful single attempt in the whole history of the decipherment of unknown writings and languages." Coming from so eminent a source, this is high praise indeed, and the fact that the feat was accomplished, as recently as 1952, by someone other than a professional philologist, certainly suggests that there is nothing to prevent would-be Champollions from exercising their ingenuity and their talents, always providing that these attributes are accompanied by a thorough knowledge of the subject of their choice.

Not a few problems are at present outstanding, some of them far from new, *e.g.*, that presented by the language of of the Etruscans (*vide infra*), which has long baffled scholars, and is seemingly little nearer solution to-day than it was 2,000 years ago. Other questions have arisen since the beginning of the present century, and at least some of them promise to be less intractable, in that they seemingly await nothing more than the discovery of additional material, unilingual or otherwise. Into this category, perhaps, can be placed a series of enigmatic inscriptions which came to light a few years ago (from 1929 onwards) at the ancient Phoenician town of Byblos. Since their publication by Maurice Dunand (*Byblia grammata*, Beyrouth, 1945), the texts have been given much attention by Dhorme, who has reported the existence of more than 100 different signs (Fig. 13). The language is assumed to be Semitic, and the oldest of the inscriptions, variously ascribed to the 13th-11th centuries B.C., was found on the massive sarcophagus prepared by King Ittobaal for his father Ahiram.

II

The recent decipherment of the Mycenaean Linear B script has left unsolved the problem presented by the Cretan Linear A and hieroglyphic writings, which are believed to express a non-Greek, non-Indo-European language. Little is known about the pre-Hellenic inhabitants of Crete, but there is evidence of their having engaged in commercial exchanges with Egypt during the Bronze Age, a contact which may well have led to the introduction of a form of hieroglyphic writing such as that to be found on the Minoan seal-stones. There is little doubt that it represents, as an independent system, the beginning of writing on the island, and it would appear to have been devised during the Early Minoan period.

As in the case of the linear script which was subsequently derived from it, two classes of the hieroglyphic writing, labelled A and B, were distinguished by Evans. Hieroglyphic A apparently served as a means of identification, while the more advanced B class came into general use during MM II, and a cursive form of it was incised on clay. Further development, which probably took place during MM III, led to the appearance of the Linear A script, about a dozen examples of which were found by Evans at Knossos. Other texts were discovered by Halbherr at the beginning of the present century, when he recovered about 150 small clay tablets from the so-called Royal Villa at Hagia Triada. These documents, all of the familiar page shape, each contain from four to nine lines of writing, which progresses from left to right. As in all word syllabic systems, three classes of signs are employed: ideograms, or word signs; syllabograms, or syllable signs; and auxiliary signs, such as a word division mark, here used in the form of a dot. Like their Mycenaean

Fig. 14. Cretan Linear A sign list (after G. P. Carratelli).

Linear B counterparts, the documents appear to be inventories, in which commodities are listed by means of ideograms, used in conjunction with seventy-five syllabic signs (Fig. 14).

III

In July, 1908, at Phaistos, in Crete, the Italian scholar Luigi Pernier discovered an inscribed terra-cotta tablet. It was roughly circular in shape, about 6 inches in diameter, and each face of the disc bore pictographic markings which were unusual in that they followed the path of a spiral. Each curve was made up of five coils, subdivided by vertical lines into sections, presumably containing words or sentences. The writing was also exceptionable in that the individual characters were not incised, but appeared to have been stamped on the disc with the aid of movable type. Stratigraphical evidence suggested that the find could be dated about 1700 B.C. (Fig. 15).

A count of the signs showed that they numbered 241 in all—118 (in 30 sections) on one face of the disc, and 123 (in 31 sections) on the other. The symbols, which were highly pictorial, were clearly representative of human and animal figures, buildings, household goods, and so on. Pernier recognised 45 different characters, which he grouped under 7 main headings, from Vegetation and Plants to Arms and Tools. In as much as living creatures were shown facing towards the right, it was assumed that the writing progressed from right to left, and that, consequently, it began at the outside and ended in the centre of the disc.

Although some of the pictures bear a resemblance to the symbols of other Cretan scripts, in the main the forms are different, and appear to represent a separate development. One of the characters, a plumed head-dress, often repeated, has been held to suggest that the disc is an importation, and some scholars have ascribed authorship to the Anatolians, though nothing like it has been found in Asia Minor, or indeed anywhere else. Until additional material does come to light, the prospects of decipherment would seem to be slight, for it would be rash to assume that the 45 signs which appear on the disc constitute the entire system. In their *Documents in Mycenaean Greek*, Ventris and Chadwick suggest

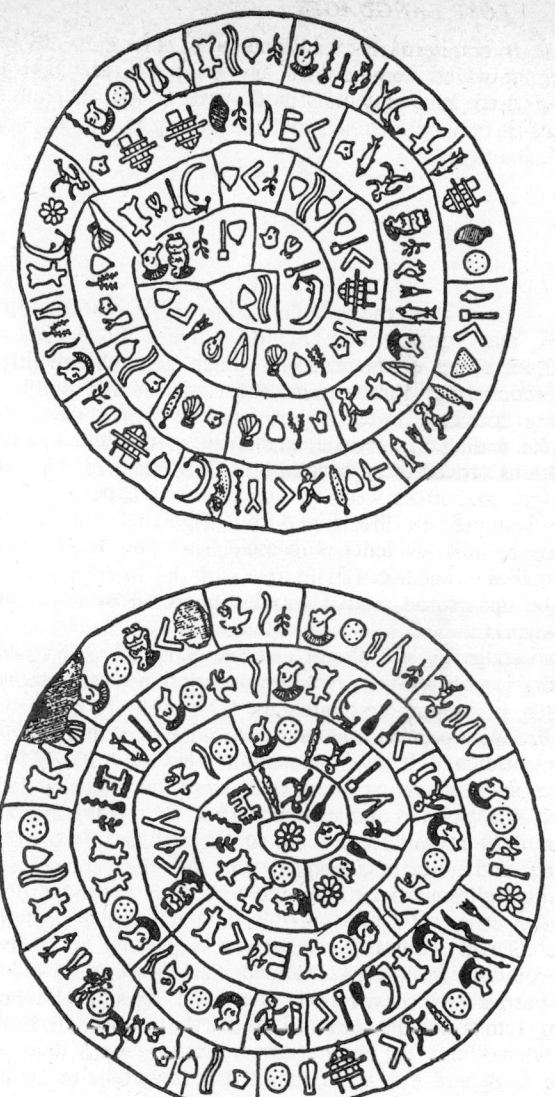

Fig. 15. The Phaistos Disc (from Sir Arthur Evans's *Scripta Minoa*, Oxford University Press, London, courtesy Macmillan and Co., Ltd., London).

that, having regard for the brevity of the inscription, the total number of signs is probably about 60, and that from this, plus the fact that individual words consist of from 2 to 5 signs, it may be assumed that the writing is syllabic, and of the Aegean type.

IV

About the middle of the 19th century, on the island of Cyprus, the Duc de Luynes happened upon examples of an unknown script which was subsequently deciphered, largely through the efforts of George Smith. The writing consisted of 56 signs, each of which stood for a syllable ending in a vowel, and most of the 500 known inscriptions proved to be written in a Greek dialect. They dated from about 700 B.C., and it was apparent that the syllabary was ill-adapted to Greek, and that originally it had been designed to suit an indigenous language. This native tongue, when it was encountered in some of the inscriptions, could not be understood, and it was distinguished by the name of Eteocyprian.

Subsequently, at Enkomi (ancient Salamis) and elsewhere on the island, a series of short inscriptions was discovered, written in unfamiliar characters. This writing, belonging to the Bronze Age, was clearly much older than that previously discovered, and it was assigned to between 1500-1150 B.C. More of these ancient inscriptions were found during 1952-3, when excavations conducted on behalf of the Department of Antiquities revealed three baked clay tablets. Two of these tablets were much damaged, but the third preserved 22 continuous lines of text on one face, and a smaller number on the other. There were 57 different signs, presumably syllabic, and individual words were separated by a division mark in the form of a short, vertical stroke.

Analysis has shown that of the 22 lines, each contains from 4 to 5 words; that the same 5-letter word is repeated on lines 3 and 10; that another, 3-letter, word appears on lines 5, 8, and 11; and that a 2-letter word is to be found on lines 4, 10, and 18. The script progresses from left to right, and according to one theory it is a descendant of Minoan-Mycenaean writing, though an attempt to read it in Greek was inconclusive, in part because of an insufficiency

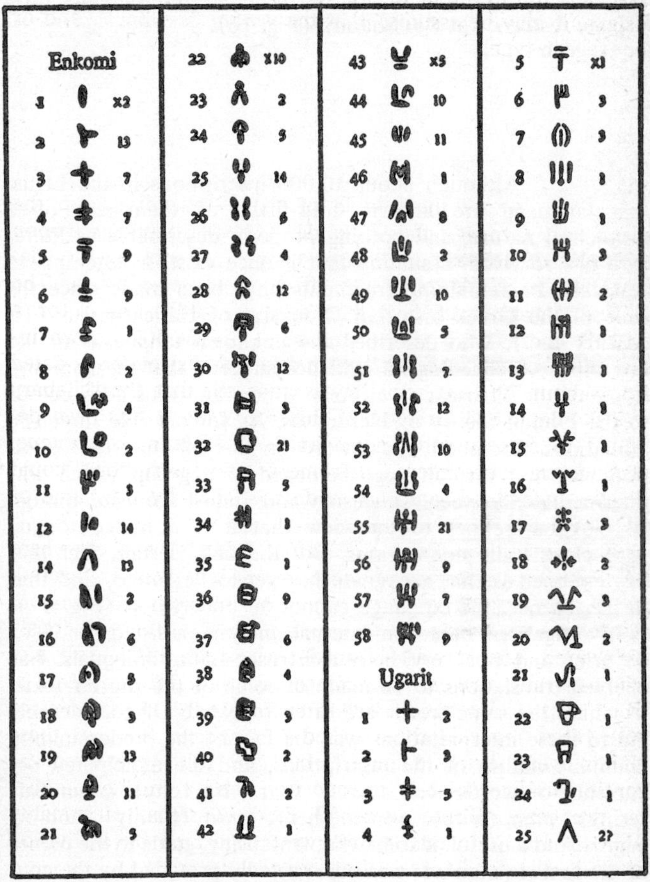

Fig. 16. Cypro-Minoan sign list, derived from Enkomi and Ugarit —small figures indicate the number of occurrences. Sign No. 13, omitted from the Enkomi list, was subsequently identified with No. 44 (from Ventris and Chadwick's *Documents in Mycenaean Greek*, The University Press, Cambridge).

of material. A possible external source of additional inscriptions has been revealed by Schaeffer, who recovered a fragmentary example of the script from the remains of a private residence at Ras Shamra (Fig. 16).

V

Although about 10,000 inscriptions in the Etruscan language are known, four-fifths of them are of a sepulchral nature, and nothing properly describable as literature has survived, assuming that it once existed. Attempts to translate the remaining fragments have been made since the time of the Greek historian Dionysius of Halicarnassus (1st century B.C.), who described the unknown tongue as unlike any other. Archaeological evidence suggests that the ancestral home of the Etruscans was Asia Minor, and thus adds colour to the Lydian theory of Herodotus. As for possible linguistic affiliations, Trombetti's last word on this all-important question was that the language belonged to a group which was intermediate between Caucasian and Indo-European, though B. Nogara inclines to the view that it is a mixed tongue with close Italic connections. But the only certain fact that has emerged is that a cognate has yet to be found, and that in its absence, the language cannot be understood (Fig. 17).

Investigations based on internal analysis, assisted by 30 or so brief and not very helpful Etrusco-Latin bilinguals, has enabled translations to be made of some of the shorter texts, in which the same words are often repeated. Of considerable aid to these interpretations was the fact of the predominantly epitaphic nature of the inscriptions, and the anticipated occurrence of words such as *avil* (year), *tin* (day), *alpan* (offering), *puia* (wife), *ati* (mother), *lautn* (family), and *ril* (age). And a useful, if somewhat tantalising, guide to the names of the first six numbers was unexpectedly provided by the contents of a tomb at Toscanella, which contained a pair of ivory dice bearing the words *mach, zal, thu, huth, ci,* and *sa*. The distribution of the numbers, however, remains a matter of conjecture, and the assumption that it follows the traditional 1-6, 2-5, 3-4 arrangement may be unfounded. Other valuable clues have been provided by recognisable paintings accompanied by the names Clutmsta (Clytemnestra) and Elina-i (Helen). But lengthy texts, such as the writing found

Fig. 17. Etruscan inscription on the Perugia *cippus* (from D. Diringer's *The Alphabet*, Hutchinson and Co. (Publishers) Ltd. London).

on the linen bandages of some mummified remains (containing as many as 500 different words), still await a satisfactory translation.

VI

Knowledge of the Mayan glyphs was lost to the world through the fanatical bigotry of Diego de Landa, second Bishop of Yucatan, who assumed office not long after the Spanish descent upon the New World at the end of the 15th century. In an attempt to stamp out all trace of the native religion, this vandal cleric ordered the wholesale destruction of Mayan records, and so zealously were his instructions put into effect that out of many hundreds of pre-Columbian illuminated manuscripts on sized-agave paper, only three are now known to exist. And with the loss of these irreplaceable documents, there also perished all knowledge and understanding of a culture which, calendrically at least, was superior to that of its destroyer.

This fact emerged when, by a strange twist of fate, a forgotten work by de Landa, written in 1566, was discovered three centuries later in the Royal Library of Madrid. It gave details of the glyphs which the Mayas had used to designate days and months, and it also contained an alleged alphabet of 27 letters. When this information was applied to the contents of some of the numerous monumental inscriptions which existed amidst the ruins of ancient Mayan cities, the calendrical data proved to be reliable. Most disappointingly, however, it quickly became apparent that the supposed alphabet was worthless, and it would seem either that the Bishop misunderstood his informants, or that he was deliberately misled by them.

The meaning of about a third of the signs is known, and from the insight thus gained, the Mayan system would appear to be predominantly ideographic (Fig. 18). The existence of phonetic elements has long been claimed by many investigators, and recent advocates of this view include the American scholar Benjamin Whorf and the Russian linguist J. V. Knorozov. But I. J. Gelb is highly sceptical of all such claims. He makes the point that a phonetic writing, if the underlying language is known, cannot long resist decipherment; that Mayathan continues to be spoken by some 350,000

Fig. 18. Mayan glyphs (The British Museum).

people in the neighbourhood of Yucatan; and that consequently, the Maya writing cannot be a phonetic system, if only because it has so successfully defied all attempts at elucidation.

VII

Evidence of the existence of a hitherto unknown civilisation which flourished in the Indus valley during the 3rd millennium B.C. was first found more than 100 years ago at Harappa, in the Montgomery district of the Punjab, though a detailed examination of the site was not undertaken until the 1920's. At this time, another mound was discovered and investigated some 450 miles away at Mohenjodaro, where the spade revealed the remains of an extensive city which had boasted brick houses of more than one storey, equipped with baths and drains.

It has been suggested that a noticeable absence of inscriptions, other than on seals, points to the use of some perishable material for archival purposes. As for the seals, of copper and stone, about 800 of these have been recovered, each containing, on average, half a dozen signs (Fig. 19). Estimations of the total number of the signs vary—G. R. Hunter has distinguished 253, S. Langdon 288, and C. J. Gadd 396 different characters, the pictorial origin of some of which is evident. The script, which appears to be mainly, but is probably not wholly, ideographic, normally reads from right to left, but on occasion the reverse direction is encountered, and sometimes boustrophedon.

From the point of view of decipherment, the writing presents a formidable problem. Absolutely nothing is known about its users—their race, their language, the names of their leading citizens, all are long forgotten. The only possible clue is a prospect of establishing Mesopotamian connections, suggested by certain significant features, *e.g.*, the existence of cylinder seals. In the meantime, Meriggi has essayed a purely ideographic interpretation, Langdon and Hunter have tried in vain to explain the script in terms of the Brahmi alphabet, Hrozný has advocated the merits of a possible Hittite solution, and M. G. de Hevesy has sought the answer on far-off Easter Island. As to this, if, as Langdon confirms, there can be no doubt as to the identity of the Indus valley writ-

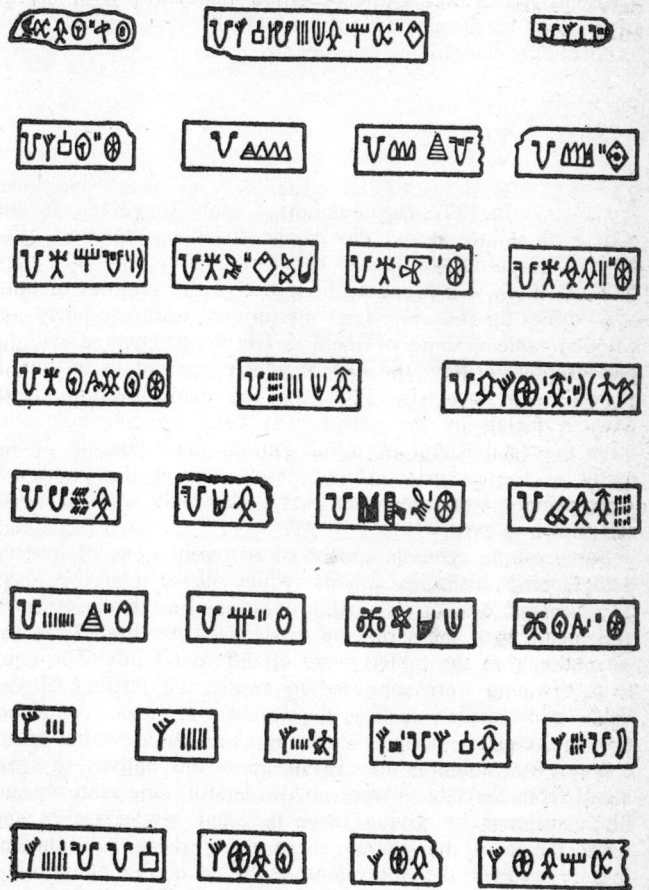

Fig. 19. Indus Valley writing (from G. R. Hunter's *The Script of Harappa and Mohenjodaro*, Routledge and Kegan Paul Ltd., London).

ing and the *rongo rongo* script, the similarity must, as he also suggests, be the outcome of an astonishing historical accident. At all events, the proposed association with Easter Island may be dismissed as geographically very unlikely, and as chronologically highly improbable.

VIII

In 1722, the Dutchman Jacob Roggeveen, in the course of sailing across the Pacific from east to west, discovered Rapa-nui, or Easter Island, the 45 square mile surface of which was found to be dotted with hundreds of outsize stone figures. No less mysterious were numbers of wooden tablets, some of them 6 feet long, covered with a pictographic writing, the like of which was not to be found elsewhere in Polynesia (Fig. 20). The name given to these unusual tablets by the natives was *kohau-rongo-rongo*, and after the establishing of a mission on the island in 1864, many of the records suffered destruction at the hands of their owners, with the result that to-day only a score or so are known to exist.

Some of the symbols consist of representations of human beings, birds, fish, and plants, while others take the form of geometric designs. On being questioned as to the purpose and meaning of the script, aged islanders vouchsafed the information that the tablets were of different kinds. The contents of some were supposed to ensure the fertility of the fields, while others, such as the *kohau o te ranga*, contained powerful charms, designed to bring about the downfall of an enemy. But attempts to prevail upon the natives to read aloud from the tablets were not successful. One man obliged his questioner by giving three different renderings of the same tablet in the course of as many days, and another merely intoned the equivalent of "This is the figure of a man; next comes the outline of a bird. . . ." Too late, it was realised that knowledge of how to read the writing had been lost.

The script, every other line of which is in an inverted position, may well be an importation. According to the Viennese scholar Robert von Heine-Geldern, the original source was China, while de Hevesy, as already noted, favours the Indus valley. Local tradition, however, suggests that the

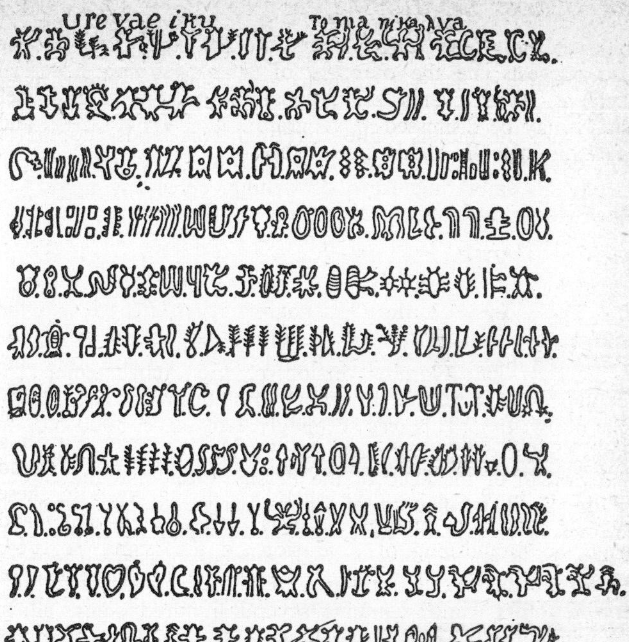

Fig. 20. Easter Island *rongo rongo* script (from T. Heyerdahl's *Aku-Aku*, Rand McNally & Co., Chicago, courtesy George Allen and Unwin Ltd., London).

script was brought to the island by 300 warriors and their families about the 12th century A.D., and moreover maintains that it was primarily intended for use by bards, who read from the tablets while chanting. This lends support to the ideas of Th. S. Barthel, who holds that the script is merely an embryonic form of writing, consisting merely of catch-words intended to serve a mnemonic purpose.

IX

The Elamite version of the Achaemenian trilinguals was preceded by what has been termed Proto-Elamite writing. This was seemingly evolved, *c.* 3000 B.C., at Susa (Shushan), a city on the Karkhev River, some 150 miles north of the head of the Persian Gulf, and the capital of the ancient kingdom of Elam. Early and late forms of the script appear to exist, the more recent example consisting of a comparatively small number of signs (between 50 and 60 have been recognised to date). The earlier writing, on the other hand, contains several hundred signs, all of them apparently ideographic (Fig. 21). Usually, though not invariably, they progress from right to left, and with few exceptions, the writing is confined to clay tablets, the contents of which appear to relate to economic matters, though, as yet, none of the signs can be safely read. It has been deduced, however, that an accompanying numerical system is probably decimal.

Whether or not the Proto-Elamite scripts are to be regarded as entirely independent inventions cannot yet be finally decided. But in view of the close proximity of the Sumerians (by whom the Elamites were on occasion defeated and subjected), this is to be looked upon as unlikely, particularly in view of the fact, as earlier recounted, that the Elamites eventually abandoned this style of writing, and adapted a much simplified form of Babylonian cuneiform to their needs. This suggests that the Proto-Elamite script may have originated in a like manner, and that in this possibility an aid to its decipherment is perhaps to be found.

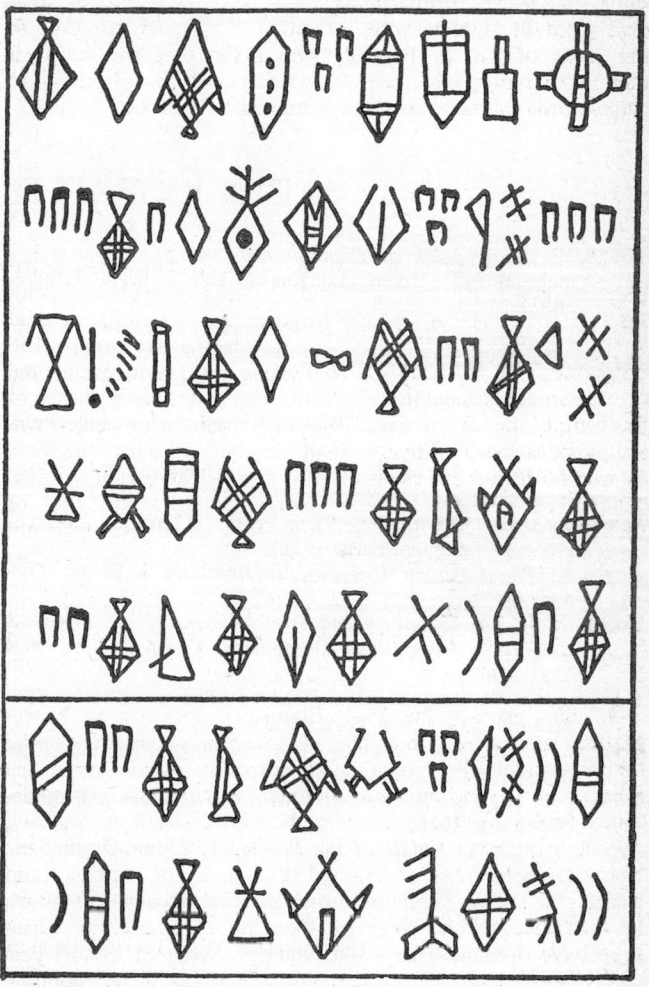

Fig. 21. Early Proto-Elamite inscription (after V. Scheil).

BIBLIOGRAPHY

Arago, F., *Biographies of Distinguished Scientific Men* (Longman, Brown, Green, Longmans, and Roberts, London, 1857)

Barton, G. A., *The Origin and Development of Babylonian Writing* (The Johns Hopkins Press, Baltimore, 1913)

Bauer, H., *Das Alphabet von Ras Schamra* (Max Niemeyer Verlag, Halle/Salle, 1932)

Bennett, E. L., *The Pylos Tablets* (Princeton University Press, Princeton, 1955)

———*A Minoan Linear B Index* (Yale University Press, New Haven, 1953)

Benveniste, E., *Grammaire Vieux-Perse* (Librairie Ancienne Honoré Champion, Paris, 1931)

Birch, S., *The Egyptian Hieroglyphs* (Bradbury & Evans, London, 1857)

Booth, A. J., *The Discovery and Decipherment of the Trilingual Cuneiform Inscriptions* (Longmans, Green & Co., New York, 1902)

Botsford, G. W., and Robinson, C. A., *Hellenic History* (The Macmillan Co., New York, 1956)

Boulton, W. H., *The Romance of Archaeology* (Sampson Low, Marston & Co. Ltd., London, 1930)

Breasted, J. H., *The Conquest of Civilization* (Harper & Brothers, New York, 1926)

Brown, J. M., *The Riddle of the Pacific* (T. Fisher Unwin Ltd., London, 1924)

Budge, E. A. W., *Cleopatra's Needle* (The Religious Tract Society, London, 1926)

———*The Rosetta Stone* (The Religious Tract Society, London, 1929)

———*The Mummy* (Cambridge University Press, Cambridge, 1893)

———*The Rise and Progress of Assyriology* (Martin Hopkinson & Co., Ltd., London, 1925)

——— *The Literature of the Ancient Egyptians* (J. M. Dent & Sons Ltd., London, 1914)
Burckhardt, J. L., *Travels In Syria and the Holy Land* (John Murray, London, 1822)
Bury, J. B., *A History of Greece* (Modern Library, New York)
Cameron, G. C., *History of Early Iran* (The University of Chicago Press, Chicago, 1936)
Ceram, C. W., *Gods, Graves, and Scholars* (Alfred A. Knopf, Inc., New York, 1952)
Conder, C. R., *Altaic Hieroglyphs and Hittite Inscriptions* (Richard Bentley & Sons, London, 1887)
Diringer, D., *The Alphabet* (Philosophical Library, New York, 1948)
Drummond, W., *Origines* (A. J. Valpy, London, 1824)
Elgood, P. G., *The Ptolemies of Egypt* (J. W. Arrowsmith Ltd., Bristol, 1938)
Erman, A., *The Literature of the Ancient Egyptians* (Methuen & Co. Ltd., London, 1927)
Evans, A., *The Palace of Minos* (Macmillan & Co. Ltd., London, 1921-35)
——— *Scripta Minoa* (Oxford University Press, London, 1909)
——— *Scripta Minoa II* (Oxford University Press, London, 1952)
Finegan, J., *Light from the Ancient Past* (Princeton University Press, Princeton, 1946)
Gadd, C. J., *The Fall of Nineveh* (British Museum, London, 1923)
Galtruchius, P., *The Poetic Histories* (Moses Pitt, London, 1672)
Gardiner, A. H., *Egyptian Grammar* (Oxford University Press, London and New York, 1957)
Garstang, J., *The Hittite Empire* (Constable & Co. Ltd., London, 1929)
Gelb, I. J., *Hittite Hieroglyphs, I, II, and III* (University of Chicago Press, Chicago, 1931, 1935, 1942)
——— *A Study of Writing* (Routledge & Kegan Paul Ltd., London, 1952)
Gordon, C. H., *Ugaritic Literature* (Ventnor Publishers, Ventnor, N. J., 1949)
Gurney, O. R., *The Hittites* (Penguin Books Ltd., Harmondsworth, 1954)
Heyerdahl, T., *Aku Aku* (Rand McNally & Co., Chicago, 1958)
Hitti, P. K., *History of Syria* (Macmillan Co., New York, 1951)
——— *Lebanon in History* (St. Martin's Press, Inc., New York, 1957)
Hunter, G. R., *The Script of Harappa and Mohenjodaro* (Kegan Paul, Trench, Trubner & Co. Ltd., London, 1934)
Jack, J. W., *The Ras Shamra Tablets* (T. & T. Clark, Edinburgh, 1935)

Johnstone, M. A., *Etruria Past and Present* (Methuen & Co., Ltd., London, 1930)

King, L. W., *Assyrian Language* (Kegan Paul, Trench, Trubner & Co. Ltd., London, 1901)

———*The Seven Tablets of Creation* (Luzac & Co., London, 1902)

———*A History of Sumer and Accad* (Chatto & Windus, London, 1910)

———*Legends of Babylon and Egypt in Relation to Hebrew Tradition* (The British Academy, London, 1918)

King, L. W., and Thompson, R. C., *The Sculptures and Inscription of Darius the Great* (The British Museum, London, 1907)

Loftus, W. K., *Travels and Researches in Chaldea and Susiana* (James Nisbet & Co., London, 1857)

Long, G. G., *The Egyptian Antiquities in the British Museum* (M. A. Nattali, London, 1846)

Luckenbill, D. D., *Ancient Records of Assyria and Babylonia* (The University of Chicago Press, Chicago, 1926)

Mackay, E., *The Indus Civilisation* (Lovat Dickson & Thompson Ltd., London, 1935)

Metraux, A., *Easter Island* (Oxford University Press, New York, 1957)

Modona, A. N., *A Guide to Etruscan Antiquities* (Leo. S. Olschki, Florence, 1954)

Montgomery, J. A., and Harris, Z. H., *The Ras Shamra Mythological Texts* (The American Philosophical Society, Philadelphia, 1935)

Moret, A., *The Nile and the Egyptian Civilisation* (Kegan Paul, Trench, Trubner & Co. Ltd., London, 1927)

Morley, S. R., *The Ancient Maya* (Stanford University Press, Stanford, 1956)

Murray, M. A., *The Splendour That Was Egypt* (Philosophical Library, New York, 1949)

Norden, F. L., *Travels in Egypt and Nubia* (Lockyer Davis & Charles Reymers, London, 1757)

Oberman, J., *Ugaritic Mythology* (Yale University Press, New Haven, 1951)

Oldham, F., *Thomas Young, F.R.S.* (Edward Arnold, London, 1933)

Paper, H. H., *The Phonology and Morphology of Royal Achaemenid Elamite* (The University of Michigan Press, Ann Arbor, 1955)

Pritchard, J. B., *Ancient Near Eastern Texts* (Princeton University Press, Princeton, 1950)

Rogers, R. W., *A History of Babylonia and Assyria* (Luzac & Co., London, 1901)

Rowley, H. H. (Ed.), *The Old Testament and Modern Study* (Oxford University Press, London, 1956)

Sayce, A. H., *The Hittites* (The Religious Tract Society, London, 1888)
Schaeffer, C. F. A., *The Cuneiform Texts of Ras Shamra-Ugarit* (The British Academy, London, 1939)
Sharpe, S., *Egyptian Hieroglyphics* (Edward Moxon & Co., London, 1861)
Simonides, C., *Hieroglyphic Letters* (David Nutt, London, 1860)
Smith, S., *Early History of Assyria* (Chatto & Windus, London, 1928)
Sprengling, M., *The Alphabet* (The University of Chicago Press, Chicago, 1931)
Sturtevant, E. H., *A Hittite Glossary* (University of Pennsylvania, Philadelphia, 1936)
——— *A Comparative Grammar of the Hittite Language* (Linguistic Society of America, Philadelphia, 1933)
Thompson, J. E. S., *The Rise and Fall of the Maya Civilization* (University of Oklahoma Press, Norman, Okla., 1956)
Ventris, M., and Chadwick, J., *Documents in Mycenaean Greek* (Cambridge University Press, Cambridge and New York, 1956)
——— "Evidence for Greek Dialect in the Mycenaean Archives," *Journal of Hellenic Studies,* LXXIII, 1953.
Weigall, A. E. P., *The Life and Times of Akhnaton* (G. P. Putnam's Sons, New York, 1923)
——— *A Short History of Ancient Egypt* (Chapman & Hall Ltd., London, 1934)
Wood, A., *Thomas Young* (Cambridge University Press, Cambridge, 1954)
Woolley, C. L., *The Sumerians* (Oxford University Press, London, 1928)
——— *A Forgotten Kingdom* (Penguin Books Inc., Baltimore, 1953)
Wright, W., *The Empire of the Hittites* (James Nisbet & Co., London, 1884)
Young, T., *Egyptian Antiquities* (John Murray, London, 1823)

INDEX

Abdashirta, 114, 136
Abraham, 117
Academie des Inscriptions et Belles-lettres, 46
Accad, 101, 103f.
Accadians, the, 65, 105, 107, 131
   language and writing of, 65f., 68, 72, 92, 102, 106, 115, 117, 120, 127f., 136, 140
Acco (Acre), 134
Achaeans, the, 136
Achaemenes, 66, 91
Achaemenidae, the, 66ff., 78, 81, 90
Achilles, 159
Adab, 103
Adana (Dnnjm), 126
Aegysthus, 145
Agamemnon, 145, 160
Ahab, 133
Ahiram, 133, 162
Ahumelech, 117
Ahura-Mazda (Ormuzd), 68, 77, 89
Akerblad, J. D., 40ff.
Aksak (Arsaces I), 78
Alalus, 128
Albright, W. F., 139, 143
Aleppo, 72, 113
Alexander the Great, 18, 30f., 42, 50, 69, 78, 106, 134
Alexandria, 33, 42, 48
   Library of, 35, 70
Aleyn, 143
Allah, 34, 70
Alphabet, the, *see* Writing
Amasis, II, 32

Amenemhet, 61f.
Amenophis III, 114f., 136
Amenophis IV (Ikhnaton), 63f., 115f., 128
Ammi-zadusa, 107
Amnisos, 153
Amon-Ra, 63, 127
Amorites, the, 104, 114, 117, 131
Amose, 63
Amqa, 127f.
An Account of Some Recent Discoveries (T. Young), 48
Anatolia, *See* Asia Minor
Anatolians, the, 65, 164
Ancient Alphabets (A.B.A. Wahshih), 41
Antony, Mark, 33
Anu, 110
Anus, 129
Apadama, the, 69
Apopi, 63
Apries, 38
Apsu, 111
Arabia, 73, 88, 131
Arabs, the, 33, 70
   language and writing of, 23, 29, 34, 40f., 56, 86, 90
Aradus (Ruad), 134f.
Aramaeans, the, 131
Aranzahas (Tigris), the, 129
Ariaramnes, 91, 93
Aristobulous of Cassandreia, 67
Armenia, 72, 87, 113
Arrian, 84

INDEX

Arsacids, the, 70
Arsames, 91, 93
Artabanus, 91
Artatama, 115
Artaxerxes I, 69, 83
Artaxerxes III, 135
Aruru, 109
Arvad (Ruad), 134f.
Arzawa, 117
Ashmolean Museum, the, 145
Ashur, 107
Ashurbanipal (Sardanapalos), 66, 76, 101, 111
Asia Minor (Anatolia), 17, 113ff., 147, 150, 164, 167
Asitavandas ('zwdt), 126
Assyria, 30, 100, 103, 115
Assyrians, the, 65, 105ff., 115, 136
  language and writing of, 58, 98f., 102
Astarte, 139
Astyages, 66
Athena, 159
Athenaeus, 76
Athens, 144
  British School of, 151
Aton, 63f.
Augustus (Octavian), 33, 37
Avarikus ('wrk), 126
Ay, 63, 128

Baal, 139f., 143f.
Babel, Tower of, 15
Babopolasser, 66
Babylon, 68f., 88, 94, 104, 107, 112f., 134
Babylonia, 27, 100, 113, 115
Babylonians, the, 19, 66, 102, 105ff., 117, 131
Bactria, 69, 88
Bactrians, the, 66
Bagdad, 72
Bankes, W. J., 48
Barbaro, G., 71
Barthel, Th. S., 176
Barthélemy, J. J., 38, 46
Bauer, H., 137, 139f.
Behistun, 68, 70, 76, 91, 97ff., 106
  Rock of, 27, 68, 89ff.
Beirut (Berytus), 134f.

Bembo, A., 89
Bengal Asiatic Society, the, 17
Bennett, E. L., 150, 152, 156
  The Pylos Tablets, 150
Berenice, 45
Berossos, 103, 106
Berytus (Beirut), 134f.
Bessus, 69
Beth Shamesh, 144
Bibhururiyas (Nibhururiyas), 128
Bidawa, 140
Birch, S., 121
Blegen, C. W., 150, 154, 160
Boghaz Keui (Hattushash), 113, 116ff., 127f.
Bolzani, G. V. P., 34
  Hieroglyphica, 34
Bombay, 74
Bonaparte, Napoleon, 38f., 46
Bonn, University of, 88
Book of the Dead, the, 30, 60
Bor, 116
Bosphorus, the, 88
Bossert, H. T., 122, 124, 126
Botta, P. E., 98, 106
Boughton, Sir W. E. R., 41
Bow-wow theory, the, 14
Breasted, J. H., 131
British Museum, the, 39, 101, 109, 116, 121
Brun, C. le, 73, 75
Brugsch, H. K., 43, 58
Buck, S. de, 53
Bulharmaden, 116
Burckhardt, J. L., 116f.
  Travels in Syria, 116
Burnouf, E., 86ff., 90, 94
  Commentaire sue le Yaçna, 87
  Mémoire sur deux inscriptions, 87f.
Burraburiash, 134
Byblia grammata (M. Dunand), 162
Byblos (Jebail), 134f., 162

Cadiz (Gades), 132
Cadmus, 133
Caesar, Julius, 33
Caesarion, 33
Calah, 101

INDEX

Çambel, H., 124
Cambridge, University of, 154
Cambyses, 67, 81
Canaan, 117, 132
Canaanites, the, 65, 131ff., 136ff.
   language and writing of, 65, 136ff., 143
Canopus, Decree of, 32f., 53
Cappadocia, 88, 94, 113
Carchemish (Jerablus), 116, 121ff., 127, 131
Carmel, Mount, 134
Cartouche, the, 38, 42, 44f., 47, 50f., 58
Castor, 159
Caylus, Vase of, 83, 85
Chadwick, J., 154f.
   "Evidence for Greek Dialect" (with M. Ventris), 154
   Documents in Mycenaean Greek (with M. Ventris), 156, 164
Chaeremon of Naucratis, 35
Chaldeans (Neo-Babylonians), the, 106
Champollion, J. F., 46ff., 83
   De l'ecriture Hieratique, 46
   Dictionnaire Egyptien, 52
   Grammaire Egyptienne, 52
   Lettre à M. Dacier, 51
   Précis du Système Hiéroglyphique, 52
Champollion, J. J., 46, 52
Chardin, Sir J., 72
Charles II, 72
Chelel Minar, 71
Chenet, G., 135
Chester, G., 145
Cicero, 18
Cincinnati, University of, 150
Clay tablets, 19, 27, 76, 98f., 103, 106f., 115, 117ff., 136, 148ff., 150, 159, 166
Clement of Alexandria, 35
   Stromateis, 35
Cleopatra I, 47
Cleopatra II, 47f.
Cleopatra III, 48
Cleopatra VII, 33

Clytemnestra (Clutmsta), 145, 168
Coffin Texts, the, 59
Collège de France, the, 87
Commentaire sur le Yaçna (E. Burnouf), 87
Conder, C. R., 121
Constantinople, 72, 74, 116
Copenhagen, 74
   International Congress of Classical Studies at, 161
   Royal Academy of, 78
Coptic, 33f., 36, 53f., 58
Copts, the, 33
Coste, P., 97
Cowley, A. E., 122, 150
Creation Epic, the, 111
Crestomathie demotique (E. Revillout), 43
Cretans, the, 146ff., 162f.
   language and writing of, 146, 148ff., 156, 162ff.
Crete, 145ff., 153, 165
Ctesias, 106
Cuneiform,
   Accadian (Babylonian), 58, 68, 74ff., 86, 115, 117f.
   Assyrian, 99f., 102, 105
   Elamite (Susian), 65, 68, 74, 92, 96ff.
   Hittite, 65, 117ff., 127
   Sumerian, 100ff.
   Ugaritic, 136ff.
Cyaxares, 66
Cyprus, 132, 135, 166f.
   Bronze Age of, 166
   Department of Antiquities, 166
Cyrus I, 91
Cyrus II, 66f., 81, 84
   tomb of, 67, 84

Dadkere Isesi (Assa), 61
Dagon, 138
Daily Telegraph, the, 109
Dakhamun, 127f.
Damanhur, 40
Damascus, 72, 116
Daniel, 143
Daniel, Book of, 112, 144
Darius I, 68ff., 81ff., 87ff., 91, 96, 106

INDEX

Darius III, 69
D'Assigny, 35
David, Psalms of, 40, 64
Davis, E. J., 116
Decerto, 76
Decipherment, technique of, 24ff.
De Cuneatis Inscriptionibus (O. G. Tychsen), 77
De l'ecriture Hieratique (J. F. Champollion), 46
Delitzsch, F., 102
Deluge, the, 109ff.
Demotic, 53f.
Determinatives, 38, 45, 56, 98, 100
Dhorme, P., 137ff., 162
Dictionnaire Egyptien (J. F. Champollion), 52
Die altpersischen Keilinschriften (C. Lassen), 88
Diodorus, 34, 69, 76
Dionysius of Halicarnassus, 168
Dionysus, 159
Dispute of a Man with his Soul, 63
Divination, 108
Divine Legation of Moses (W. Warburton), 38
Documents in Mycenaean Greek (M. Ventris and J. Chadwick), 154, 164
Domitian, 37
Domuztepe, 124
Dorians, the, 145, 147, 159
D'Origny, P. A. L., 37
Dörpfeld, W., 147
Dow, S., 159
Drangians, the, 66
Duauf, Instruction of, 61
Dunand, M., 162
  Byblia grammata, 162
Duperron, A., 76, 80
  Zend Avesta, 76, 82, 86
Dussaud, R., 135

Ea (Enki), 110f.
East India Company, the, 73, 90
Easter Island (Rapa-nui), 172f.
Ecbatana, 68f.
Eden, Garden of, 15, 111
Edomites, the, 131

Egypt, 14, 29ff., 67, 69ff., 88, 113, 127f., 131f., 134, 136, 146
Egyptian Grammar (A. H. Gardiner), 54
Egyptian Sage, Admonitions of an, 61
Egyptians, the, 20, 28
  language and writing of, 20, 28ff., 53ff.
El (Elohim), 139, 142ff.
Elam, 98, 103, 175
Elamites, the, 65f., 104, 176f.
  language and writing of, 65f., 68, 73, 92, 96ff., 106, 176f.
Elvand, Mount, 87, 90, 93
Encyclopedia Britannica, the, 45, 47
Enkhosnepaaton, 128
Enki (Ea), 110f.
Enkidu, 109
Enkomi (Salamis), 166
Epano Englianos, 150
Ephron, 117
Erech, 109f.
Eridu, 103
Erman, A., 53
Esdraelon, Plain of, 134
Etruria, 150
Etruscans, the, 21, 161, 168
  language and writing of, 21, 26, 161, 168f.
Euphrates, the, 94, 103, 111, 114, 122, 127
Euyuk, 116
Evans, Sir A., 145ff., 150, 151, 154, 162
  Scripta Minoa, 148
  The Palace of Minos, 149
"Evidence for Greek Dialect" (M. Ventris and J. Chadwick), 154
Exodus, Book of, 51
Ezekiel, Book of, 133

Fasa, 84
Fertile Crescent, the, 131
Figueroa, G. de S., 71
Fiorillo, 80
Flaminian Obelisk, the, 37
Flandin, E., 97
Flower, S., 73f.
Forrer, E., 120, 122, 124, 140

INDEX

Fort Rashîd (St. Julien), 39
Fourier, J. B., 46
Frank, C., 122
Frederic, V., 73
French Asiatic Society, the, 94
Freret, N., 37

Gabinus, A., 33
Gadd, C. J., 172
Gades (Cadiz), 132
Galilee, 134, 144
Galtruchius, P., 35
   The Poetic Histories, 35
Gardanne, 89
Gardiner, Sir A. H., 54
   Egyptian Grammar, 54
Gaugamela, 69
Gautama, 67
Gebelin, C. de, 37
Gelb, I. J., 20, 122ff., 133, 161, 170
   A Study of Writing, 21
   Hittite Hieroglyphs, I, II, III, 122
Genesis, Book of, 111, 144
George III, 39
German Oriental Society, the, 117
Germanicus, 33
Gibraltar, Straits of, 132
Gilgamesh, 109ff., 128
Gleye, A., 121
Goetze, A., 143
Gordon, A., 37
Göttingen, University of, 80, 85
Gouvea, A. de, 71
Gozan, 107
Grammaire Egyptienne (J. F. Champollion), 52
Grapow, H., 53
Greece, 14, 145ff.
   Bronze Age of, 145ff., 149, 159
   Iron Age of, 159
Greeks, the, 21, 69, 133, 159
   language and writing of, 16, 32f., 39, 133, 147ff., 153, 159
Greko-Roman period, the, 31, 53, 58
Grenoble, Academy of Sciences, 46

Grote, G., 145
Grotefend, G. F., 80ff., 89ff., 94, 96
Guignes, C. L. J. de, 38f.
Gurgam, 122
Gutium, the, 103

Hadish, the, 69
Hagia Triada, 162
Halbherr, 162
Haleb, 122
Halévy, J., 102
Hall of a Hundred Columns, the, 69
Halle, University of, 77, 137
Hama (Hamath), 116, 120, 122, 124
Hamadan, 87, 90f.
Hamilton, W., 116
Hammer-Purgstall, Baron von, 41
Hammurabi, 104, 112f., 130
Hanover, Lyceum of, 80
Harappa, 172
Hatti (Hittim, Kheta), the, 113ff., 127f.
Hattushash (Boghaz Keui), 113, 116ff., 127f.
Hattushilish III, 127
Haukal, Ibn, 70
Hebrews, the, 65, 102, 106f., 112, 131, 133, 142f.
   language and writing of, 15f., 65, 112, 138, 142
Hebron, 117
Hector, 159
Heeren, A. H. L., 78
Heidelberg, University of, 88
Heine-Geldern, R. von, 174
Helen (Elina-i), 168
Heliopolis, 37
Hellespont, the, 69
Hemaka, 30
Hera, 159
Herbert, Sir T., 72
Hercules, Pillars of, 132f.
Herder, J. G., 78
Hermapion, 37
Hermes, 14, 159
Herodotus, 29, 34, 68, 83, 88, 91, 106, 113, 132, 147, 168
Heth, Sons of, 117
Hevesy, M. G. de, 172

Hiddekel, the, *see* Tigris
Hieroglyphica (G. V. P. Bolzani), 34
Hieroglyphika (Horapollo), 35
Hieroglyphs,
  Cretan, 146, 149, 154, 162
  Egyptian, 20, 30f., 34ff., 54ff., 75
  Hittite, 27, 116, 120ff.
Hincks, E., 96, 98, 100f.
Hittites (Hittim), the, 60, 65, 114ff., 127
  language and writing of, 27, 113, 116ff.
Holtzmann, A., 96
Homer, 134, 147, 159
Homophones, 20, 45, 49, 56, 99f.
Horapollo, 35
  Hieroglyphika, 35
Horites, the, 117, 131
Hrozný, B., 103, 118f., 122, 124, 152, 172
Hunter, G. R., 172f.
Hurriya, 142f.
Hüsing, 98
Huyot, J. N., 50
Hyde, T., 76
Hyksos, the, 63, 136
Hymettos, 147
Hystaspes, 68, 82ff., 85, 91, 106

Ideograms (word signs), 19f., 56, 98, 100, 105, 123, 156, 162
Ikhnaton (Amenophis IV), 63f., 115f., 128
India, 14, 17, 72, 76, 88, 90, 97
Indo-Europeans, the, 17f., 66
Indra, 14
Indus, the, 66, 172, 174
Institut de France, the, 135
Iran, 66
Isaiah, Book of, 133, 144
Ishtar, 110
Isis, 35, 48
Israel, 89, 133
Israelites, the, 131, 144
Issus, 69, 134
Istakhr, 71
Ittobaal, 162

Ivriz, 116

Jaanhama, 140
Jaatlinu, 140
Jablonski, P. E., 37
Jebail (Byblós), 134f., 162
Jebusites, the, 117
Jensen, P., 121f.
Jerablus (Carchemish), 116, 121ff., 127, 131
Jerusalem, 72, 137, 139
  École Biblique, 137
Jessup, S., 116
Jeyhan (Pyramos), the, 124
Jidda, 74
Job, Book of, 133, 143
Johnson, J. A., 116
Jones, Sir W., 17
Josephus, 35, 134
Journal of Hellenic Studies, the, 154
Julamerk, 87

Kadesh, 60, 115
Kampfer, E., 65, 73
Karatepe, 124ff.
Karkhev, the, 176
Karnak, 45, 127
Kemal, Mustapha, 24
Keret, 142f.
Kermanshah, 90f., 93
Kheta (Hittites), the, 60, 65, 114ff., 127
Kheuf, 36, 62
Khorsabad, 99
Kinneir, J. M., 89
Kircher, A., 36ff.
Klaproth, J., 52
Knorozov, J. V., 170
Knossos, 146, 148, 150, 152f., 156, 159, 162
Knudzton, J. A., 117
Kober, A. E., 150ff.
Koch, J. G., 37
Koran, the, 70
Korinthos, 147
Kouyunjik, *see* Nineveh
Kugler, F. X., 107
Kulaks, the, 107
Kumarbis, 129
Kur, the, 67, 68, 71
Kurds, the, 87

Labarnash (Tabarnash), 113
Lagash, 103
Lagus, 31
Land of No Return, the, 110
Landa, D. de, 170
Langdon, S., 172f.
Language(s),
  agglutinative, 15
  application of, 13
  classification of, 15f.
  evolution of, 16, 23
  inflectional, 15f.
  isolating, 15
  number of, 15
  origins of, 14ff.
  relationships among, 16f., 29
Larsa, 101, 103
Lassen, C., 88f., 94
  Die altpersischen Keilinschriften, 88
Latakia (Laodicea), 135
Layard, Sir H., 98, 101, 106, 109
Lebanon, 127, 132, 134
Lepsius, R., 52f.
Letronne, J. A., 49
Lettre à M. Dacier (J. F. Champollion), 51
Lettre à M. le professeur H. Rosellini (R. Lepsius), 52
Leviathan, 143
Lewis, Sir G. C., 76
Libya, 30
Lichtenstein, 86
Lithuania, 18
Loftus, W. K., 101
Longperrier, H. A. de, 99
Lucas, P., 36
Luvians, the, 113
Luynes, Duc de, 166
Lydians, the, 66, 168
Lyktos, 153

Madrid, Royal Library of, 170
Malcolm, Sir J., 90
Mandeslo, J. S., 72
Manetho, 30, 35, 51, 103
Marcellinus, A., 37
Marduk, 111f.
Margians, the, 66
Mariette, F. A. F., 59
Mark, St., 33
Marsham, J. D., 37

Martin, J. S. St., 85, 94, 98
Maspero, G., 53, 59
Mattiwaza, 127
Maya, the, 170
  language and writing of, 170f.
Medes (Mada), the, 66
Media, 87f.
Megiddo, 114
Mellink, M. J., 126
Mémoire sur deux inscriptions (E. Burnouf), 87f.
Mémoires sur diverses Antiquities (S. de Sacy), 76
Memphis, 39, 61
  Decree of, 24, 39ff., 46ff., 51
Menes, 29, 36
Men-kau-Re (Mykerinos), 58
Mercati, 34
Meriggi, P., 122, 124, 172
Mervdasht, Plain of, 68
Mesha, 133
Meyer, E., 147
Meyer, W., 85
Millin's *Magasin Encyclopedique*, 83
Minet-el-Beida, 135f.
Minos, 146
Minotaur, the, 147
Mitanni, 114f., 120, 127
Mnemonic devices, 18, 176
Moabite Stone, the, 133
Mohammed, 116
Mohenjodaro, 172
Mokha, 74
Montezuma, 16
Monumenti d'Egitto (H. Rosellini), 52
Mordtmann, A. D., 98, 121f.
Morgan, J. de, 111
Morier, J. J., 84
Münden, 80
Münter, F. C. C., 78ff., 87
Murghab, 71, 78, 84
Mursilis I, 113
Mursilis II, 127f.
Mycenae, 135f., 145, 148, 154
Myers, Sir J. L., 149, 154
  Scripta Minoa II, 149, 153
Mykene, 147

Nabataeans, the, 131
Naksh-i-Rustam, 69, 71, 77, 96

INDEX 189

Naram-sin, 103
Nebuchadrezzar, 134
Necho, 132
Nibhururiyas (Bibhururiyas), 128
Niebuhr, C., 36, 73ff., 77ff., 85, 87f.
  Voyage en Arabie, 74, 78
Nile, the, 18, 29, 32, 38, 114, 132, 136, 146
Nineveh, 66, 76, 101, 107, 109
Ninhursag, 111
Nin-sun, 109
Niqmadda (Nqmd), 140
Noah, 85, 134
Nogara, B., 168
Norden, F. L., 36
Norris, E., 94, 98, 100f.
Nubayrah, 40

Octavian (Augustus), 33, 37
OEbares, 68
Old Testament, the, 106, 111ff., 116, 133, 143f.
On Isis and Osiris (Plutarch), 35
Onomatopoetic theory, the, 14
Oppert, J., 100, 102
Ormuzd (Ahura-Mazda), 68, 77, 89
Osiris, 35, 38
Otter, J., 89
Ouseley, Sir W. G., 84

Pabel, 142
Palace of Minos, The, (A. Evans), 149
Palermo Stone, the, 133
Palestine, 14, 62, 114f.
Palin, Count B. de, 40
Pamphilian Obelisk, the, 37, 41
Papyrus, 18, 27, 30, 41, 133, 159
  Casati, 47
  Ebers, 60
Parnassos, 147
Parthians, the, 66, 78
Parviz, K. (Chrosroes II), 70
Pasargadae, 67, 84
Passeri, G., 26
Patizithes the Magian, 67
Pausanias, 145
Pehlevi, 70, 77ff., 80f.

Peiser, F. E., 122
Pelusium, 67
Peoples of the Sea, the, 115
Pepi, 61
Peretti, F. (Sixtus V), 37
Perizzites, the, 117
Pernier, L., 164f.
Persepolis, 69ff., 78, 80, 84, 96
Persia, 27, 30, 71, 73, 84, 88, 93, 96
Persian Gulf, the, 65, 103, 131, 176
Persians (Parsa), the, 66ff., 76, 134
  language and writing of, 17, 67, 68f., 71ff.
Petrie, Sir W. M. F., 30
Phaenebythis, 35
Phaistos, 153, 164
Phaistos Disc, the, 24, 164f.
Philae, Island of, 34, 48
Philae Obelisk, the, 47f.
Philippe, King Louis, 97
Philippus, 35
Phoenicia, 114f., 132ff.
Phonemes, 22
Phonograms, 20, 56, 123
Pictograms, 19, 21f., 102
Plutarch, 35, 78
  On Isis and Osiris, 35
Pococke, R., 36
Poetic Histories, The (P. Galtruchius), 35
Polvar, the, 68, 71
Polyphones, 20, 99f.
Pooh-pooh theory, the, 14
Porter, Sir R. K., 85, 89
Poseidon, 159
Précis du Système Hiéroglyphique (F. J. Champollion), 52
Pritchard, J. B., 127
Psalms, Book of, 143
Psamtik III, 67
Ptahhopte, 61
Ptcria, 113
Ptolemy I, 31, 45
Ptolemy II, 30
Ptolemy III, 32, 53
Ptolemy V, 32, 39f., 47f.
Ptolemy VI, 47
Ptolemy VII, 32, 47f.
Ptolemy XI, 33

INDEX

Ptolemy XII, 33
Ptolemy XIII, 33
Punt, 29
Pur-Sagail, 107
Pylos, 148, 150, 152, 160f.
Pylos Tablets, The (E. L. Bennett), 150, 154
Pyramid Texts, the, 36, 59
Pyramos (Jeyhan), the, 124

Ra (Re), 51
Rabana, 140
Radio-carbon dating, 30
Rameses, 51
Rameses II, 60, 115, 127
Ras Shamrah (Ugarit), 134ff., 140, 144, 168
Rask, R. C., 86
Rassam, H., 109
Rawlinson, Sir H. C., 90ff., 97ff., 121
Red Sea, the, 132, 143
Revillout, E., 43
  Crestomathie demotique, 43
River:
  Aranzahas, 129
  Euphrates, 94, 103, 111, 114, 122, 127
  Indus, 66, 172f., 174
  Jeyhan, 124
  Karkhev, 176
  Kur, 67, 68, 71
  Nile, 18, 29, 32, 38f., 114, 132, 136, 146
  Polvar, 68, 71
  Pyramos, 124
  Sabbatius, 36
  Tigris, 103, 111, 129
Roggeveen, J., 174
Rosellini, H., 52
  Monumenti d'Egitto, 52
Rosetta, 32, 39
Rosetta Stone, the, 25, 39ff., 46ff., 51
Royal Asiatic Society, the, 94, 100
Royal Irish Academy, the, 98
Royal Society, the, 72
Ruad (Aradus), 134f.
Rusch, R., 121
Sabbatius, the, 36
Sabitu, 110

Sacy, S. de, 40, 42, 46, 76f., 80f., 83
  Mémoires sur diverses Antiquities, 76
Sana, 74
Sarangia, 88
Sarcey, Count de, 97
Sardanapalos (Ashurbanipal), 66, 76, 101, 111
Sargon of Accad, 103
Sargon (Sharrukin), 99, 116
Saros, the, 108
Sassanids, the, 70f.
Saulcy, L. C. de, 98
Sayce, A. H., 98, 116, 121f.
Schaeffer, C. F. A., 135, 140, 168
Schliemann, H., 145
Schultz, F. E., 87
Schumacher, J. H., 37
Scripta Minoa (A. Evans), 148
Scripta Minoa II (J. L. Myers), 149, 153
Sebennytos, 30
Sekenere, 63
Seleucids, the, 70
Semiramis, 76
Semites, the, 117, 131ff.
  language and writing of, 29, 96, 100f., 136ff., 162
Sesusri I, 61
Sethe, K., 53
Seti I, 37, 115
Seyfarth, G., 52
Shabdiz, 71
Shalmaneser V, 89
Shem, 86
Shipwrecked Sailor, the, 62
Shiraz, 71ff.
Shubbiluliu, 114f., 127f., 136
Shurippak, 110
Sidon (Saida), 134f.
Simonides, C., 52
Simyra (Sumra), 134f.
Sinuhe, the Tale of, 62
Sipylos, 116
Sixtus V (Felice Peretti), 37
Smerdis, 67, 81
Smith, G., 109, 122, 166
Smyrna, 121
Snefru, 134
Society for Antiquaries, the, 39, 43

Sogdiana, 88
Solomon, King, 71
Somaliland, 29
Speech, human, 13, 18
Spiegelberg, W., 53
Spohn, F. A. W., 52
Stern, L., 53
St. Julien (Fort Rashîd), 39
Storm god, the, 129
Strabo, 67, 76
Stromateis (Clement of Alexandria), 35
Sturtevant, E. H., 120
Sumer, 101, 104
Sumerians, the, 102ff., 106f., 176
   language and writing of, 100ff.
Sundwall, J., 149, 152
Sur (Tyre), 69, 134f.
Surat, 76
Susa (Shushan), 69, 88, 98, 111, 176
Syllabograms, 20f., 65, 105, 123f., 133, 149f., 162, 166
Syria, 33, 36, 60, 73, 113ff., 132

Tabarnash (Labarnash), 113
Tabor, Mount, 144
Tachara, the, 69
Tacitus, 33
Takht-i-Jamshid, 71f., 74, 78
Talbot, W. H. F., 100
Tanis, 53
Tarchundaraus, 117
Tarkondemos Boss, the, 121
Tasisus, 129
Taurus Mountains, the, 124
Teispes, 66, 91, 94
Telepinush, 114
Tell el-Amarna Letters, the, 115, 117, 127, 134
Teshub, 136
Texier, C., 116
Thebes (Egypt), 33, 63
Thebes (Greece), 159
Theseus, 159
Thompson, R. S., 121
Thompson, Sir H., 53
Thracians, the, 115
Thucydides, 147
Tiamat (Tehom), 111
Tiglath-pileser I, 100, 136
Tigris, the, 103, 111, 129
Tigro-Euphrates valley, the, 76, 131
Tiryns, 159
Tondern, 77
Toscanella, 168
Transliteration, 28
Travels in Syria (J. L. Burckhardt), 116
Trojan War, the, 145
Trombetti, A., 15, 16, 168
Troy, 145, 147
Tudkhaliash II, 114
Tunni, 122
Tushratta, 115
Tutankhamon, 128
Tutmosis, 51
Tutmosis I, 114
Tutmosis III, 114, 134
Tychsen, O. G., 77ff.
Tychsen, T. Ch., 37
Tylissos, 153
Tyre (Sur), 69, 134f.
Tyrians, the, 134

Udi, 30
Udum, 142
Ugarit (Ras Shamra), 134ff., 140, 144, 168
Ullikummis, the Song of, 128
Ur, 103ff.
Uriah, 117
Ur-Nammu, 103
U (ra)-hi-li-na-sa, 124
Ut-Napishtim, 110f.

Valle, P. della, 71f.
Van, 87
Varro, 18
Venidad Sade, the, 77
Ventris, M., 152ff., 161
   Documents in Mycenaean Greek (with J. Chadwick), 156, 164
   "Evidence for Greek Dialect" (with J. Chadwick), 154
Venus Tablets, the, 107
Virgin's Stream, the, 36f.
Virolleaud, C., 135, 137ff.
Vossichen Zeitung, the, 139
Voyage en Arabie (C. Niebuhr), 74, 78

Wace, A. J., 159
Wahshih, A. B. A., 41
  Ancient Alphabets, 41
Warburton, W., 38
  Divine Legation of Moses, 38
Warka (Uruk), 103
Wenamon, 63
Westergaard, N. L., 96, 98
Western Asia, 66, 76, 102, 114
Whorf, B., 170
Winckler, H., 117
Word Signs (ideograms), 19f., 56, 98, 100, 105, 123, 156, 162
Wright, W., 116
Writing,
  alphabetic, 20ff.
  boustrophedon, 21, 120, 172
  ideographic, 19, 65, 149, 163, 171
  materials, 18f.
  origins of, 19
  phonetic, 20ff., 105, 123f., 137, 170
  pictographic, 19ff., 65, 104
  syllabic, 20f., 65, 105, 123f., 133, 149f., 162, 166

Writing, A Study of (I. J. Gelb), 21

Xerxes, 69f., 82ff., 85, 87, 91, 106

Yahweh, 14, 34, 143f.
Yakut, 70
Yasna, the, 87
Yassib, 142
Yemen, the, 74
Yo-ho-ho theory, the, 14
Young, Sir T., 17, 41ff., 47ff., 54
  An Account of Some Recent Discoveries, 48

Zarathushtra (Zoroaster), 76
Zend, 70, 77, 78f., 85ff.
Zend Avesta (A. Duperron), 76, 82, 86
Zend Avesta, the, 86
Zeus, 159
Ziggurats, 103
Zoega, G., 38, 46
Zohak, 71
Zuliyas, 130